K Harriman

P9-DOG-940

Field Detectives

Investigating Playground Habitats

Author
Suzy Gazlay

Editor
Betty Cordel

Illustrator
Margo Pocock

Desktop Publisher
Roxanne Williams

Content Consultant
Kirk A. Janowiak

Acknowledgments

Maria Abuelas
Linda Behringer
Care Butler, Margaret Castelazo
Betty Cordel
Michael Guelker-Cone
Pam Stryker, Gerlinde Wirzfeld-Olvera

Jeffery Smith Bryant
Education Director
Monterey Bay Aquarium — Monterey, California

Kirk A. Janowiak
Biology/Ecology Instructor
Delphi Community High School — Delphi, Indiana

Michael Kunz
Professor of Biology
Fresno Pacific University — Fresno, California

This book contains materials developed by the AIMS Education Foundation. **AIMS** (**A**ctivities Integrating **M**athematics and **S**cience) began in 1981 with a grant from the National Science Foundation. The non-profit AIMS Education Foundation publishes hands-on instructional materials (books and the monthly *AIMS* magazine) that integrate curricular disciplines such as mathematics, science, language arts, and social studies. The Foundation sponsors a national program of professional development through which educators may gain both an understanding of the AIMS philosophy and expertise in teaching by integrated, hands-on methods.

Copyright © 1998 by the AIMS Education Foundation

All rights reserved. No part of this work may be reproduced or transmitted in any form or by any means —graphic, electronic, or mechanical, including photocopying, taping, or information storage/retrieval systems — without written permission of the publisher unless such copying is expressly permitted by federal copyright law. The following are exceptions to the foregoing statements:

- A person or school purchasing this AIMS publication is hereby granted permission to make up to 200 copies of any portion of it, provided these copies will be used for educational purposes and only at that school site.

- An educator providing a professional development workshop is granted permission to make up to 35 copies of student activity sheets or enough to use the lessons one time with one group.

Schools, school districts, and other non-profit educational agencies may purchase duplication rights for one or more books for use at one or more school sites. Contact the AIMS Education Foundation for specific, current information. Address inquiries to Duplication Rights, AIMS Education Foundation, P.O. Box 8120, Fresno, CA 93747-8120.

ISBN 1-881431-74-6
Printed in the United States of America

I Hear
and
I Forget,

I See and I
Remember,

I Do
and I
Understand

Chinese Proverb

© 1998 AIMS Education Foundation

Field Detectives

Field Detectives

Introduction

We share the world with an abundance of fascinating plants and animals. Students don't have to go far to meet many of these organisms face to face. Habitats are everywhere, not only in the richness of wilderness areas and parks, but also close at hand wherever plants and animals live, including the familiar territory of the school playground.

The needs and relationships of plants and animals living on the school grounds are basically the same as those observed in habitats all over the world. All living things need food, water, air (oxygen), shelter, and space in order to survive and reproduce. Plants also need light, using energy from the sun to make their own food. Animals get their food and energy by eating plants or other animals that eat plants. Physical conditions within a habitat such as temperature, light, water, and soil also determine which organisms will be able to survive there.

The publication *Field Detectives* is designed to encourage students to look closely at the diverse habitats in and around their school playground. The students become detectives as they search for evidence of life and clues to the natural world around them. They investigate relationships found within all habitats, regardless of size or location.

As the students sharpen their investigative skills, they will discover many clues to understanding the diverse community of plants and animals living out their lives within or near the playground habitat. This understanding and experience can then be applied to other habitats both nearby and far away.

Throughout *Field Detectives*, classes studying playground habitats are encouraged to compare notes with students in other locations who are also investigating their own playgrounds. A special discussion area has been set up for this purpose on the Internet at this site:

http://www.aimsedu.org/discussion/science.html

Project 2061 Benchmarks for Science Literacy*

AIMS is committed to remaining at the cutting edge of providing curriculum materials that are user-friendly, educationally sound, developmentally appropriate and aligned with the recommendations found in national education reform documents.

The Nature of Science

Scientific Inquiry

🐜 *People can often learn about things around them by just observing those things carefully, but sometimes they can learn more by doing something to the things and noting what happens.*

🐜 *Scientific investigations may take many different forms, including observing what things are like or what is happening somewhere, collecting specimens for analysis, and doing experiments. Investigations can focus on physical, biological, and social questions.*

🐜 *Tools such as thermometers, magnifiers, rulers, or balances often give more information about things than can be obtained by just observing things without their help.*

The Scientific Enterprise

🐜 *A lot can be learned about plants and animals by observing them closely, but care must be taken to know the needs of living things and how to provide for them in the classroom.*

The Physical Setting

Processes that Shape the Earth

🐜 *Animals and plants sometimes cause changes in their surroundings.*

🐜 *Change is something that happens to many things.*

🐜 *... Soil is made partly from weathered rock, partly from plant remains — and also contains many living organisms.*

The Living Environment

Diversity of Life

🐜 *A great variety of kinds of living things can be sorted into groups in many ways using various features to decide which things belong to which group.*

🐜 *All organisms, including the human species, are part of and depend on two main interconnected global food webs. One includes microscopic ocean plants, the animals that feed on them, and finally the animals that feed on those animals. The other web includes land plants, the animals that feed on them, and so forth. The cycles continue indefinitely because organisms decompose after death to return food material to the environment.*

Cells

   🐜 Magnifiers help people see things they could not see without them.

   🐜 Most living things need water, food, and air.

Interdependence of Life

   🐜 Animals eat plants or other animals for food and may also use plants (or even other animals) for shelter and nesting.

   🐜 Changes in an organism's habitat are sometimes beneficial to it and sometimes harmful.

   🐜 For any particular environment, some kinds of plants and animals survive well, some survive less well, and some cannot survive at all.

   🐜 In all environments — freshwater, marine, forest, desert, grassland, mountain, and others — organisms with similar needs may compete with one another for resources, including food, space, water, air, and shelter. In any particular environment, the growth and survival of organisms depend on the physical conditions.

   🐜 Insects and various other organisms depend on dead plant and animal material for food.

   🐜 Living things are found everywhere in the world. There are somewhat different kinds in different places.

   🐜 Organisms interact with one another in various ways besides providing food. Many plants depend on animals for carrying their pollen to other plants or for dispersing their seeds.

Flow of Matter and Energy

   🐜 Almost all kinds of animals' food can be traced back to plants.

   🐜 Food provides the fuel and the building material for all organisms. Plants use the energy from light to make sugars from carbon dioxide and water. This food can be used immediately or stored for later use. Organisms that eat plants break down the plant structures to produce the materials and energy they need to survive. Then they are consumed by other organisms.

   🐜 Over the whole earth, organisms are growing, dying, and decaying, and new organisms are being produced by the old ones.

   🐜 Plants and animals both need to take in water, and animals need to take in food. In addition, plants need light.

   🐜 Some source of "energy" is needed for all organisms to stay alive and grow.

The Human Organism

Human Identity

🐜 *People need water, food, air, waste removal, and a particular range of temperatures in their environment, just as other animals do.*

The Designed World

Agriculture

🐜 *Most food comes from farms either directly as crops or as the animals that eat the crops. To grow well, plants need enough warmth, light, and water...*

For students in the early grades, the emphasis should overwhelmingly be on gaining experience with natural and social phenomena and on enjoying science. Abstractions of all kinds can gradually make their appearance as students mature and develop an ability to handle explanations that are complex and abstract. This phasing-in certainly applies to generalizations about the scientific world view, scientific inquiry, and the scientific enterprise.

That does not mean, however, that abstraction should be ignored altogether in the early grades. By gaining lots of experience doing science, becoming more sophisticated in conducting investigations, and explaining their findings, students will accumulate a set of concrete experiences on which they can draw to reflect on the process. At the same time, conclusions presented to students (in books and in class) about how scientists explain phenomena should gradually be augmented by information on how the science community arrived at those conclusions. Indeed, as students move through school, they should be encouraged to ask over and over, "How do we know that's true?" (page 4)

*American Association for the Advancement of Science. *Benchmarks for Science Literacy*. Oxford University Press. New York.

National Science Education Standards*

Science as Inquiry

Abilities Necessary to Do Scientific Inquiry

- Plan and conduct a simple investigation.

- Employ simple equipment and tools to gather data and extend the senses.

Understandings about Scientific Inquiry

- Simple instruments, such as magnifiers, thermometers, and rulers, provide more information than scientists obtain using only their senses.

- Scientists develop explanations using observations (evidence) and what they already know about the world (scientific knowledge). Good explanations are based on evidence from investigations.

Life Science

The Characteristics of Organisms

- Organisms have basic needs. For example, animals need air, water, and food; plants require air, water, nutrients, and light. Organisms can survive only in environments in which their needs can be met. The world has many different environments, and distinct environments support the life of different types of organisms.

Organisms and Their Environments

- All animals depend on plants. Some animals eat plants for food. Other animals eat animals that eat the plants.

- An organism's patterns of behavior are related to the nature of that organism's environment, including the kinds and numbers of other organisms present, the availability of food and resources, and the physical characteristics of the environment. When the environment changes, some plants and animals survive and reproduce, and others die or move to new locations.

Populations and Ecosystems

- Populations of organisms can be categorized by the function they serve in an ecosystem. Plants and some micro-organisms are producers — they make their own food. All animals, including humans, are consumers, which obtain food by eating other organisms. Decomposers, primarily bacteria and fungi, are consumers that use waste materials and dead organisms for food. Food webs identify the relationships among producers, consumers, and decomposers in an ecosystem.

For ecosystems, the major source of energy is sunlight. Energy entering ecosystems as sunlight is converted by producers into stored chemical energy through photosynthesis. It then passes from organism to organism in food webs.

The number of organisms an ecosystem can support depends on the resources available and abiotic factors, such as quantity of light and water, range of temperature, and soil composition ...

Earth and Space Science

Properties of Earth Materials

Soils have properties of color and texture, capacity to retain water, and ability to support the growth of many kinds of plants, including those in our food supply.

Soil consists of weathered rocks, decomposed organic material from dead plants, animals, and bacteria. Soils are often found in layers, with each having a different chemical composition and texture.

Science and Technology

Understanding about Science and Technology

People have always had questions about their world. Science is one way of answering questions and explaining the natural world.

Science in Personal and Social Perspectives

Changes in Environments

Environments are the space, conditions, and factors that affect an individual's and a population's ability to survive and their quality of life.

During the elementary grades, children build understanding of biological concepts through direct experience with living things, their life cycles, and their habitats. ... Making sense of the way organisms live in their environments will develop some understanding of the diversity of life and how all living organisms depend on the living and nonliving environment for survival. Because the child's world is closely associated with home, school, and immediate environment, the study of organisms should include observations and interactions within the natural world of the child. (page 128)

*National Research Council. *National Science Education Standards*. National Academy Press. Washington, D.C. 1996.

xi   © 1998 AIMS Education Foundation

Curriculum and Evaluation Standards
for School Mathematics*

Mathematics as Problem Solving

🐜 *Develop and apply strategies to solve a wide variety of problems*

Mathematics as Communication

🐜 *Relate physical materials, pictures, and diagrams to mathematical ideas*

Mathematics as Reasoning

🐜 *Recognize and apply deductive and inductive reasoning*

Mathematical Connections

🐜 *Use mathematics in other curriculum areas*

🐜 *Apply mathematical thinking and modeling to solve problems that arise in other disciplines, such as art, music, psychology, science, and business*

🐜 *Use mathematics in their daily lives*

Number Sense and Numeration

🐜 *Construct number meanings through real-world experiences and the use of physical materials*

Computation and Estimation

🐜 *Compute with whole numbers, fractions, decimals, integers, and rational numbers*

Patterns and Functions

🐜 *Describe and represent relationships with tables, graphs, and rules*

Geometry and Spatial Sense

🐜 *Develop spatial sense*

Measurement

🐜 *Understand the attributes of length, capacity, weight, mass, area, volume, time, temperature, and angle*

🐜 *Develop the process of measuring and concepts related to units of measurement*

🐜 *Make and use measurements in problems and everyday situations*

🐜 *Extend their understanding of the process of measurement*

🐜 *Estimate, make, and use measurements to describe and compare phenomena*

Statistics

🐜 *Collect, organize, and describe data*

🐜 *Construct, read, and interpret displays of data*

🐜 *Formulate and solve problems that involve collecting and analyzing data*

🐜 *Systematically collect, organize, and describe data*

🐜 *Make inferences and convincing arguments that are based on data analysis*

Students should have many opportunities to observe the interaction of mathematics with other school subjects and with everyday society. ... This integration of mathematics into contexts that give its symbols and processes practical meaning is an overarching goal of all the standards. It allows students to see how one mathematical idea can help them understand others, and it illustrates the subject's usefulness in solving problems, describing and modeling real-world phenomena, and communicating complex thoughts and information in a concise and precise manner. (page 84)

*National Council of Teachers of Mathematics. *Curriculum and Evaluation Standards for School Mathematics*. NTCM. Reston, VA. 1989.

 © 1998 AIMS Education Foundation

The Inside Story Habitats...

A habitat is the place where a plant or animal lives and can get every thing that it needs. Every living thing must have food, water, and oxygen. It needs shelter for protection from harsh conditions and to help it avoid being eaten by something else. Living things also need enough space to grow or move, hunt, and play.

In addition, each living thing has its own specific needs concerning the amount of sunlight it requires and the range of temperature and humidity it can tolerate. The habitat provides for the everyday needs of the particular plants and animals that live in it. The conditions in a habitat must also make it possible for each new generation to get a good start in life.

Habitats come in all sizes and types of conditions. Some may be huge, such as vast deserts, grasslands, or far-reaching stretches of forests. Some may be quite small, such as a pond, a backyard, or a damp area along a stone wall. Habitats may have different areas within them which make it possible for certain living things to thrive but keep others from doing well. For example, life forms living in the top of a tree are usually quite different than those that dwell around the base of its trunk or burrow deep in the ground beneath its roots. Smaller areas of a habitat in which the temperature, humidity, light, and other conditions are significantly different from the rest of the habitat in general are called microhabitats. Some kinds of living things may be better adapted to conditions within a microhabitat than to that of the whole area. Moss often prefers the damper, shadier north side of a tree; certain insects and microorganisms thrive in damp leaves on the forest floor but cannot survive in dry leaves nearby.

Some living things are found only in certain habitats that meet their very specific needs. Others may be tolerant of a wide range of conditions and thus be able to live successfully in many different types of habitats. The silkworm which eats only mulberry leaves is found in very few places in nature, but the rat, which eats almost anything, can thrive in all sorts of different habitats all over the world.

Animals may visit neighboring habitats to satisfy a particular need, much as people might go shopping in another town to find a certain item, but most live out the majority of their lives in the habitat that best suits their needs. Some, such as amphibians and migratory animals, may make a major change in habitat at some point in their lives according to their life-cycle pattern or need for certain food or climate conditions.

1

© 1998 AIMS Education Foundation

GOOD LOOKING

Topic
Evidence of Life

Key Question
What evidence of plant and animal life can be found around the school grounds?

Focus
Clues can be found giving evidence that living things are present or have been around even when the organisms themselves no longer can be seen.

Guiding Documents
Project 2061 Benchmark
- *Living things are found everywhere in the world. There are somewhat different kinds in different places.*

NRC Standard
- *Environments are the space, conditions, and factors that affect an individual's and a population's ability to survive and their quality of life.*

Science
Environmental science
    habitats
Life science
    plants
    animals

Integrated Processes
Observing
Collecting and recording data
Comparing and contrasting
Inferring

Materials
For each group of students:
    lapboard or clipboard
    student page duplicated on four colors, preferably light and dark shades of two different colors
    transparent tape or stapler
Optional:
    field guide(s) to help identify plants and animals
    hand lenses
    Discovery Scopes®

Background Information
   Most students can readily list plants and animals they have observed in a certain area: birds, insects, trees, grass. Aside from being able to see a plant or animal itself, it takes a bit of detective work to discover some of the organisms that live in an area, as well as those who have been there but are no longer around. Some life forms are so tiny or well hidden that only the most discerning observer can find them: tiny insects crowded together under a single leaf or a fragile sprout on its way to its full size of only a few millimeters tall.

   Good detective work will turn up larger plants and animals too. A grassy field may actually include a diverse collection of different plant varieties. Animals often move out of sight as humans approach, but they leave evidence of life behind. Sometimes the clues are in the form of shelter, such as nests, holes in ground or bark, webs, or ant hills. Sometimes the evidence is food: chewed leaves, insects caught in a spider's web, remains of an animal's meal. Other clues include footprints or traces of paths an animal has traveled, such as flattened grass or slime trails of a snail or slug. Bird and animal droppings, called scat, provide additional evidence as to which creatures have made use of this habitat.

Management
1. Mysteries and detective work are known to be highly motivating. Throughout these activities, do everything possible to create a mystery atmosphere and encourage the students to become "Field Detectives" involved in collecting evidence.
2. Before starting this activity, arrange for a "mystery guest" or two, a person or persons well-known to the students, to visit the room when the students are not there and leave some piece of evidence. Some suggestions include:
    music teacher–musical instrument
    another staff member–trademark hat, scarf, etc.
    librarian–current book being read aloud
    custodian–empty waste basket, light bulb replaced
    messenger from office–notice or memo posted
3. If, as you begin this activity, your students notice the planned evidence of your mystery guest right away, just move on through *Procedure 2* and continue.
4. Encourage students to take the lead in the search for evidence of life on the playground. However, if your school grounds appear somewhat barren, explore on your own ahead of time to identify three or four especially good places to find animal life.
5. If your school is regularly sprayed for insect control, you may have to choose another location to study or arrange that a section of the playground is not sprayed during this study.
6. Generate guidelines for respecting organisms that live in an area. Encourage the students to be careful not to destroy the surroundings in an attempt to find something. Make clear your rules for behavior

and establish a method for calling a "find" to everyone's attention without disturbing it more than necessary.

7. For the playground part of the activity, divide the class into groups of three or four students. Equip each group with a clipboard or lapboard, (see *Easy-to-Make Equipment*) paper, and pencil so that everyone can contribute to recording what animals (and evidence of animal life) are found.

8. The record keeping begun in this activity in the form of links on a chain should become an ongoing project. Duplicate the student page on four different colors. If possible use dark and light shades of two colors for the four choices (i.e. light green for plant life, dark green for evidence of plant life, etc.). Keep a supply of strips on hand. As the students better learn *how* to look, they will continue to add new discoveries to their group's chain. New life forms will also appear with the passing of time and changes in weather and seasons.

Tab | Date: 3-3 Notes: Bug holes in the mud.

Procedure

1. Ask the students to look around the room and tell you who is there and how they know. [I can see each person.] Ask who has been there but isn't there now including evidence to show that this person really has been in the room. [Mia is sick today so she isn't at her desk.]

2. If the item left behind by the mystery guest has not yet been noticed, tantalize the students with clues such as "I can tell that someone else has been here. Who else can tell?" and continue until they can identify who was there and how they know. Start again with different clues showing that someone else has been there. Continue with the mystery game, encouraging the students to take the lead and propose a new mystery, while you and the rest of the class follow the clues to solve the mystery.

3. Generate a discussion of what kinds of evidence could show that something alive had been in a certain place. Guide the students to think about what evidence of life they might be able to find on the playground. Brainstorm an informal list of some good places to start looking, emphasizing that they will think of many more as they continue to investigate.

4. Take the class to the playground. Gather in a central location and ask "Who's here?" After several responses ask, "Who isn't here?" (what living things have been here but cannot themselves be seen). Cite specific evidence regarding "who isn't here" and discuss.

5. Ask each team to choose a particular area to observe and study more closely on an ongoing basis. The area should be clearly defined, such as

a certain tree, the area within a meter of a back-stop, or a flower bed. Send each team with a lap board to its target location to list, describe, or draw all living things and evidence of life they can find. Assure them that the goal is to find a variety of clues and living things, not necessarily to be able to identify what they find.

6. Take a group tour and encourage each team to share which living things and clues they have found in their area. Back in class, establish a key to show which color represents each category (animal life, evidence of animal life, plant life, evidence of plant life). Have each team record its information on appropriately colored links and begin constructing a team chain. Encourage the students to continue adding links to their team's chain as they make new discoveries in the days and weeks to come.

Discussion

1. How were you able to tell that someone had been in your classroom but was no longer there? If you were not in the room, what clues would be there so others would know you had been there?

2. What were some of the evidences of life that you found? Where were some particularly good places to look for clues?

3. What clues were most surprising to you?

4. Where would you like to look for clues next? Why?

5. When your class left the playground, what clues did you leave that would show you had been there?

Extensions

1. Refer to the *Bibliography* for suggestions for resource books about your location. Visit your local library or natural history center for information to help identify the plants and animals the students are observing.

2. Have each group make a map of the habitat area they have chosen to study. Display the maps along with the chains and use them for reference in subsequent activities.

Curriculum Correlation

Literature

Dendy, Linda. *Tracks, Scats, and Signs.* NorthWord Press, Inc. Minocqua, WI. 1995.
- Written for forest, field, and pond habitats, but the clues, explanations, and illustrations are applicable to any search for evidence of life.

Robertson, Kayo. *Signs along the River.* Roberts Rinehart, Inc. Niwot, CO. 1986.
- A gentle encouragement to look for "signs," the evidence of life along the river. The story is told as much in the illustrations as in the text.

Home Link

Be a detective! Solve the mystery of who is at your house or in your yard (or who isn't there any more) in addition to your family. List all clues you can find.

GOOD LOOKING

Tab

Date:
Notes:

Tab

Date:
Notes:

Tab

Date:
Notes:

Tab

Date:
Notes:

4

© 1998 AIMS Education Foundation

Telltale Clues

Topic
Using Deductive Reasoning

Key Questions
1. What can we learn about other people by looking at objects that are important to them?
2. What can we find out about living creatures by looking at evidence from their daily lives?

Focus
We can use deductive reasoning to learn about living things, including other people, as we examine the clues they leave behind.

Guiding Documents
Project 2061 Benchmark
- *Scientific investigations may take many different forms, including observing what things are like or what is happening somewhere, collecting specimens for analysis, and doing experiments. Investigations can focus on physical, biological, and social questions.*

NRC Standards
- *Scientists develop explanations using observations (evidence) and what they already know about the world (scientific knowledge). Good explanations are based on evidence from investigations.*
- *People have always had questions about their world. Science is one way of answering questions and explaining the natural world.*

NCTM Standard
- *Recognize and apply deductive and inductive reasoning.*

Science
Environmental science
   habitats

Integrated Processes
Observing
Classifying
Collecting and recording data
Comparing and contrasting
Inferring

Materials
For the class:
   teacher-prepared bag of objects (see *Management 6* and *Procedures 1 and 3*)
For each student:
   plain paper lunch bag

Background Information
A detective needs to be able to *deduce* information, that is, to use reasoning to put together bits and pieces of evidence to tell the story of what may have happened. The famous Sherlock Holmes was a master at solving mysteries by means of deductive thinking.

Deductive reasoning can also help us determine the everyday stories of many living things. We humans surround ourselves with clues such as the objects we collect and enjoy having around us. Animals also leave behind clues as they carry out the activities and processes of life: remains of a meal, waste products, changes to the environment such as bent or broken vegetation, subtle signs of where they are living or hiding, and more. Even though the organism may have moved on or even died, a careful and persistent observer can find and interpret such clues to determine who has been in the area and to tell some part of the story of its life.

In this lesson students will construct stories about other students from "clues" (objects) brought to school. This same type of deductive reasoning will then be applied to the plant and animal evidence they observed in the lesson *Good Looking*.

Management
1. Discourage the students from choosing valuable or irreplaceable objects to put in their bag. A drawing can represent an object of value or one too large for the bag.
2. You may wish to send home a note explaining the activity.
3. Determine some way of identifying the collections so that you alone will be able to tell whose is whose.
4. Students may work in teams of two. Each team should investigate two different bags so that everyone's collection is used.
5. Encourage the students to keep the descriptions positive and not critical, especially since they may be read aloud.
6. For demonstration purposes, put together your own bag representing yourself or a member of your family.
7. For the team-written stories, you may wish to have a recorder write for the team and a reporter read the story to the class.
8. Two student pages are included. They are designed to go together to make one larger scene. You may also choose to use one for this activity and the other as a follow-up activity such as writing about the evidence observed.

          © 1998 AIMS Education Foundation

Procedure

Part 1

1. The day before you plan to do this activity, explain to the students that they will be providing the clues for a mystery that some of their classmates will try to solve. Give each student a paper bag with directions to take it home and put five objects in it. The objects should represent things that are important to that individual: a favorite toy or collected item, a favorite food, a picture of a pet, a representative of a hobby, etc. The students should not tell anyone what they put in their bags.

2. In class, collect the bags. Discuss with the students different ways of using clues to figure out the story of what happened in a mystery. Point out that the kind of skill involved (deductive reasoning) is something that is very useful and improves with practice.

3. Tell the students that they will be trying to *deduce* everything they can about the person whose clues are in the bag. Generate a list of things they would like to try to find out about their mystery person. At this point they should not be concerned so much with the name of the person as with what that person is like and what kinds of things he or she enjoys doing. Demonstrate with a bag you have prepared, guiding the students to make observations, and move into making deductions about the person whose bag it is.

4. Have each team brainstorm to decide how they are going to go about this task and make a list of strategies. They should add to this list throughout the activity as new ideas occur.

5. Give each team a bag and tell them to follow their strategies to find out everything they can about the person it represents. Encourage them to list any information they can justify, including the piece(s) of evidence supporting those deductions.

6. When they have analyzed the clues as completely as possible, ask them to write a descriptive account about the person who put the objects in the bag.

7. Have volunteers read their stories aloud, asking the class to guess who is being described. Give the teams the opportunity to meet with the person whose clues they had in order to fill in any pieces of information and discuss the results.

Part 2

1. Remind the students of the different "evidences of life" they discovered in *Good Looking*. Look at some of the clues that are now part of your paper chain. Discuss ways in which these clues are similar to those the students selected to tell the story of their daily life.

2. Give each student team a copy of the student page(s). Explain that although the drawing does not show the critters that have lived in or passed through the area pictured, those animals have left behind all sorts of clues. There are also clues concerning plant life. Each team should examine the picture closely to discover as many clues as possible, then discuss and decide how to interpret them. Challenge them to work together to develop a story about what has occurred in the pictured habitat, using deductions based upon the clues they have found.

3. Give the students the opportunity to share their stories with the whole class and compare the deductions they made about the various clues.

Discussion

1. Which piece(s) of evidence told you the most about your mystery person? Was there anything in the bag that was not very helpful?

2. Were any of the clues confusing? If so, what could have helped to make the evidence clearer?

3. Did you and your partner always agree about the meaning of the clues? How did you defend your opinions?

4. Do you think you were able to get an accurate picture of the person you were trying to learn about just from these clues? What additional evidence might have been helpful to have? What could have made this task easier?

5. If you were going to put together another bag of objects representing you, what changes (if any) would you make? Why?

6. How were the team stories about the drawings alike? How were they different? Since you were all looking at the same evidence, how do you account for the differences?

Extensions

1. Have the class assemble a time capsule collection representing the culture of your classroom or school. If possible, box it appropriately and bury for another class to dig up in 25 or 50 years.

2. Draw different habitats showing evidence of occupation.

Curriculum Correlation

Social Studies

1. Some of the information we have about other cultures or people in history comes from clues in the form of objects left behind. Make a list of such objects pertaining to the people or period of history you are studying.

2. Visit a local museum and construct "stories" from the clues that are displayed.

Literature

Read aloud a Sherlock Holmes mystery or another good detective story using deductive reasoning.

Fitzsimmons, Cecilia. *Nature's Hidden Worlds: Animal Habitats*. Raintree Steck-Vaughn Publishers. Austin, TX. 1996.
- Sharp observational skills are needed to solve these puzzles illustrating various global habitats, accompanied by informative text and detailed illustrations.

Stock, Catherine. *Where Are You Going, Manyoni?* Morrow Junior Books. New York. 1993.
- Abundant evidence of life to look at and more to find in the beautiful illustrations depicting a young African girl's two-hour trek to school.

Young, Caroline. *The Big Bug Search*. Usborne Publishing Ltd. London. 1996.
- Nearly 100 critters from a dozen habitats are hiding on each two-page spread. About 200 different varieties are highlighted overall, each with a pertinent fact. Answers included. Also available: *The Great Animal Search* (17 habitats, 300 different animals)

Math

Introduce or practice math problems using deductive reasoning. For example: In a class of 29 students, if 16 students are boys, how many are girls?

Home Link

Talk to other family members about which five objects they would choose to represent themselves. Are any of the objects the same as the ones you chose?

 © 1998 AIMS Education Foundation

© 1998 AIMS Education Foundation

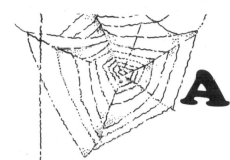

A Special Plot

Topic
Habitats

Key Question
What lives in one small plot on the school playground?

Focus
Close observation of a small section of the school playground reveals a variety of plants and animals carrying out their normal lives or just passing through.

Guiding Documents
Project 2061 Benchmarks
- *Living things are found everywhere in the world. There are somewhat different kinds in different places.*
- *For any particular environment, some kinds of plants and animals survive well, some survive less well, and some cannot survive at all.*

NRC Standards
- *Employ simple equipment and tools to gather data and extend the senses.*
- *Environments are the space, conditions, and factors that affect an individual's and a population's ability to survive and their quality of life.*

NCTM Standards
- *Develop spatial sense*
- *Collect, organize, and describe data*

Math
Measurement
   linear
Mapping
Counting and tallying
Venn diagrams

Science
Environmental science
   habitats
Life science
   plants
   animals

Integrated Processes
Observing
Classifying
Predicting
Collecting and recording data
Comparing and contrasting
Inferring

Materials
For each team of students:
   4 golf tees or 4 large nails (5 cm or more)
   piece of strong string or yarn, 140 cm long
   student pages
   hand lenses and/or DiscoveryScopes®
   clipboard, lapboard, or similar hard surface
   chart paper
   markers or crayons
Optional:
   hammer (if the ground is very hard)
   resource books to help identify plants and animals
   microscope

Background Information
In this activity, students use a hand lens as they continue their quest to find evidence of life. This time the focus is on one very small section of the playground, unique in its particular combination and arrangement of living organisms, yet part of the bigger picture of the entire field or playground. While the emphasis is on finding evidence of life and some of the living organisms themselves, students will also get a close view of the diversity and complexity of life at ground level.

Management
1. Encourage students to hold the hand lens close to one eye and move their head close to the area or object they are observing. If they have not had prior experience using a hand lens, allow additional time for them to explore and become accustomed to using this tool of science. You may wish to add a hand lens activity for this purpose (see *Extensions*).
2. Select an area of study best suited for your class. For best results, choose an area with a healthy combination of plant life, animal life, and soil. For simplicity, have each team of two students study a plot on the grassy part of the playground or in a field. Another option would be to have the students choose varied plots in such places as shade under trees and bushes, damp stretches along a wall or fence, flower beds, planted areas in direct sun, etc.

3. Try to find areas that are somewhat protected from being disturbed. Negotiate with the groundskeeper so that your observation area does not get mowed while you are studying it. If this is non-negotiable, begin your study after the area has been mowed; then be sure to remove the nails or tees before the mower comes through again.

4. If the ground is very hard, you may need to use nails instead of golf tees.

5. Remove the string if it poses a safety hazard. If the golf tees or nails are driven very firmly into the ground, they should remain to mark the plot without the string. A little cornstarch sprinkled at each corner will also help mark the location.

6. If your students have not had prior experience with mapping, show them how to draw objects in location on a map and give them some practice before beginning this activity. Two versions of the first student page, with and without grid line guides, are included here. Choose the one most appropriate for your class.

7. Be sure to encourage the students to add any new living discoveries or evidences of life to their chains from *Good Looking.*

8. It is not essential to identify the plants and animals found, only to describe or code them in such a way (words and pictures) that they can be recognized.

Procedure
Part 1

1. Have the students work with a partner, facing each other for several seconds to memorize what they see. Then ask them to turn their backs and each change just one thing about their own appearance (such as remove a watch or ring). Have them face each other again and see if they can identify the change within a minute. Play several rounds; then discuss the strategies they used to improve their observation skills.

2. Remind the students of the importance of all clues, both large and small, in solving a mystery, as they experienced in *Good Looking* and *Telltale Clues.* Inform them that today they will be focusing on very small clues in their quest for living things.

3. Give each student team four golf tees or nails, a piece of string, the student activity sheets and a clipboard. Take them to the area that you have selected for them to study (see *Management 2*).

4. Each team should pick a place to study. Have them mark the spot by laying the paper on the ground to determine the plot they will be studying. Direct them to push a golf tee or nail halfway into the ground at each corner of the paper, then pick up the paper.

5. Leaving a 10 cm tail, have them wrap the string once or twice around one of the tees, continuing around the rectangle and wrapping each tee in turn. When the rectangle has been framed, the ends of the string should be tied together.

6. Once the plot has been established, allow the students to spend some time observing and getting to know it, looking for clues as to who has been there as well as who is there now. Urge them to be gentle and not to dig or tear up the plot in their quest.

7. Have each team make a map of their plot (first activity page), sketching both the location of any plant or animal form they see and the location of any clues they find. Animals should be sketched in the spot where they were first observed. Evidence of life should also be drawn where it is seen. Tell the students to use stippling (dots) to show the grass rather than trying to draw each individual plant. Any larger or unusual plants should be shown.

8. On the second activity sheet, have the students sketch several plants and/or animals they observe, counting the number of each they can find in their plot. They should record the tally in the lower right corner of each sketch space.

9. Direct them to take a good look at the dirt in their plot, both with and without a hand lens, and describe it in a few carefully chosen words. Also have them look for any nonliving materials (rocks, dirt clods, garbage, etc.) and dead materials (sticks, dead insects, etc.) These should also be added to the map.

Part 2

1. Back in the classroom, ask the students to list the different plants and animals (and evidence) they have found.

2. Have each team work with another team to develop a large Venn diagram with two circles, one for each team's plot, showing the living things and evidence of life they found. Use four different colors of marker or crayon to designate plant life, animal life, and evidence of each. You may wish to coordinate the colors with those you are using in the paper chain begun in *Good Looking.* Display the diagrams where all can see and draw some conclusions about which animals are found generally throughout the playground habitat and which may be found only in certain places.

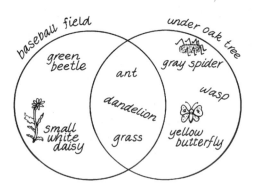

Discussion

1. How were you able to describe certain living things so that others could recognize them?
2. What were some of the evidences of life that you found? Where were some particularly good places to look for clues?
3. Were there any animals that were found by all or most groups? Were there any that were seen only in one or two places? Why do you think some animals are able to live in lots of different places while others seem more limited?
4. What did you observe about the soil in your plot? Do you think it is good soil for plants? Explain your answer.
5. What was the easiest part about making the map of your plot? What was the hardest part? What could you do to make it easier?
6. What do you think would happen to the things living in your plot if it rained for a whole week? What do you think would happen if it snowed? How might a very strong wind affect it?
7. If your plot is in an area that is cared for (mowed, watered, pruned, etc.), how might it be different if it were allowed to grow wild and not cared for? If it is in a wild area, how might it be different if someone cared for it like a garden?

Extensions

1. Extend the grid lines to accommodate coordinate labels. Label one side with consecutive numbers and the other side with consecutive letters. Have the students list the plants and animals shown on their map and locate them by coordinates (for example: ant hill 7,d; dandelion 2,b; fuzzy-leaf plant 3,d; sow bug 5,e, and so forth).
2. Have the students visit their plots again in a few days, weeks, or throughout the year. Copy the original maps so the students can compare or add to them as they observe changes in their plot over time. Discuss the changes as well as those things that stay the same.
3. Look even more closely at the plants and animals through microscopes.
4. Invite local agricultural, gardening, and nursery professionals or hobbyists to help identify and talk about plants, animals, and soils.
5. For additional activities exploring the use of a hand lens, see "Mealworms Under Glass" and "Night Crawlers" from AIMS publication *Magnificent Microworld Adventures*.

Curriculum Correlation

Resources and references

Johnson, Kipchak. *Worm's Eye View*. The Millbrook Press. Brookfield, CT. 1991.

- With appealing whimsical attitude, this guide covers the whole range of critters and relationships found in a backyard habitat. Includes encouragement to set up a "wildlife refuge" in backyard — or playground!

Silver, Donald M. *One Small Square: Backyard*. W. H. Freeman & Co. New York. 1993.

- The perfect companion to this activity: describes the ecology around, above, and below the ground.

Language Arts

Write "Who Was Here?" riddles giving clues to a mysterious visitor for others to solve.

Technology

Post a message at the AIMS Field Detectives Discussion Area web site (http://www.AIMSedu.org/discussion/science.html). Describe what you found in your special plots and compare to what other students in other geographic locations found in theirs.

Home Link

Ask the students to observe a habitat at or near their home for a period of time. They can look in their yard or a vacant lot, or find a spot as small as the area under and around a planter. Encourage them to make a map and keep notes recording the different plants and animals they find.

A Special Plot

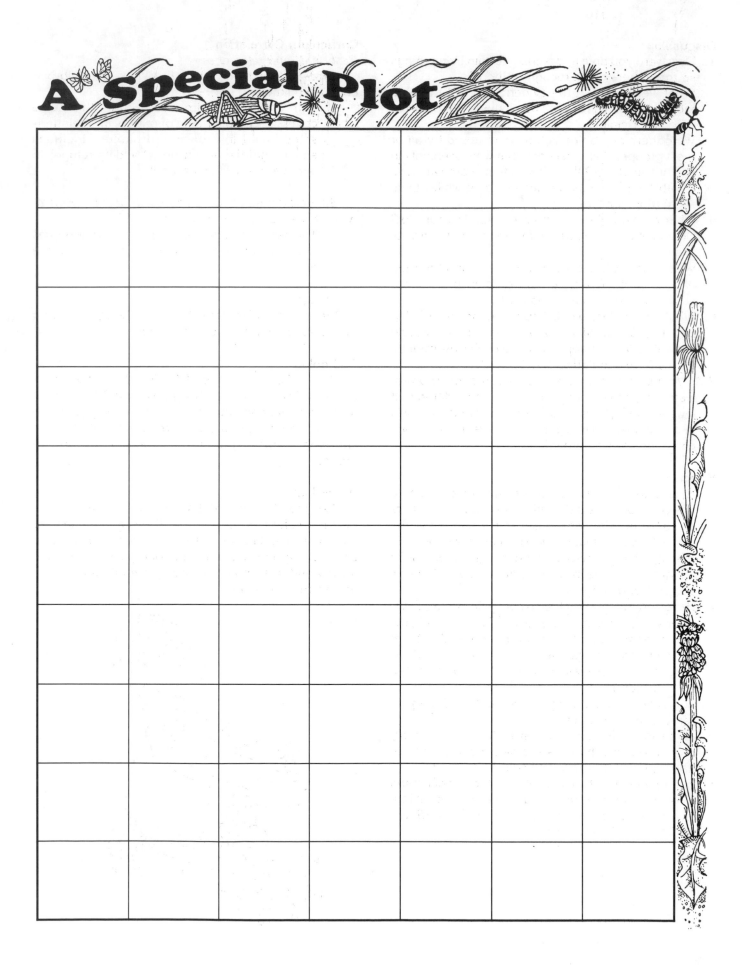

A Special Plot

14

© 1998 AIMS Education Foundation

A Special Plot

Observers

Draw and describe

Close-up of the dirt

15

© 1998 AIMS Education Foundation

Floor Samples

Topic
Non-living Components of a Habitat

Key Question
How does the surface influence what can live in a habitat?

Focus
A habitat includes both living and nonliving elements. The type and condition of the surface helps determine what lives in a habitat.

Guiding Documents
Project 2061 Benchmark
- *Living things are found everywhere in the world. There are somewhat different kinds in different places.*

NRC Standard
- *Organisms have basic needs. For example, animals need air, water, and food; plants require air, water, nutrients, and light. Organisms can survive only in environments in which their needs can be met. The world has many different environments, and distinct environments support the life of different types of organisms.*

Science
Environmental science
   habitats

Integrated Processes
Observing
Classifying
Collecting and recording data
Comparing and contrasting
Generalizing

Materials
For each group of students:
   isopods (pillbugs, sowbugs) or other small critters
   plastic or paper cups to hold isopods
   hand lenses
For the class:
   chart paper
   markers
Optional:
   potatoes (for potato traps – see *Management 2*)
   knife

Background Information
The surface material forming the foundation of a habitat gives significant clues as to which plants and animals can survive there. Some surfaces provide suitable material and accessible water to nurture plant growth (when conditions of light and temperature are also favorable). The plants in turn provide food, shelter, and sometimes an additional source of moisture for various animals. Some surfaces have a texture that can provide shelter for critters needing a place to escape a predator or wait out the heat of the day. Some surfaces are unable to support plant growth and serve mainly as a thoroughfare for animals going about their daily lives. Very few areas, even those on the school playground, are totally devoid of all life forms.

In a playground situation, the surface often varies while other conditions are nearly the same. Different soil types support different varieties of plant life; different types of plant life attract and support different types of animal life. Thus plants growing in the mixture of sand and soil near a sandbox may differ from those growing nearby in soil alone, even though both areas receive the same amount of sunlight and water.

In this activity, students are encouraged to become more aware of what is underfoot. They should be guided to understand that different surfaces serve different purposes and meet different needs, and that the type of surface is a determining factor in whether an area is densely populated, supports just a few organisms, or used only by a sporadic traveler.

Management
1. If finding fragments of surfaces such as cement or blacktop is a problem, you or the students may need to bring samples from another location.
2. Be sure of a reliable source for isopods (or whatever critters you use). See *Easy-to-Make Equipment* for instructions for making a simple potato trap. Have the critters collected and ready in a cup.
3. Direct the students not to leave isopods in an area where they are not likely to survive (for example, in direct sunlight).
4. Encourage detailed observation and record keeping of the behavior of the isopods.
5. You may wish to have a back-up container of critters in case some escape.
6. If needed, model the careful handling of an isopod before beginning this activity.

Procedure
1. Tell the students that detectives are sometimes called "gumshoes" and ask if anyone knows how they got that name. [from wearing rubber-soled shoes to enable them to walk without being heard] After ideas have been shared, point out that surfaces are important to detectives in other ways besides being able to sneak around without being caught! Ask the class to think of examples of ways that surfaces might make a detective's job easier or more difficult. [some surfaces will show fingerprints, others won't; some will catch fiber or hair, etc.]

2. Discuss the importance and influence of surfaces in our daily lives, especially floor coverings. Ask students how the surfaces they are living or working on affect their lives. Draw on their experiences at home and camping for observations.

3. Brainstorm a list of every floor covering in the school (door mats, carpet squares, wood, linoleum, etc.), identify the use of each type, and organize the list accordingly. Discuss multiple uses and the reasons for developing and choosing various types of coverings. Guide the students to recognize that among other factors, floor coverings are chosen to suit specific uses.

4. Ask the students to think about the different "floor" (surface) coverings on the playground and around the school and the purpose of each. Generate a list of all the playground surface coverings the students can think of. Visit the playground to add to the list. Older students can be encouraged to be very specific, i.e. *sandy soil, rocky soil, hard-packed dirt* rather than just *dirt*; *asphalt* or *cement* rather than *pavement*.

5. Choose five or six very different surfaces on the playground, including both natural and human-made. Send student teams with hand lenses to observe living things and evidence of life at each location. Use a scale of one to three to describe abundance of plant life, with *one* representing barren and *three* characterizing dense growth. (older students may prefer a scale of one to five.)

6. Have the teams collect small samples of each of the surfaces and glue them to the recording page(s). These pages may also be used to record a description of the surface and the scale of abundance.

7. Encourage the students to think about why a living thing might be found on a certain type of surface but not on another. [type/condition of soil; moisture; availability of food; shelter from heat, weather, predators] Is this a place where the animal lives or is it just passing through? Guide the students to draw conclusions concerning the different types of surface coverings and the life they support.

8. Send each group with its isopods (or other critter) to visit an identified area for a designated period of time, turning a critter loose and observing its behavior. Ask them to evaluate if this would be a good habitat for this creature to live in. Point out that animals may visit an area in their constant search for food or temporary shelter, but they will not spend their whole lives there unless all of their life needs can be met.

9. Return the critters either to where they were found or to a terrarium where they can be properly cared for.

Discussion

1. What would happen if different floor covers around school were switched — for example, carpet traded for asphalt, doormats for the gym floor?

2. Dirt floors in buildings are common in many parts of the world. What would be some advantages and disadvantages of living on a dirt surface?

3. Imagine that you are living on the school playground and that the playground is your floor. What surface coverings would you prefer for various activities of your daily life? Explain your choices.

4. If you had to stand all day, what kind of covering would you want on the floor? What type of coverings would be best for cooking? … for sleeping?… for in-line skating? Think of several possibilities for each and give reasons for your thinking.

5. Tell which of the different playground surfaces you think would be best for supporting life in a habitat. Which would be worst? Explain your thinking.

6. How can you tell if a creature such as your isopod is comfortable in a particular habitat?

7. Based on this experience, describe what you think would be an ideal habitat for isopods (or whatever you used) to live in, where they would get everything they need.

Extensions

1. Have students think of animals that do not live on the ground and collect information about the surfaces they use.

2. Use hand lenses or microscopes to compare and contrast the surface material of each area studied.

3. Separate the surface samples on the student pages. Sort and classify them in a variety of ways.

Curriculum Correlation

Art

1. Make a collage of various materials showing different surface textures.

2. Choose a natural habitat and draw a side view cross section of it. Use samples of the surface and soil layers and pressed leaves of representative plants to show the different parts.

3. Use blank paper and an unwrapped crayon or soft pencil to make rubbings of various surfaces.

Literature

Bourgeois, Paulette. *The Amazing Dirt Book.* Addison Wesley Publishing Company, Inc. Reading, MA. 1990.
- Everything anyone could possibly want to know about dirt: household, garden; history; science.

Dunrea, Olivier. *Deep Down Underground.* Aladdin Books (Macmillan). New York. 1993.
- A delightful, whimsically illustrated counting book describing living things encountered by a mole digging deeper into the earth. Written in Scottish vernacular.

Home Link

Ask the students to survey their homes and make a list of every type of floor covering they can find, as well as its purpose. Have the students bring the lists to school to compare and contrast, both with each other and with the list they generated at school.

Floor Samples

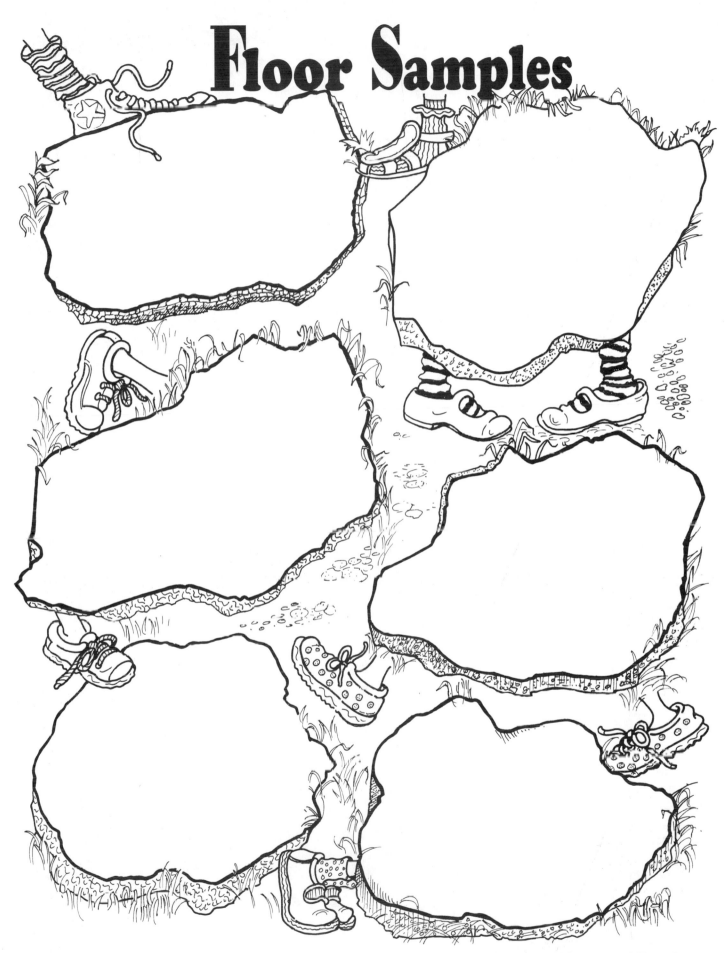

18

© 1998 AIMS Education Foundation

A Watched Pot

Topic
Importance of Soil in a Habitat

Key Question
What will happen to a soil sample when it is dug up, watered, and cared for?

Focus
Soil often contains seeds waiting to sprout until conditions are favorable for growing.

Guiding Documents
Project 2061 Benchmarks
- *People can often learn about things around them by just observing those things carefully, but sometimes they can learn more by doing something to the things and noting what happens.*
- *Living things are found everywhere in the world. There are somewhat different kinds in different places.*
- *Plants and animals both need to take in water, and animals need to take in food. In addition, plants need light.*

NRC Standard
- *Organisms have basic needs, which for animals are air, water, and food. Plants require air, water, and light. Organisms can only survive in environments in which they can meet their needs. The world has many different environments, and distinct environments support the life of different types of organisms.*

Science
Environmental science
  habitats
Life science
  plants
  animals

Integrated Processes
Observing
Predicting
Collecting and recording data
Comparing and contrasting
Generalizing
Inferring

Materials
For each group:
  small flower pots or containers with drainage holes
  hand lenses and/or DiscoveryScopes®
  cups or watering can
  trowel or sturdy spoon

For the class:
  tape
  paper fasteners
  lined paper
  yarn
Optional:
  microscopes
  pleated coffee filters
  colored paper

Background Information
What may look like dry, lifeless dirt to a casual observer may actually be a community of life waiting for the right conditions to occur. Microscopic life forms such as bacteria are typically present almost everywhere, but beyond that, the soil may also contain life in embryo form such as animal eggs and plant seeds. Unless it has been sterilized (as in the case of most types of commercial potting soil) or treated thoroughly with herbicides and pesticides, very little soil is truly lifeless, no matter how dry and dead it may appear.

Most children have experienced the process of putting a seed in soil, watering it, and watching a plant grow. This process goes on constantly in nature without human intervention. Plants rely on wind, water, and animals to disperse their seeds. The seeds wait wherever they land until the conditions are favorable for growth. This supply of waiting seeds is appropriately known as a "seed bank." Depending on the type of seed, the seed may be in the "bank" for a year or two, a decade, or even several centuries!

Sometimes the wait is seasonal. In places where the ground is very cold or frozen, the new cycles will not begin until the soil warms up or thaws. Some seeds must go through a period of being cold or they will never sprout at all. Often it is water that has been lacking. When the rains begin or water otherwise comes in, the life forms within the soil begin to emerge. Sometimes it has to do with being exposed to light, as may happen if the soil is disturbed or turned over. Sometimes the wait involves recovery from a disaster, such as a fire or flood. In fact, the seeds of certain plants such as redwoods and bishop pines may lie waiting for many years, but they will not sprout unless set into action by the heat of a fire. Some seeds actually need to have their hard covering cracked or chipped, such as happens when they are nibbled by an animal, before the seed can sprout!

Management
1. You will need soil samples taken from a variety of locations for this activity. Collect some samples from the school grounds or visit a natural area and collect there. Label the pots so you will be able to identify them.
2. For best results, use samples from locations near established growth areas such as flower beds, fields, or vacant lots. Be sure the area has not been treated for weed control.

3. This activity should be done outdoors as much as possible. Bring the containers inside at night or over the weekend if they need protection, but keep them outside in the sunlight at least on school days.
4. It may take several weeks to get results. Be sure that the pots are kept damp and monitored closely every day. Meanwhile, go on to other activites.
5. Three- or four-inch flower pots work well for this activity, as do milk cartons or disposable cups with drainage holes poked in the bottom.
6. If the dirt is so fine that it washes out of the drainage holes, line the container with a pleated coffee filter or add a few marbles or pebbles to the bottom.
7. Soak the contents of the pots really well on the first few days. From then on, keep them moist but not soggy.
8. Duplicate the pot pieces on cardstock or heavy paper. Cut lined 8 1/2 x 11 inch paper in fourths to fit the journal.
9. Journals may be used for individual or group recording.

Procedure
1. Tell the students that they are beginning a new detective case: finding out some of the secrets hidden in basic, ordinary, everyday, dirty dirt!
2. Equip each group with a container and a trowel or spoon. Tell them to find an area of dirt and collect a sample, filling the container loosely to about an inch below the rim.
3. Ask the students to think about what sorts of things they expect to be in their dirt sample. See if they can detect any signs of life at all. Discuss the different conditions that encourage plants and animals to live in dirt.
4. If the discussion has not already come around to the need for water, guide it in that direction. Suggest that all the pots be watered and left in the sunlight to see what happens to them.
5. Have the students construct their *Watched Pot* journal. They should observe and water the containers each day, recording any changes (new clues) they notice. Discuss new developments and compare the samples taken from different locations.
6. As various seedlings sprout, ask the students to offer suggestions as to how they got there and why they had not sprouted before. Have them draw or construct paper plants in the "pot" of their journal to represent the growth they see.
7. Go back to the area where the samples were collected. Have the students look around at all the things that are growing. Ask them to share what they know about how all those plants got there and look for clues concerning the origin of the small plants now appearing in their dirt sample.
8. Ask them to think back about the various critters they have observed so far. If any animals have appeared in the dirt samples since the beginning of this activity, ask the students to infer how they might have gotten there.

Discussion
1. What did you expect to happen when you began watching this pot? Did any of the results surprise you?
2. What were the first clues that you observed? How did your clues compare to those noticed by others in the class?
3. How can you explain the mystery of where the plants in your pot came from? How could you prove your explanation?
4. A good detective has to dig up clues. In the process sometimes new clues are unearthed and brought to light. How does this compare to what you did when you dug up dirt and filled your container? What were some of the changes you made in the conditions surrounding your dirt? How do you think those changes affected organisms living or waiting in the dirt?
5. Did you see any seeds in your soil sample when you started? What evidence do you have that seeds were there? How do you think they got there? What clues could you find to prove your case?
6. What other places would you look for soil samples to try next? What do you think might happen?

Extension
Set up an investigation to test variables. Use several samples from the same site but provide different amounts of water, put some in sun and some in shade, some in different temperatures, etc.

Curriculum Correlation
Social Studies
Research to find out more about various discoveries of seeds dating back hundreds of years and the efforts of scientists to get these seeds to sprout. Include the Internet in your search if available.

Technology
Check the *Field Detectives* discussion area on the Internet. Post your results and compare them to other postings there. Be sure to include your geographic region.

Literature
Lauber, Patricia. *Seeds Pop Stick Glide*. Crown Publishers. New York. 1981.
• A well-suited resource to help students understand the origin and journey of the seeds they now see sprouting in their pots.

Overbeck, Cynthia. *How Seeds Travel*. Lerner Publications. Minneapolis. 1982.
• Photographs and detailed text trace various paths taken and adaptations used by seeds en route to a place to grow.

Home Link
Have the students repeat the investigation with soil samples collected from their backyards and neighborhoods. Compare the results.

A Watched Pot

21

© 1998 AIMS Education Foundation

A Watched Pot

1. Cut the snails and the front and back journal covers along the solid lines.

2. Fold the tabs of the front cover pieces toward the back along the broken lines. Tape the folds to the back side of the journal's back cover.

3. Staple several pieces of lined paper to the inside of the journal.

4. Use paper fasteners to attach the snails to the outside of the front cover pieces where marked.

5. Wrap a piece of yarn or string around the snails to close your journal when not in use.

Back Cover of the Journal

22

© 1998 AIMS Education Foundation

Comfort Clues

Topic
Physical Conditions in a Habitat

Key Question
How does temperature vary within a habitat?

Focus
Temperatures vary within a habitat. Temperature is one of the physical conditions influencing which plants and animals live in a particular location.

Guiding Documents
Project 2061 Benchmarks
- *Tools such as thermometers, magnifiers, rulers, or balances often give more information about things than can be obtained by just observing things without their help.*
- *For any particular environment, some kinds of plants and animals survive well, some survive less well, and some cannot survive at all.*

NRC Standards
- *Simple instruments, such as magnifiers, thermometers, and rulers, provide more information than scientists obtain using only their senses.*
- *Environments are the space, conditions, and factors that affect an individual's and a population's ability to survive and their quality of life.*

NCTM Standard
- *Compute with whole numbers, fractions, decimals, integers, and rational numbers*

Math
Calculating averages
Calibrating a scale
Measuring
    temperature

Science
Environmental science
    habitats
Life science
    plants
    animals

Integrated Processes
Observing
Predicting
Collecting and recording data
Comparing and contrasting
Applying
Generalizing

Materials
For each group:
thermometer
writing materials
calculators, optional

Background Information
It is important for a detective to be able to determine the circumstances surrounding certain key events which may lead to the solution of a mystery. In the habitat, too, circumstances are important factors influencing which organisms are able to live in which location. Temperature, sunlight, water, air (quality and movement), and rock/soil type are all important non-living influences to be observed and taken into consideration. The particular combination of these conditions encourages success for some plants and animals while determining that other organisms cannot survive in a certain spot or area.

Students may be surprised to realize that the temperature can vary even within a short distance. Such variation is due to a combination of factors including amount of sunlight, movement of air, reflection or radiation of heat from nearby surfaces, and the cooling effect of moisture given off by leaves (transpiration). Even the distance from the ground can be significant since soil temperature generally changes more slowly than the surrounding air and thus has a heating or cooling effect.

Every organism has limits concerning extremes of temperature it can tolerate. The conditions it prefers fall within these limits. Students will not be able to determine limits by measurements taken in the course of a single day. They can, however, observe and measure the variance of temperature and other physical conditions within the habitat and think about why some places might be warmer or cooler than others. They can also add to their understanding of why some organisms might prefer a particular location over a neighboring area.

Management
1. If no students are wearing sweaters or jackets in class, or if you have a school policy preventing this, take a survey of long or short sleeves, the type of jacket worn to school (if at all), or some other variation of dressing for warmth or coolness.
2. Students should already be familiar with the basics of calculating averages and using thermometers.
3. For meaningful results, record the temperature of at least eight locations within the classroom.
4. Thermometers should be left undisturbed for several minutes before reading and recording a temperature.

5. Have student teams calibrate their paper thermometers in Celsius or Fahrenheit to match the instrument they used. If this is too time-consuming for younger learners, calibrate the black-line master before duplicating it. (When there is a choice, Celsius is the preferred temperature scale for scientific use.)

Procedure

1. Take a quick survey of the students to find out how many at that moment are wearing coats, sweaters, or jackets in class. Discuss why different students have chosen to dress more or less warmly, guiding the conversation to understanding that a comfortable temperature may be warmer or cooler for some students than for others.

2. Ask the students to identify the areas of the room they perceive to be warmer or cooler than the rest of the room in general. Measure the actual temperature in each location. Determine the average temperature of the classroom and organize the data according to which areas are average, warmer, or cooler than average. Discuss what factors in the classroom environment could affect the temperature.

3. Ask different students to point out where they would most like to sit in the classroom. Encourage them to make their selection for other reasons than to sit near a friend. Ask them to explain the reasons for their choice and list their responses. Point out that some of the reasons they may have mentioned (light, temperature, comfort, convenience to things they need) are the very reasons that some animals live in certain areas but not in others; also why plants grow better in particular locations.

4. Explain to the students that looking at the physical conditions in a habitat is a lot like collecting circumstantial evidence in a mystery: these conditions influence the life and activity that occur in that location. Tell them that they will be collecting such circumstantial evidence at several locations on the playground.

5. Challenge each team to try to find a warm place and a cool place on the playground. Encourage them to choose locations no one else has chosen. Take the class to the playground, set whatever limits are necessary, and send them to take the first temperature measurement. (Here's one way to hang a thermometer off the ground if needed.)

6. While waiting for the thermometers to stabilize, have each team look for and list whatever plants and animals they see in the area they are measuring, being careful not to let their shadows fall across the thermometers in direct sunlight.

7. Direct each team to calculate the average of the two temperatures they recorded. Ask them to select a location that appears to be between the extremes of the other two sites and measure the temperature there to see how close it comes to the average of their other two readings.

8. Back in the classroom, ask each team to calibrate the scale of the paper thermometers to match the tool they used and color to show the degrees recorded, one for each of the three sites.

9. Collect the data from each group and calculate the average temperature of the entire study area. Have each team mark their thermometers to show the average, comparing that measurement to the measurements they recorded.

10. Display the activity sheets. Discuss the data displayed and encourage the students to infer connections between the temperature, sunlight or shade, and the plants and animals observed.

Discussion

1. Are you a person who likes to wear a jacket even when others don't or are you someone who is often running around without a jacket when everyone is talking about how cold they are? Which creatures did you observe that seemed to prefer being warm? ... cold?

2. Which areas had the lowest temperatures recorded? ... the highest? What reasons can you think of for these results?

3. Was there an area or areas that seemed not to have much animal life? How could this be explained looking at its physical conditions compared to the other areas?

4. Think back to the behavior of the isopods (or other critters) you observed in the activity *Floor Samples*. What connections can you make between their behavior and the temperature, amount of direct sunlight, and type of surface? What generalizations could you make about the type of habitat (including surface, light, and temperature) an isopod might prefer?

5. Think about a pet cat or dog. Where does it go to get warm? ... to keep cool? Where are you likely to find a cat in winter? Where is a dog likely to go in summer? Where do you go to get warmer or to cool off?

6. Instructions for aquariums and terrariums often suggest keeping them away from windows or direct sunlight. Why is this important advice?

Extensions

1. Repeat the survey at regular intervals or in different seasons and compare.

2. Determine the median and mode for each set of data collected, as well as for the total area.

3. Survey a vacant lot or local park in a similar fashion.

Home Link

Have the students predict where the warmest and coolest spots might be in their bedroom and/or their home, giving reasons to back up their predictions. Loan the thermometers in turn so they can collect data to bring back to class and compare.

Comfort Clues

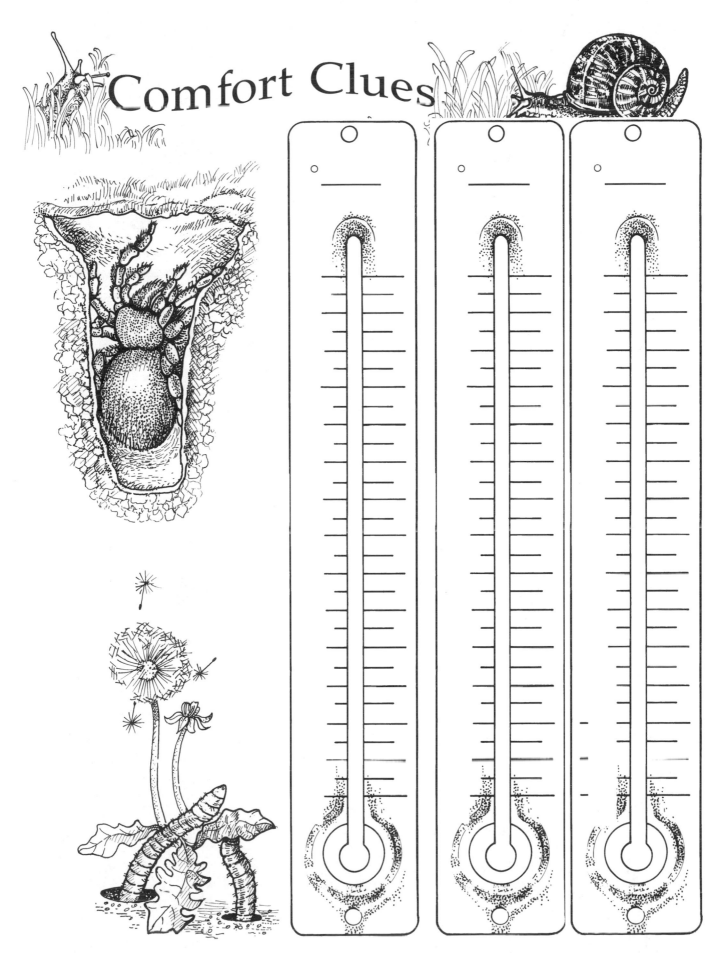

© 1998 AIMS Education Foundation

FISHING for CLUES

Topic
Basic Needs Supplied by Habitats

Key Questions
What are the basic needs that a habitat must provide?

Focus
Students identify the basic needs of all living things and determine how those needs are met for themselves and for other organisms.

Guiding Documents
Project 2061 Benchmarks
- *Most living things need water, food, and air.*
- *Plants and animals both need to take in water, and animals need to take in food. In addition, plants need light.*
- *People need water, food, air, waste removal, and a particular range of temperatures in their environment, just as other animals do.*

NRC Standard
- *Organisms have basic needs, which for animals are air, water, and food. Plants require air, water, and light. Organisms can only survive in environments in which they can meet their needs. The world has many different environments, and distinct environments support the life of different types of organisms.*

Science
Environmental science
  habitats

Integrated Processes
Observing
Comparing and contrasting
Applying
Generalizing

Materials
For each student:
  cardstock
  coloring materials
  tape or glue
  paper fastener
  toothpick
  10 cm thread
  paper clip

For each group:
  2-3 sheets of chart paper
Optional:
  assortment of natural living or once-living objects or models (pine cone, small plant or leaf, realistic plastic animal, etc.)
  yarn, fabric (see *Management 4*)

Background Information
As students explore a habitat, they should look for five essential clues — food, water, air (oxygen), shelter, and space — to determine how that particular area supplies everything that is needed by each type of plant and animal that lives there. Some of the clues may be less obvious than others (a challenge for a good detective!), but all must be present in some combination for each organism that lives in that habitat.

People have the same needs as other living things. Students should come to understand that they also must have food, water, air, shelter and space in order to survive, and that the specific source for obtaining each of these things may not be exactly the same for everyone. In addition they should add to their understanding of how other living things are able to get what they need to survive.

The word *air* is used here to describe a basic need which is actually for *oxygen*, a component of air. You may choose to substitute the word *oxygen* for air in this and subsequent activities, as appropriate to the developmental level of your students. Also, be aware that there are a few living things that are exceptions. For example, anaerobic bacteria do not need air. Keep in mind that plants and many animals need light in addition to the essentials emphasized here.

Management
1. For best results, duplicate the structure template and figure on cardstock or glue the paper to cardstock.
2. Students may suggest, bring in, or make models of various living things to place on the structure, or the teacher may supply them. Pictures could also be used.
3. Include both plants and animals as organisms to be discussed.
4. Yarn, fabric, and other such decorations could be added to the figures to resemble the student.
5. Labels are included for use at your discretion.

Procedure

1. Have the students work in small groups to list everything they can think of that they would need in order to live. Post the lists so that everyone can see. Discuss the difference between the things that are "wants" and the things that are truly "needs." Guide the discussion to encourage students to understand that their direct needs are food, water, air (oxygen), shelter, and space.

2. Explain to the students that a detective on the job comes to the scene of the mystery and "fishes" for clues. A habitat detective exploring the territory "fishes" for clues by observing and thinking and putting together pieces of evidence to "catch" the information he or she wants to find.

3. Tell the students that the structure they are making is a way to remember the most important clues to look for in a habitat: food, water, air, shelter, and space. Have them follow the directions for making the figure and structure, adding the name of each of life's essentials to a side of the structure.

4. Instruct each student to bend the feet of the figure and reinforce it with a bent paper clip. Tell them to use the paper fastener to secure the feet to the structure so that it can turn freely.

5. Direct the students to turn the figure so that the fish hangs over the *food* side. Then ask them to think about how their own need for food is met. Encourage a variety of responses. Then direct them to turn the figure so the fish hangs over another side and discuss how that need is met. Repeat until all sides have been done.

6. Ask each group to select one structure to represent a "typical" student in the class, placing it in the center of a large piece of paper. Use the shape of the structure to guide dividing the paper into five sections. Ask the students to write briefly how each of the needs are typically met, recording their answers directly on the paper close to the base of the structure.

7. Provide some natural objects, or objects which represent living things, or let the students go outside to gather some. Have them remove the figure and place an object on the structure in the center of the paper. Direct each team to discuss

how the habitat meets the needs of that organism (or the organism it represents: for example, a pine cone represents a pine tree; a leaf represents that type of plant). Have them draw lines parallel to and below their initial responses to record the new information.

8. Repeat with other natural objects. After several rounds, discuss the similarities and differences in the ways that the habitat meets the needs of various living things.

Discussion

1. Which needs are the easiest for you to get in your everyday life? Which ones take more effort on your part?

2. Do your classmates get what they need from their environment the same way you do? Were any needs met in nearly the same ways? What were some of the more unusual responses? Can some of your needs be taken care of in more than one way? Explain.

3. Are your needs met in different ways when you are at home than when you are at school? What about when you are outside, especially if you are in a park or a natural area?

4. What situations can you think of where one or more of your needs was not met? What did you do about it? What would happen to a plant or animal in a situation where it could no longer get something that it needed?

5. As you discussed the different natural objects, what similarities did you find in how the habitat supported them? Were there any whose needs would be hard to meet? How would this apply to where such an organism could live?

Extensions

1. Encourage the students to collect information about a variety of living things and how their needs are met. Challenge the class to design a game in a team quiz-show format using the information that has been gathered.

2. Build a folded paper dodecahedron, or use a cube or blank die as a random selector. Label the sides with the categories used on the support structure and design a game. One possibility: one player or team names a familiar plant or animal. The other rolls the random selector and answers how the need is met for whatever side comes up.

Curriculum Correlation

Music

Sing *Homing in on Habitats*

Home Link

Encourage the students to take the structure home and demonstrate it to their family, perhaps showing how the needs of a sibling or family pet are met.

© 1998 AIMS Education Foundation

Fishing for Clues

1. Write **FOOD, WATER, AIR, SHELTER,** or **SPACE** in each trapezoid.
2. Cut along all solid lines. Fold tabs to the back along the broken lines.
3. Glue or tape the tabs to the back of the next segment.
4. Cut out the figure and decorate it to look like yourself.
5. Fold the base of the figure upward along the broken lines so it will stand.
6. Use a bent paper clip to help the figure stand straight.
7. Glue or tape the hands of the figure together holding a toothpick fishing pole.
8. Use a paper fastener to attach the feet of the figure to the structure.
9. Cut out the fish and use thread to hang it from the fishing pole.

Fishing for Clues

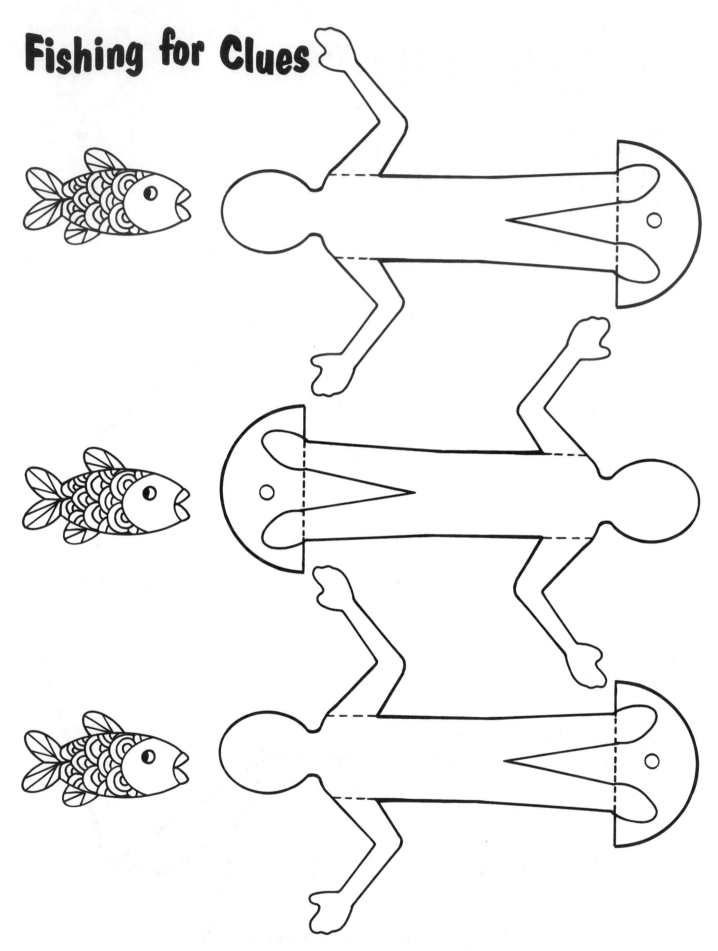

Fishing for Clues

FOOD	WATER	AIR	SPACE	SHELTER
FOOD	WATER	AIR	SPACE	SHELTER
FOOD	WATER	AIR	SPACE	SHELTER
FOOD	WATER	AIR	SPACE	SHELTER
FOOD	WATER	AIR	SPACE	SHELTER

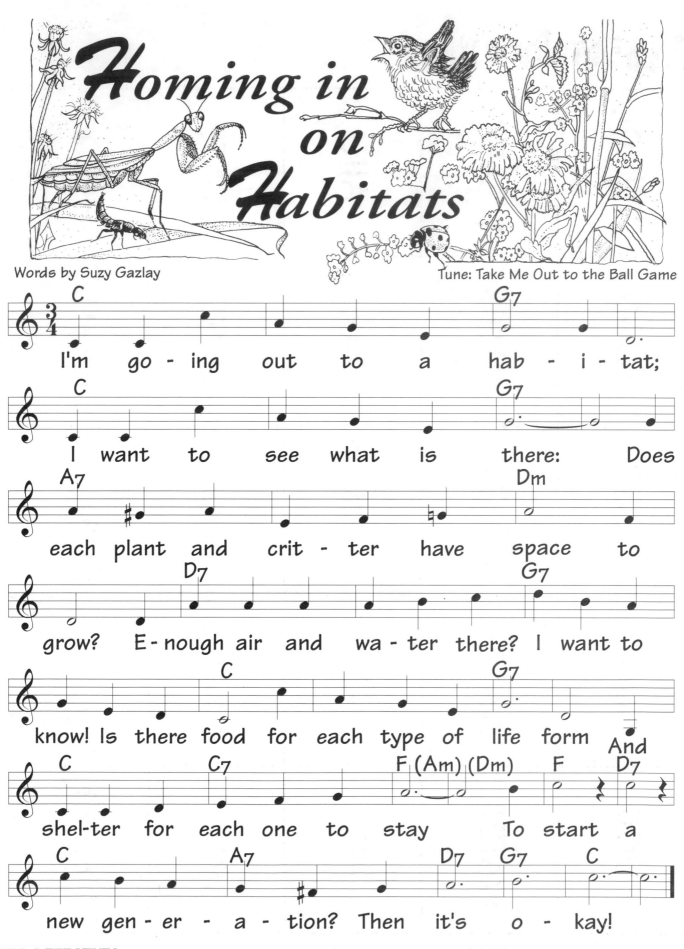

Homing in on Habitats

Words by Suzy Gazlay

Tune: Take Me Out to the Ball Game

I'm go - ing out to a hab - i - tat;
I want to see what is there: Does
each plant and crit - ter have space to
grow? E - nough air and wa - ter there? I want to
know! Is there food for each type of life form
shel - ter for each one to stay To start a
new gen - er - a - tion? Then it's o - kay!

 © 1998 AIMS Education Foundation

Home Away From Home

Topic
Setting Up a Terrarium

Key Question
How can you best design a terrarium to be as much as possible like a natural habitat?

Focus
A terrarium can be designed, balanced, and maintained to model a natural habitat.

Guiding Documents
Project 2061 Benchmarks
- *A lot can be learned about plants and animals by observing them closely, but care must be taken to know the needs of living things and how to provide for them in the classroom.*
- *Most living things need water, food, and air.*
- *Plants and animals both need to take in water, and animals need to take in food. In addition, plants need light.*

NRC Standard
- *Organisms have basic needs, which for animals are air, water, and food. Plants require air, water, and light. Organisms can only survive in environments in which they can meet their needs. The world has many different environments, and distinct environments support the life of different types of organisms.*

Science
Environmental science
   habitats
Life science
   plants
   animals

Integrated Processes
Observing
Predicting
Collecting and recording data
Comparing and contrasting
Applying
Generalizing

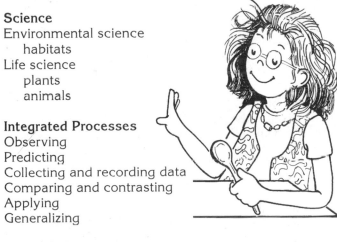

Materials
Terrarium container(s) with lid(s) (see *Easy-to-Make Equipment*)
Collecting containers
Trowels or small shovels
Spray bottle
Clean gravel

Optional:
buckets
tarp
plywood to fit under glass terrarium
black construction paper

Background Information
After the previous activities, the students probably have a good idea of the most common plants and animals that live on the playground, as well as a general understanding of what surfaces, temperature, and other conditions they prefer. In this activity they will be designing and setting up a terrarium habitat as a window of life in a particular area of the playground.

It is important to emphasize that the terrarium include all of the essential elements of a habitat: food, water, air, shelter, space, plus light. If living things are put together randomly without care for providing for their needs on a long term basis, the result is simply "bugs in a jar," not a terrarium habitat. All organisms will need food and water in order to become established in their new home. Animals will need a place to hide similar to what they have been used to. A successful terrarium habitat will support the life cycles of the organisms living there, enabling at least some of the plants and animals to reproduce during the time it is set up. Some organisms will become part of the food chain for other inhabitants.

Students may be strongly tempted to collect plants and animals from everywhere on the playground. Avoid mixing organisms from diverse microhabitats even though they are all found on the same playground. Moisture-loving plants and animals from a wet, shady spot in a planter will not do well in dry, sandy soil from the playing field. Encourage students to stock the terrarium only with the types of organisms they have actually observed in the area the terrarium represents.

It takes time for a terrarium habitat to become balanced and established. The process of setting it up will take several days, and that is only the beginning. Plan to maintain the terrarium during the rest of your study of habitats; perhaps even longer if student interest continues. Subsequent activities in *Habitats* will include *The Terrarium Connection* to help the students apply what they are learning to this small window on the natural world.

Management
1. You may wish to have small groups of students each design, set up, and maintain their own terrarium. If the class is setting up multiple terrariums, you may want to designate different areas of the playground to different groups.

2. Refer to the *Easy-to-Make Equipment* section for suggestions concerning putting together easy and inexpensive terrariums, containers, and lids.
3. *Who's Who in the Habitat* contains helpful hints and guidelines for meeting the needs of a variety of plants and animals commonly found on school playgrounds. The *Bibliography*, Internet, and your local library or natural history resource center have additional information.

Procedure
1. Have the students work in small groups to plan a terrarium that would represent some of the plant and animal life found close to the ground on the playground or around the school.
2. Encourage them to use the information and impressions they have gained in their careful detective work surveying the playground for evidence of life and essential elements of a successful habitat. Included in their design should be the physical arrangement of the terrarium, the varieties of plants and animals they would like to observe, and a plan for providing for the needs of the organisms: space, air, water, food, and shelter. Remind them that the plants also need light.
3. Have the class set up at least one of the designed terrariums (or a combination of compatible ideas) and maintain it throughout their study of habitats.
4. Make use of some of the suggestions for constructing small-critter live traps (see the *Easy-to-Make Equipment* section) or have the students design their own.
5. Be sure the students collect food that the animals will eat. Keep the terrarium supplied with a constant source of water or moisture.
6. Encourage close observation of the various critters and plants living in the terrariums. When possible, have the students count populations and measure growth. Prompt them to be on the lookout for evidence of change.
7. Have them compare the living conditions and the sources for the necessities of life among these, other terrariums that may be accessible, and the playground itself. Encourage them to keep an ongoing record, frequently recording thoughts, observations, and questions.

Discussion
1. Explain the terrarium design your group proposed. What are its strongest points? What changes would you make after seeing or hearing the designs done by other groups?
2. What are the basic needs of plants and animals living in the habitat represented by the terrarium you set up? How are those needs supplied in the natural world? How will they be supplied in the terrarium?
3. Which plants and animals in the terrarium do you predict might be eaten by other inhabitants? Why do you think so?

4. Which need is the easiest to supply? Which is the hardest? Explain.
5. What changes do you observe in the terrarium soon after setting it up? What changes do you think might happen in the future?
6. How is the terrarium similar to the natural habitat? How is it different?
7. What other organism(s) could also live in your terrarium? What organisms would not be able to survive there? Why not?

Extensions
1. Set up additional terrariums or aquariums to represent other habitats.
2. Draw or paint close-up portraits of the different plants and animals living in the terrarium. Find out all you can about each one. Display the information on a bulletin board or in a binder near the terrarium.
3. Visit an aquarium, museum, or even the local pet store. Analyze the terrariums/aquariums/displays to determine if all the needs would be met for the organisms living or pictured there.
4. Begin a class collection of photographs from magazines depicting different types of habitats. Look for evidence of life and sources for needs of the inhabitants being met.

Curriculum Correlation
Literature

James, Betsy. *Mary Ann.* Dutton Children's Books. New York. 1994.
- A young girl keeps a praying mantis in a terrarium, learning about its needs and life cycle. Contains good, practical information for everyone who will want to keep a critter after reading this story!

Merrill, Jean. *The Girl Who Loved Caterpillars.* Philomel. New York. 1992.
- Retelling the twelfth century Japanese tale of a free-spirited young girl who pursued her interest in spite of pressure from her family and culture.

Social Studies

Discuss the possibilities of what different habitats might be like in other communities, states, countries, or civilizations you are studying. Encourage the students to look for clues in the resources (books, films, videos, etc.) you are using.

Home Link
Ask the students to report on how they supply the needs of any pets they have. Encourage them to look at aquariums at home and describe them as a habitat.

33 © 1998 AIMS Education Foundation

Home Away From Home

What would live in a terrarium representing your playground? Plan and explain how your terrarium habitat would meet the needs of the plants and animals living in it.

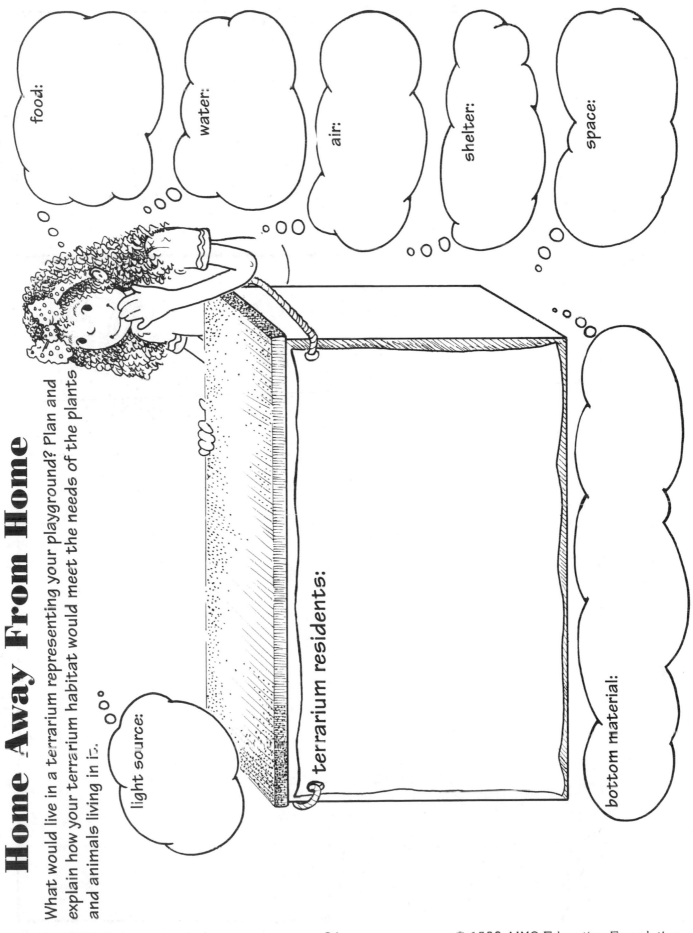

food:

water:

air:

shelter:

space:

light source:

terrarium residents:

bottom material:

Terrarium Design

Draw your plan for a terrarium.

top view

side view

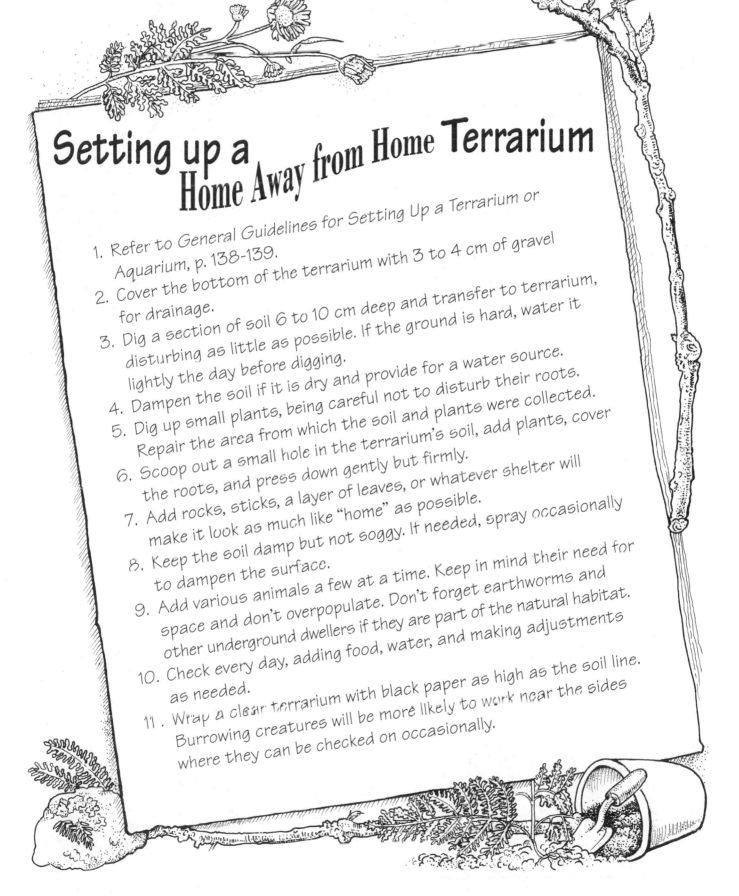

Setting up a Home Away from Home Terrarium

1. Refer to General Guidelines for Setting Up a Terrarium or Aquarium, p. 138-139.

2. Cover the bottom of the terrarium with 3 to 4 cm of gravel for drainage.

3. Dig a section of soil 6 to 10 cm deep and transfer to terrarium, disturbing as little as possible. If the ground is hard, water it lightly the day before digging.

4. Dampen the soil if it is dry and provide for a water source.

5. Dig up small plants, being careful not to disturb their roots. Repair the area from which the soil and plants were collected.

6. Scoop out a small hole in the terrarium's soil, add plants, cover the roots, and press down gently but firmly.

7. Add rocks, sticks, a layer of leaves, or whatever shelter will make it look as much like "home" as possible.

8. Keep the soil damp but not soggy. If needed, spray occasionally to dampen the surface.

9. Add various animals a few at a time. Keep in mind their need for space and don't overpopulate. Don't forget earthworms and other underground dwellers if they are part of the natural habitat.

10. Check every day, adding food, water, and making adjustments as needed.

11. Wrap a clear terrarium with black paper as high as the soil line. Burrowing creatures will be more likely to work near the sides where they can be checked on occasionally.

The Inside Story Food Chains...

Do you know where your meals come from? Of course you do, when you stop to think about it. You've probably helped buy food, carry groceries, or even cook. Perhaps you eat fruit or vegetables from your garden. You probably enjoy going out to a restaurant. You've noticed that special smell that tells you someone is baking bread, cookies, or some other treat. These are just some of the clues that let you know not only where your meals come from, but also how they are prepared and even when they are ready to eat. It's good to know that someone in your family, the cafeteria staff, a restaurant cook, or YOU are able to buy or grow food and prepare it so you can get what you need to eat.

It is very different for plants and animals. Like all living things, they must have nourishment in order to have energy, grow, and stay healthy, but no one prepares meals for animals in the wild. They spend much of their time searching for whatever type of food they require: plants, other animals, or both. Plants can't go to find food, so they make their own, using energy from the sun, water, and other nutrients. This process is called *photosynthesis*.

All plants and animals, living or dead, are potential food for somebody else. Thus a caterpillar munching on a leaf makes a good snack for a frog; the frog is a great meal for a snake; the snake is dinner for a hawk. The leaf, caterpillar, frog, snake, and hawk are all links in a type of food relationship called a *food chain*.

The main source of energy in a habitat is sunlight. During the process of making its own food, a plant stores some of the sun's energy. When an animal eats a plant, it also gets some of the energy from the plant, using some and storing the rest. In this way energy is passed along the food chain each time something is eaten.

Think about eating a tuna sandwich. With each bite you are getting some of the energy made by wheat plants as they were growing and forming grain, which was then ground into flour to make your bread. Do you like lettuce or sprouts on your sandwich? If so, you are getting more energy from another plant. You get energy from the tuna too, but it comes to you less directly because it has passed through several links of a food chain. Perhaps before it was caught, the tuna ate a herring. The herring dined on tiny saltwater animals which ate microscopic ocean organisms that use photosynthesis to make their own food. The energy from these organisms was passed along each link of that food chain to you!

A food chain shows the order of who eats what. It also helps us see that some of the energy stored in a plant or animal is transferred to whoever eats it. Food chains can be as short as two links. Chains longer than four or five links are not as common, but they do occur.

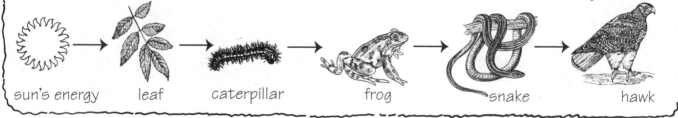

sun's energy   leaf   caterpillar   frog   snake   hawk

The Inside Story

Producers and Consumers, Decomposers, Herbivores, Carnivores, Omnivores...

Each organism living in a habitat belongs to one of three feeding levels. The first level consists of green plants that make their own food using energy from the sun.

The second level includes the plant-eating animals, the herbivores.

The third level is that of meat-eating animals, the *carnivores*. Sometimes this level is divided to show another level for the carnivores that eat other carnivores.

Omnivores, animals which eat both plants and animals, can be found in either the second or third levels. Their position changes depending upon what they eat. Most people are omnivores, as are bears, mockingbirds, turtles, and many other creatures. When you ate that tuna sandwich, you were an omnivore feeding at two different levels!

Green plants, the organisms in the first level, are called *producers* because they produce their own food. The animals at the other levels are called *consumers* because they consume other organisms to get the food and energy they need.

A very important job is done by *decomposers*, a special type of consumer. These plants and animals break down dead plants and animals, as well as waste materials left from the process of living, returning it to the soil where it can be used by plants to make food.

An animal's size is not connected to its place in a food chain. Many people think of carnivores as large hunting animals such as a lion or wolf. In the community of small animals living in leaf litter, the carnivores are insects only a centimeter or two in length. Fleas, ladybird beetles, dogs, and tigers are all carnivores. A herbivore may be as small as an aphid or as large as a cow or giraffe.

Consumers and producers come in all sizes. Giant baleen whales eat microscopic plankton. Tiny insects eat massive trees. Comparatively large coyotes eat both small rodents and other animals close to their own size. Thirty-pound hyenas and microscopic bacteria are both decomposers with the important task of processing dead plants and animals and returning nutrients to the soil. No matter what size, each living thing has its own important place in the food chains in the habitat.

Here's the Scoop...

The Inside Story
Food Webs and Pyramids

Food relationships within a habitat are complicated. Most organisms eat and are eaten by at least two other organisms. Omnivores change levels, eating both first-level plants and second- or even third-level animals. This network of feeding relationships in the habitat is called a food web. A food chain can be thought of as a strand within the food web.

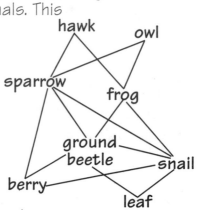

It usually takes a comparatively large amount of food at one level to support the life of a creature at the next level. Think about the food you need. In a single meal, how much of the food you eat comes from plants and how much comes from animals? Remember that the animals also needed to eat plants or other animals. Did you have cereal this morning, or toast, or pancakes? These foods are made from grain, the seeds of certain plants. Sugar, syrup, and jam are plant products too. Did you have an egg? The chicken that laid the egg needed grain to eat. Your milk came from a cow that ate a lot of grass. Look at all the plants and animals in the different food chains that contributed to your breakfast!

If you were to list the plants and animals that are part of the food chains leading to you, the greatest number would be in the first level (producers). In addition to all the plants and plant products you eat directly, remember the plants that are food for the various animals that are part of your diet. For example, even though you most likely don't eat much grass yourself, you probably eat products that come from grazing animals. If you organize your list in a picture or chart to show how many individuals lead up to what you eat, the shape might be what is called an ecological pyramid. It would show the most individuals (plants) at the bottom in the producer level and the fewest (carnivores) at the top among the consumers.

Pyramids are a good way to show food relationships in a habitat. Often the results will show many individuals at the lower levels and fewer at the top. In some habitats such as a redwood forest, comparatively few trees (producers) can support a much greater number of consumers because of the huge size of the trees and the comparatively small size of the herbivore critters. In this situation, the ecological pyramid better describes the amount of material rather than numbers of individuals.

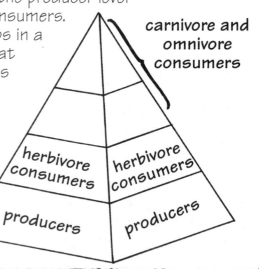

Life in the Food Chain

Topic
Food Chains and Webs

Key Question
What are some of the food chains and webs found on the playground and around school?

Focus
All living things on the playground are part of various food chains which are links to overall food webs.

Guiding Documents
Project 2061 Benchmarks
- *A great variety of kinds of living things can be sorted into groups in many ways using various features to decide which things belong to which group.*
- *Almost all kinds of animals' food can be traced back to plants.*

NRC Standards
- *All animals depend on plants. Some animals eat plants for food. Other animals eat animals that eat the plants.*
- *Populations of organisms can be categorized by the function they serve in an ecosystem. Plants and some micro-organisms are producers — they make their own food. All animals, including humans, are consumers, which obtain food by eating other organisms. Decomposers, primarily bacteria and fungi, are consumers that use waste materials and dead organisms for food. Food webs identify the relationships among producers, consumers, and decomposers in an ecosystem.*

NCTM Standards
- *Collect, organize, and describe data*
- *Make inferences and convincing arguments that are based on data analysis*

Math
Graphing
Calculating
Problem solving

Science
Environmental science
   habitats
     food chains and webs
Life science
   plants
   animals

Integrated Processes
Observing
Classifying
Collecting and recording data
Comparing and contrasting
Generalizing

Materials
For the class:
   leaf showing insect damage (see *Procedure 1*)
For each group of students:
   set of food chain cards (see *Management 1*)
Optional:
   extra 3 x 5 cards
   reference materials (see *Bibliography*)
   drawing materials

Background Information
The playground is a complete habitat with its own food chains and webs. Each plant and animal has a place on at least one chain and probably many more. In this activity, students will learn about the food chains and webs on the playground area they have been observing. They will also become more familiar with the terms *omnivore, carnivore, herbivore, consumer, producer,* and *decomposer.* Please refer to *The Inside Story: Food Chains; Producers and Consumers, Decomposers, Herbivores, Carnivores, Omnivores; Food Webs and Pyramids* for more detailed information about these relationships.

The plants and animals in this activity were chosen because they are fairly common on most playgrounds. Some may be similar to but not exactly the same species found in a particular area. Teachers and students are encouraged to add cards to the set, amend information to make it more accurate for a certain local species, or eliminate any cards that do not apply to the location being studied. As the cards are adapted to reflect the plants and animals the students are most familiar with, the games and activities will be even more effective. Keep in mind that predators such as the hawk and owl have broad territories and may feed on animals elsewhere who have found a meal on the playground. Thus they may be part of a playground food chain without ever visiting the school.

Food chains frequently overlap and are sometimes difficult to define clearly because of food preferences. An animal may eat a certain plant or animal only if its preferred food is not available. Some foods, such as ladybird beetles, may be eaten only occasionally because the predator finds out how terrible they taste and learns to leave them alone. The most typically preferred food choices are listed first in the "Eats" category of the consumer cards.

The lists on the cards reflect food chains known to exist. If the students observe a link in the chain that is not listed, it should be added to the extra cards. Local experts may also be able to provide more precise information concerning particular species.

Sometimes the feeding habits and food choices change with the life cycle. For example, a tadpole eats water plants (some also eat small water animals), but the adult frog is a carnivore, eating only insects and other animals. Plant-eating caterpillars become adult moths and butterflies who may eat nectar or nothing at all. For purposes of simplicity, the food chains in this activity reflect only the illustrated life stage of each animal.

Management

1. Mount the cards on construction paper or tagboard before cutting apart. Laminate if possible for greater durability. Mounting each complete set on a different color or pattern will help when stray cards are found or sets are mixed.
2. You may wish to reduce the size of the cards and make transparencies for the overhead projector instead of using a set taped or pinned to a board for demonstration purposes.
3. Students should work in groups of three or four for the initial activity.
4. You may wish to make a set of cards for each student to facilitate playing of games (also see *Home Link*).

Procedure

1. Use the overhead projector to show the class a leaf with evidence of insect damage. Ask them to list possible scenarios to explain the damage. If they are familiar with the Clue™ game, the questioning could follow that pattern: "I think the caterpillar did it in the area near the soccer field with its mouth."
2. Ask the students for ideas of ways they could find out who eats what in the playground habitat. Refer to evidence gathered in earlier lessons and list some of the clues the class has noticed.
3. Give each group of students a set of cards. Explain that the cards show some of the typical plants and animals on a school playground. Ask each group to sort the cards in any way they agree upon and share the thinking behind their decision. If no one chooses to sort according to *producer* or *consumer (or decomposer)*, or *omnivore, herbivore, carnivore*, discuss the categories they have chosen and then ask them to sort another way according to some of these categories. Use the opportunity to teach, discuss, and reinforce understanding of the terms.

4. Direct one student in each group to choose a card showing an insect or other invertebrate. Ask the other members to find another card that represents a plant or animal eaten by that animal. If the second card is also an animal, tell them to find one more card showing something that is eaten by the second animal, and so on. Then ask them to find (if possible) a card representing something that eats the first animal, continuing until the list is complete. Explain that what they have put together is called a *food chain*, showing what an organism eats as well as what it is eaten by.

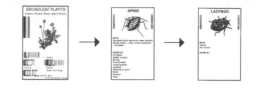

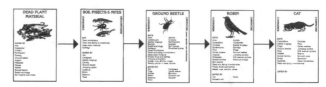

5. One at a time, list or display each group's food chain on the board (or overhead projector) where all can see. Ask the class to comment on similarities and differences. Be sure they notice that each chain begins with green plants and that the chains can be different lengths. Also call attention to the same organisms that appear in different chains. Ask the students to explain how something can be in several places, encouraging them to recognize that they also eat many different kinds of food coming from both plant and animal materials.
6. Challenge the class to look for relationships connecting two different chains. For example, a mouse eating a cricket in one chain could also eat grain in another chain or nuts in yet another. Use a marker or chalk to draw connections to show additional links among the food chains displayed. Explain that the whole process of who eats what is so interwoven that we call it a *food web*. A food chain can be thought of as simply one link of a food web.
7. Introduce another mystery: Who ate the caterpillar? Ask the students to go through the cards and pull out any that are possible suspects. Discuss which of these clues might lead to the most likely culprit(s), considering what they have observed on their playground.
8. Present yet another mystery: A hungry cricket has just arrived on the playground and is likely to stay. What food possibilities might have brought it there? Again, have the students display the cards showing possible choices. Have them put the cards in order to show what they think would most likely be eaten, based on the availability of that food type in the playground habitat.

9. Encourage the students to continue posing such mystery questions to the rest of their group until they are more familiar with the cards and demonstrate an understanding of the food chain relationships.

10 Choose from the following activities and games, both now and in the future, to give the students further practice in working with playground food chains.

Sorting and Classifying Activities

- Group in one-or two-circle Venn diagrams (depending upon the developmental level of the students). Some possible categories to start with include:

    One circle — producers; insects; carnivores; vertebrates …

    Two circles — herbivores/invertebrates; carnivores/vertebrates; mammals/omnivores …

- Organize the cards according to how many predators are listed for each organism. Arrange the cards to form a representational graph. Transfer the information to a graph of your own design. Organize the cards again to show the number of organisms eaten, graphing the data. Compare the results. Discuss the reasons that some cards are left out either way.
- Find as many chains as possible for two, three, four, five links. Graph the results.
- Make a dichotomous key using all the cards.
- Organize the cards as follows according to their shortest possible chain: producer; one link to producer (herbivores); two links to producers; three links to producers, and so forth. Display the data as a bar graph, a circle graph, or both.
- Set a specific time period and survey the playground, tallying the number of individuals spotted for each card. Organize the resulting data in a variety of ways.
- Encourage the students to come up with their own means of displaying the data in the cards.

Chain Gang
Two or three players
Rules similar to dominoes

Deal five cards to each player. Put the rest face down in a pile. Turn over the first card and place in the middle of the table for a starting point.

To play, the player must match the card with another next to it in a food chain, i.e. an organism that either eats or is eaten by the organism pictured. The card is placed touching either three-inch side of the starting card. If the player cannot play, he/she must draw from the pile until a card is drawn that can be played. The next player can match either card that has a three-inch side exposed.

The winner is whoever is out of cards first. If no more cards can be drawn and all players still have cards, the winner is whoever has the fewest cards left.

Web War
Two players
Rules similar to the card game "War"

All cards are dealt out evenly. Each player holds his or her cards face down in a stack. Each player turns over a card at the same time. If the organism pictured on one card is a consumer of the organism pictured on the other, the person holding that card gets both, adding them to the bottom of his or her stack. If the cards are from unrelated food chains, they go back to the bottom of each person's stack.

However, any time either of the spider cards or the daddy longlegs card comes up (not necessarily at the same time), a "Web War" is called. Both players stack two cards face down and a third card face up. If one is a consumer of the other, the person holding that card gets all the cards from that particular "Web War." If the two cards are unrelated, each player turns over one more card, and so on until the "war" is won.

Gain a Chain
Two to four players
Rules somewhat similar to the card game "Go Fish"

Deal five cards to each player. The remaining cards are put in a stack face down in the middle of the playing area. The goal is to connect as many food chains as possible before the cards in the pile are gone.

Each player in turn asks the person on his/her left for a specific card: "Do you have an earthworm?" If the player does, he or she must give the card to the person who asked. If he or she does not have the card, the response is "Find Food." In that case, the player who asked draws the top card from the pile.

The only time a second turn is earned is if the player draws the card he/she asked for. The card must be shown immediately, before being placed in the hand.

The game ends when someone is told to "Find Food" and takes the last card from the stack. Players organize their cards according to food chains. They get one point for every card that is in a food chain with just one other card; two points for every card in a chain with two others; three for each card in a chain with three others, and so forth. Each card can only be counted in one chain, so there is both strategy and math involved in determining which arrangement will result in the most points.

Variation: Cards are counted for points in every food chain connection that can be made in the player's hand. In this case, do not give points unless at least three links in the chain are present (lots of strategy; even more math).

Chain Builders
Two players or two teams
The opposing players try to build complete food chains.

Put all the cards face down in the center of the playing area. The first player or team draws one card

 © 1998 AIMS Education Foundation

and puts it face up where all can see. The other player or team does likewise. The game continues with the players or teams taking turn drawing cards. As each new card is drawn, the player or team lays it down with another card that could be in the same food chain. As the game progresses, the cards on each side can be rearranged to form different chains. When all the cards have been drawn, each player or team tries to arrange the cards on their side to form chains to give them the most possible points.

Scoring:
2 points each for cards in a complete food chain (from producer to highest-level consumer with no predators)
1 point each for cards in an incomplete food chain
0 points for isolated cards

Variation:
Use two decks of cards each with different backing material. Each team begins with its own deck. The teams take turns drawing cards one at a time but work together to build complete food chains. They may place cards in a chain begun by the other team as well as their own. Players may not move cards once they are placed in a food chain. The game ends when all cards have been drawn once.

Scoring (use different backing to determine ownership of cards)
1 point for each card correctly placed in a food chain, complete or incomplete
0 points for isolated cards
Subtract 1 point for a card placed in a chain where it doesn't belong

Consumer Concentration
Two to four players
The setup is like the traditional concentration game, but the matches are different.

Lay out the cards face down on the table in neat rows and columns. Each person in turn flips over two cards. If they are a "linking pair" — two cards that are next to each other in a food chain — the player picks up the cards to keep. If not, the cards are turned back face down. [Note: to be a linking pair, the two organisms may not have anything else on the food chain between them. A hawk and a mouse are a linking pair, but a hawk and grain are not.] If a linking pair is found, that player gets another turn. If not, it is the next player's turn.
The game ends when all the cards are gone or when all players agree that there are no more linking pairs left on the table. The winner is the player with the most cards.

A Web of Cards
Hand each student a single card (giving some thought to which cards are used) and form a living food web. Have the students face the center of the group with the producers near the center and the carnivores around the outside edge. You may wish to have a representation of the sun in the middle to remind students that producer plants get their energy from the sun and pass it along to everything that eats them.
Run pieces of yarn or string from each consumer to each of the organisms it consumes. When all the links are made, talk about the experience and how it feels to have so many connections. Carefully remove a single student and all his/her connections to see the impact of a single change.
Older students in particular may wish to lay down the strings and cards right where they were standing and move to the outside of the Web to get a different perspective.

More Games
Encourage the students to make up their own games to share, using the cards, adding to them, or designing something on their own.

Discussion
1. What were some of the most common categories suggested to sort the cards? What were some of the most unusual?
2. Which organisms seem to appear most often in the playground food chains? What reasons do you think might explain this? Which organisms don't seem to appear as frequently? Why do you think this is so?
3. Do you appear in the playground food chain? Is there anything on any of the cards that you might eat?
4. Which organisms seem to be the most picky eaters? Do you think this makes it easier or harder for them to survive on your playground? Explain.
5. Which organism is eaten by the most different kinds of consumers? How do you think it manages to survive when it is such a popular food?
6. Which producer is most common on your playground? How would the playground habitat be different if it no longer grew there?
7. Which animal is most common in your playground habitat? If it were no longer there, what plants would be affected? What other animals would be affected? Would they be able to survive without it? Give reasons for your answer.

Extension
Challenge the students to research and design cards for a different habitat or ecosystem, particularly one that is nearby or one that they have studied.

 © 1998 AIMS Education Foundation

Curriculum Correlation

Math

Use these cards to generate math problems: How many more omnivores than carnivores? What percent of the consumers are herbivores? Encourage the students to make up problems for others to solve.

Technology

Scan the cards into the computer so the students can organize them in different ways, or create food chains, and print the results.

Music

Learn "Food Chain Song." Make up different verses to illustrate other food chains.

Literature

Kitchen, Bert. *When Hunger Calls.* Candlewick Press. Cambridge, MA. 1994.
- Fascinating and unusual perspective on food chains focusing on 12 predators and the intriguing ways they capture their prey.

Lauber, Patricia. *Who Eats What?* HarperCollins. New York. 1995.
- Simple, clear explanation of food chains and webs emphasizing the position of humans at the top level. Especially good for younger learners.

Home Link

Make a set of cards for each student to take home to play the games with his or her family.

Terrarium Connection

What food chains are already present in the terrarium?

Which of the organisms in the terrarium are consumers? Which are producers? Which are decomposers? How do you know?

Which plants or animals might be safer in the terrarium because they are away from their natural predator(s)? Explain.

Have any of the plants or animals been eaten so far? What has been done to replace what has been eaten?

What substitute foods could you try to use instead of what might be found naturally in the playground habitat?

How do you think you might be able to tell if all of the critters are getting the food they need?

 © 1998 AIMS Education Foundation

ANT

CONSUMER

OMNIVORE (some species are HERBIVORES)

EATS (varies by species and location)
Fleshy fruits and berries
Grasses and grains
Soil insects
Dead and dying invertebrates

Caterpillars	Snails and slugs
Earthworms	Scarab beetles
Dead vertebrates	Garbage
Dead plant material	Crickets
Broadleaf plants	Isopods

Seeds, nuts, acorns, cones
Woody plants — trees, shrubs

EATEN BY

Daddy longlegs	Earthworm
Earwig	Frog
Ground beetle	Jumping spider
Mouse	Orb-weaver spider
Robin	Sparrow
Toad	

© 1998 AIMS Education Foundation

APHID

CONSUMER

HERBIVORE

EATS
Broadleaf plants (especially roses, plantain)
Woody plants — trees, shrubs (especially
  fruit trees)

EATEN BY
Centipede
Daddy longlegs
Earwig
Ground beetle
Jumping spider
Ladybug
Orb-weaver spider
Robin
Sparrow
Toad

© 1998 AIMS Education Foundation

CAT

CONSUMER

CARNIVORE

EATS

Mice	Flies
Sparrows	Garter snakes
Robins	Jumping spiders
Crickets	Screech owls
Frogs	Squirrels
Caterpillars	Daddy longlegs
Ground beetles	Orb-weaver spiders
Rabbits	Scarab beetles
Snails	Dead vertebrates
Dead and dying invertebrates	

EATEN BY

© 1998 AIMS Education Foundation

CATERPILLAR

CONSUMER

HERBIVORE

EATS
Broadleaf plants
Woody plants — trees, shrubs
Seeds, nuts, acorns, cones
Grasses and grains
Fleshy fruits and berries
Dead plant material

EATEN BY

Ant	Cat
Centipede	Earwig
Frog	Garter snake
Ground beetle	Jumping spider
Mouse	Raccoon
Robin	Screech owl
Sparrow	Squirrel
Toad	

© 1998 AIMS Education Foundation

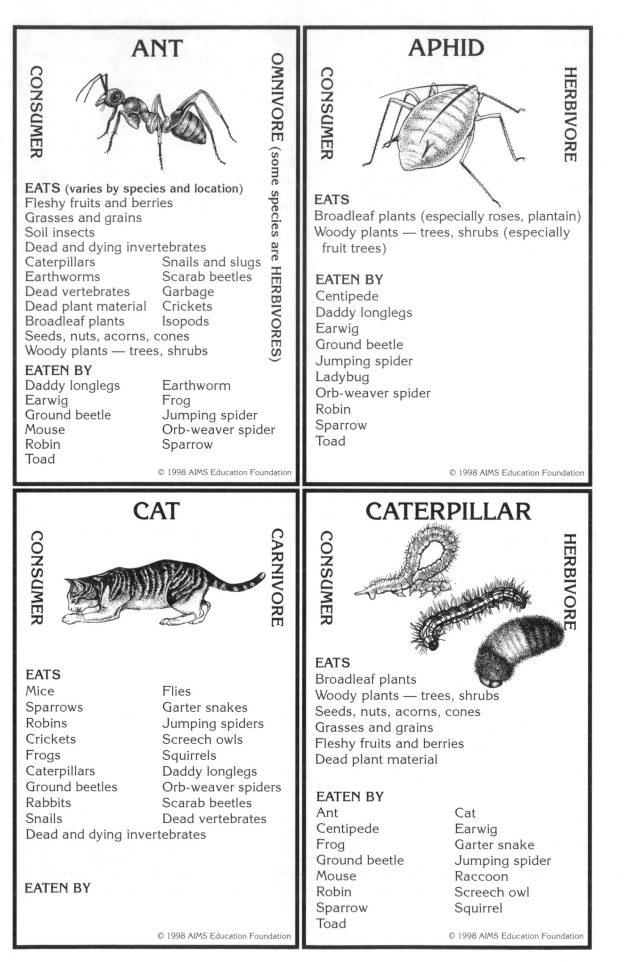

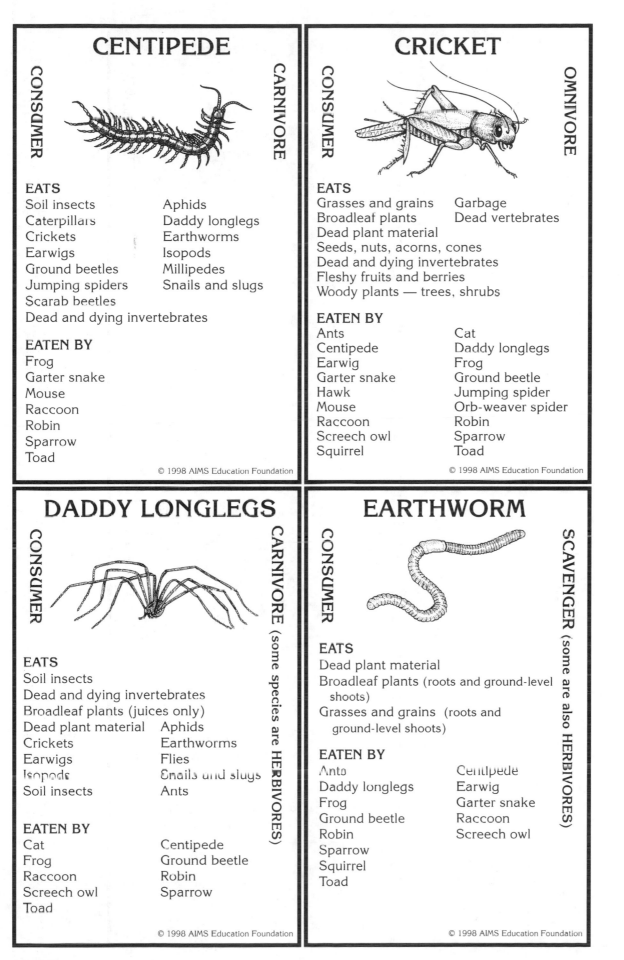

CENTIPEDE

CONSUMER

CARNIVORE

EATS

Soil insects
Caterpillars
Crickets
Earwigs
Ground beetles
Jumping spiders
Scarab beetles
Dead and dying invertebrates

Aphids
Daddy longlegs
Earthworms
Isopods
Millipedes
Snails and slugs

EATEN BY

Frog
Garter snake
Mouse
Raccoon
Robin
Sparrow
Toad

© 1998 AIMS Education Foundation

CRICKET

CONSUMER

OMNIVORE

EATS

Grasses and grains
Broadleaf plants
Dead plant material
Seeds, nuts, acorns, cones
Dead and dying invertebrates
Fleshy fruits and berries
Woody plants — trees, shrubs

Garbage
Dead vertebrates

EATEN BY

Ants
Centipede
Earwig
Garter snake
Hawk
Mouse
Raccoon
Screech owl
Squirrel

Cat
Daddy longlegs
Frog
Ground beetle
Jumping spider
Orb-weaver spider
Robin
Sparrow
Toad

© 1998 AIMS Education Foundation

DADDY LONGLEGS

CONSUMER

CARNIVORE (some species are HERBIVORES)

EATS

Soil insects
Dead and dying invertebrates
Broadleaf plants (juices only)
Dead plant material
Crickets
Earwigs
Isopods
Soil insects

Aphids
Earthworms
Flies
Snails and slugs
Ants

EATEN BY

Cat
Frog
Raccoon
Screech owl
Toad

Centipede
Ground beetle
Robin
Sparrow

© 1998 AIMS Education Foundation

EARTHWORM

CONSUMER

SCAVENGER (some are also HERBIVORES)

EATS

Dead plant material
Broadleaf plants (roots and ground-level shoots)
Grasses and grains (roots and ground-level shoots)

EATEN BY

Ants
Daddy longlegs
Frog
Ground beetle
Robin
Sparrow
Squirrel
Toad

Centipede
Earwig
Garter snake
Raccoon
Screech owl

© 1998 AIMS Education Foundation

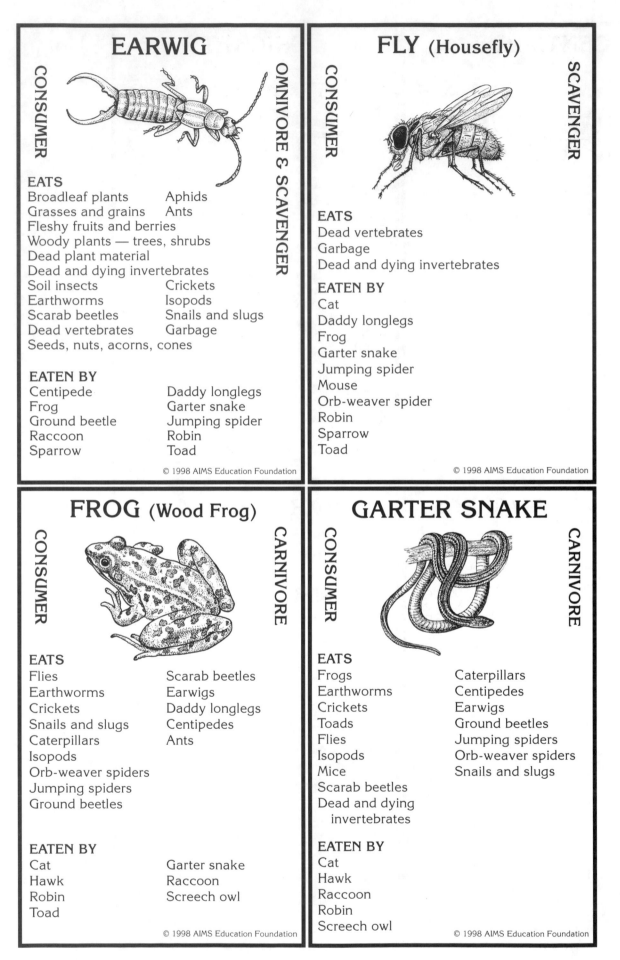

EARWIG

CONSUMER

OMNIVORE & SCAVENGER

EATS

Broadleaf plants	Aphids
Grasses and grains	Ants
Fleshy fruits and berries	
Woody plants — trees, shrubs	
Dead plant material	
Dead and dying invertebrates	
Soil insects	Crickets
Earthworms	Isopods
Scarab beetles	Snails and slugs
Dead vertebrates	Garbage
Seeds, nuts, acorns, cones	

EATEN BY

Centipede	Daddy longlegs
Frog	Garter snake
Ground beetle	Jumping spider
Raccoon	Robin
Sparrow	Toad

© 1998 AIMS Education Foundation

FLY (Housefly)

CONSUMER

SCAVENGER

EATS

Dead vertebrates
Garbage
Dead and dying invertebrates

EATEN BY

Cat
Daddy longlegs
Frog
Garter snake
Jumping spider
Mouse
Orb-weaver spider
Robin
Sparrow
Toad

© 1998 AIMS Education Foundation

FROG (Wood Frog)

CONSUMER

CARNIVORE

EATS

Flies	Scarab beetles
Earthworms	Earwigs
Crickets	Daddy longlegs
Snails and slugs	Centipedes
Caterpillars	Ants
Isopods	
Orb-weaver spiders	
Jumping spiders	
Ground beetles	

EATEN BY

Cat	Garter snake
Hawk	Raccoon
Robin	Screech owl
Toad	

© 1998 AIMS Education Foundation

GARTER SNAKE

CONSUMER

CARNIVORE

EATS

Frogs	Caterpillars
Earthworms	Centipedes
Crickets	Earwigs
Toads	Ground beetles
Flies	Jumping spiders
Isopods	Orb-weaver spiders
Mice	Snails and slugs
Scarab beetles	
Dead and dying invertebrates	

EATEN BY

Cat
Hawk
Raccoon
Robin
Screech owl

© 1998 AIMS Education Foundation

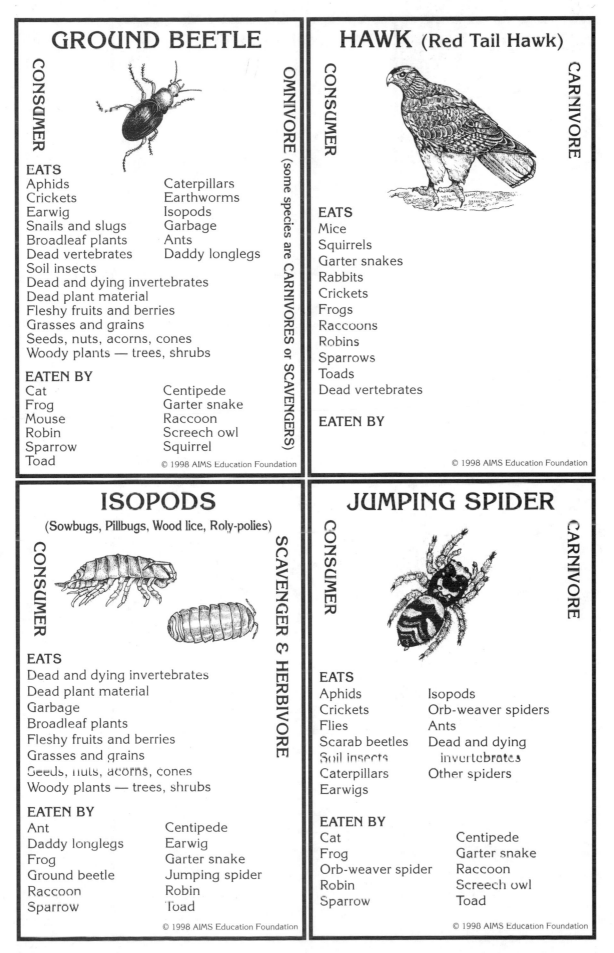

GROUND BEETLE

CONSUMER

OMNIVORE (some species are CARNIVORES or SCAVENGERS)

EATS

Aphids	Caterpillars
Crickets	Earthworms
Earwig	Isopods
Snails and slugs	Garbage
Broadleaf plants	Ants
Dead vertebrates	Daddy longlegs

Soil insects
Dead and dying invertebrates
Dead plant material
Fleshy fruits and berries
Grasses and grains
Seeds, nuts, acorns, cones
Woody plants — trees, shrubs

EATEN BY

Cat	Centipede
Frog	Garter snake
Mouse	Raccoon
Robin	Screech owl
Sparrow	Squirrel
Toad	

© 1998 AIMS Education Foundation

HAWK (Red Tail Hawk)

CONSUMER

CARNIVORE

EATS
Mice
Squirrels
Garter snakes
Rabbits
Crickets
Frogs
Raccoons
Robins
Sparrows
Toads
Dead vertebrates

EATEN BY

© 1998 AIMS Education Foundation

ISOPODS

(Sowbugs, Pillbugs, Wood lice, Roly-polies)

CONSUMER

SCAVENGER & HERBIVORE

EATS
Dead and dying invertebrates
Dead plant material
Garbage
Broadleaf plants
Fleshy fruits and berries
Grasses and grains
Seeds, nuts, acorns, cones
Woody plants — trees, shrubs

EATEN BY

Ant	Centipede
Daddy longlegs	Earwig
Frog	Garter snake
Ground beetle	Jumping spider
Raccoon	Robin
Sparrow	Toad

© 1998 AIMS Education Foundation

JUMPING SPIDER

CONSUMER

CARNIVORE

EATS

Aphids	Isopods
Crickets	Orb-weaver spiders
Flies	Ants
Scarab beetles	Dead and dying
Soil insects	invertebrates
Caterpillars	Other spiders
Earwigs	

EATEN BY

Cat	Centipede
Frog	Garter snake
Orb-weaver spider	Raccoon
Robin	Screech owl
Sparrow	Toad

© 1998 AIMS Education Foundation

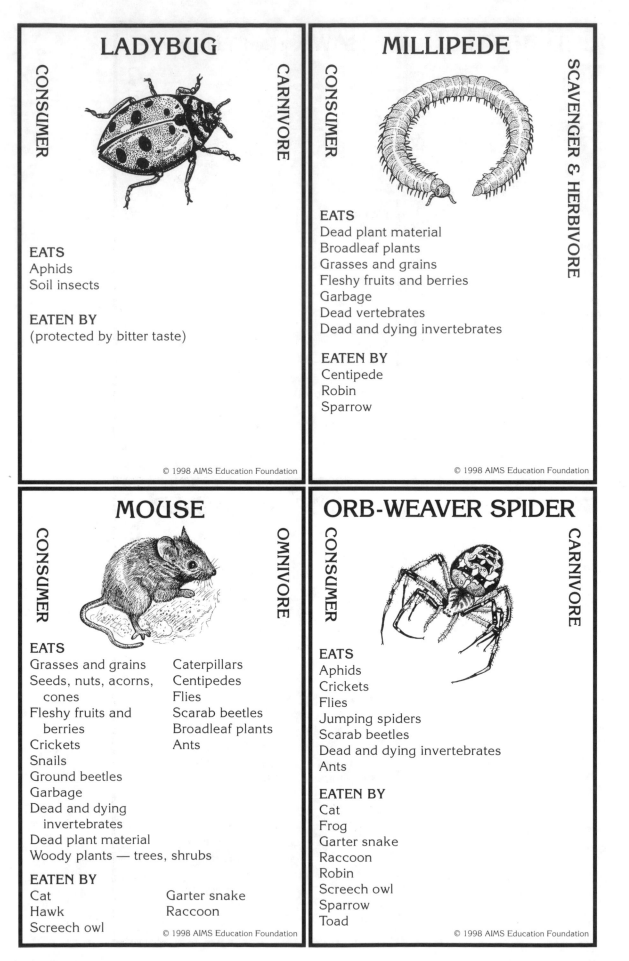

LADYBUG

CONSUMER · CARNIVORE

EATS
Aphids
Soil insects

EATEN BY
(protected by bitter taste)

© 1998 AIMS Education Foundation

MILLIPEDE

CONSUMER · SCAVENGER & HERBIVORE

EATS
Dead plant material
Broadleaf plants
Grasses and grains
Fleshy fruits and berries
Garbage
Dead vertebrates
Dead and dying invertebrates

EATEN BY
Centipede
Robin
Sparrow

© 1998 AIMS Education Foundation

MOUSE

CONSUMER · OMNIVORE

EATS
Grasses and grains
Seeds, nuts, acorns, cones
Fleshy fruits and berries
Crickets
Snails
Ground beetles
Garbage
Dead and dying invertebrates
Dead plant material
Woody plants — trees, shrubs
Caterpillars
Centipedes
Flies
Scarab beetles
Broadleaf plants
Ants

EATEN BY
Cat
Hawk
Screech owl
Garter snake
Raccoon

© 1998 AIMS Education Foundation

ORB-WEAVER SPIDER

CONSUMER · CARNIVORE

EATS
Aphids
Crickets
Flies
Jumping spiders
Scarab beetles
Dead and dying invertebrates
Ants

EATEN BY
Cat
Frog
Garter snake
Raccoon
Robin
Screech owl
Sparrow
Toad

© 1998 AIMS Education Foundation

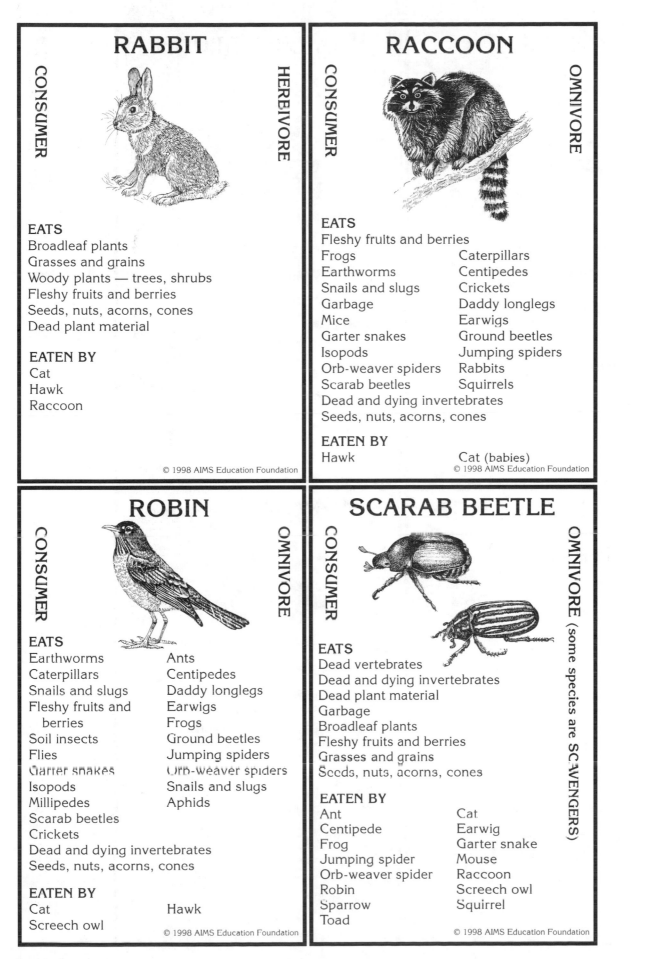

RABBIT

CONSUMER — HERBIVORE

EATS
Broadleaf plants
Grasses and grains
Woody plants — trees, shrubs
Fleshy fruits and berries
Seeds, nuts, acorns, cones
Dead plant material

EATEN BY
Cat
Hawk
Raccoon

© 1998 AIMS Education Foundation

RACCOON

CONSUMER — OMNIVORE

EATS
Fleshy fruits and berries
Frogs   Caterpillars
Earthworms   Centipedes
Snails and slugs   Crickets
Garbage   Daddy longlegs
Mice   Earwigs
Garter snakes   Ground beetles
Isopods   Jumping spiders
Orb-weaver spiders   Rabbits
Scarab beetles   Squirrels
Dead and dying invertebrates
Seeds, nuts, acorns, cones

EATEN BY
Hawk   Cat (babies)

© 1998 AIMS Education Foundation

ROBIN

CONSUMER — OMNIVORE

EATS
Earthworms   Ants
Caterpillars   Centipedes
Snails and slugs   Daddy longlegs
Fleshy fruits and   Earwigs
   berries   Frogs
Soil insects   Ground beetles
Flies   Jumping spiders
Garter snakes   Orb-weaver spiders
Isopods   Snails and slugs
Millipedes   Aphids
Scarab beetles
Crickets
Dead and dying invertebrates
Seeds, nuts, acorns, cones

EATEN BY
Cat   Hawk
Screech owl

© 1998 AIMS Education Foundation

SCARAB BEETLE

CONSUMER — OMNIVORE (some species are SCAVENGERS)

EATS
Dead vertebrates
Dead and dying invertebrates
Dead plant material
Garbage
Broadleaf plants
Fleshy fruits and berries
Grasses and grains
Seeds, nuts, acorns, cones

EATEN BY
Ant   Cat
Centipede   Earwig
Frog   Garter snake
Jumping spider   Mouse
Orb-weaver spider   Raccoon
Robin   Screech owl
Sparrow   Squirrel
Toad

© 1998 AIMS Education Foundation

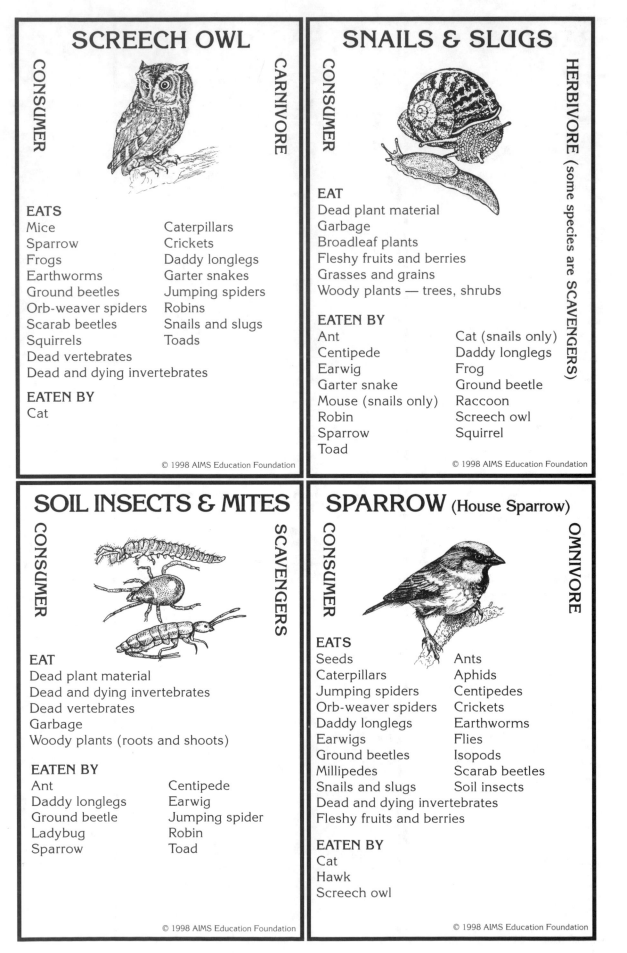

SCREECH OWL

CONSUMER

CARNIVORE

EATS

Mice
Sparrow
Frogs
Earthworms
Ground beetles
Orb-weaver spiders
Scarab beetles
Squirrels
Dead vertebrates
Dead and dying invertebrates

Caterpillars
Crickets
Daddy longlegs
Garter snakes
Jumping spiders
Robins
Snails and slugs
Toads

EATEN BY

Cat

© 1998 AIMS Education Foundation

SNAILS & SLUGS

CONSUMER

HERBIVORE (some species are SCAVENGERS)

EAT

Dead plant material
Garbage
Broadleaf plants
Fleshy fruits and berries
Grasses and grains
Woody plants — trees, shrubs

EATEN BY

Ant
Centipede
Earwig
Garter snake
Mouse (snails only)
Robin
Sparrow
Toad

Cat (snails only)
Daddy longlegs
Frog
Ground beetle
Raccoon
Screech owl
Squirrel

© 1998 AIMS Education Foundation

SOIL INSECTS & MITES

CONSUMER

SCAVENGERS

EAT

Dead plant material
Dead and dying invertebrates
Dead vertebrates
Garbage
Woody plants (roots and shoots)

EATEN BY

Ant
Daddy longlegs
Ground beetle
Ladybug
Sparrow

Centipede
Earwig
Jumping spider
Robin
Toad

© 1998 AIMS Education Foundation

SPARROW (House Sparrow)

CONSUMER

OMNIVORE

EATS

Seeds
Caterpillars
Jumping spiders
Orb-weaver spiders
Daddy longlegs
Earwigs
Ground beetles
Millipedes
Snails and slugs
Dead and dying invertebrates
Fleshy fruits and berries

Ants
Aphids
Centipedes
Crickets
Earthworms
Flies
Isopods
Scarab beetles
Soil insects

EATEN BY

Cat
Hawk
Screech owl

© 1998 AIMS Education Foundation

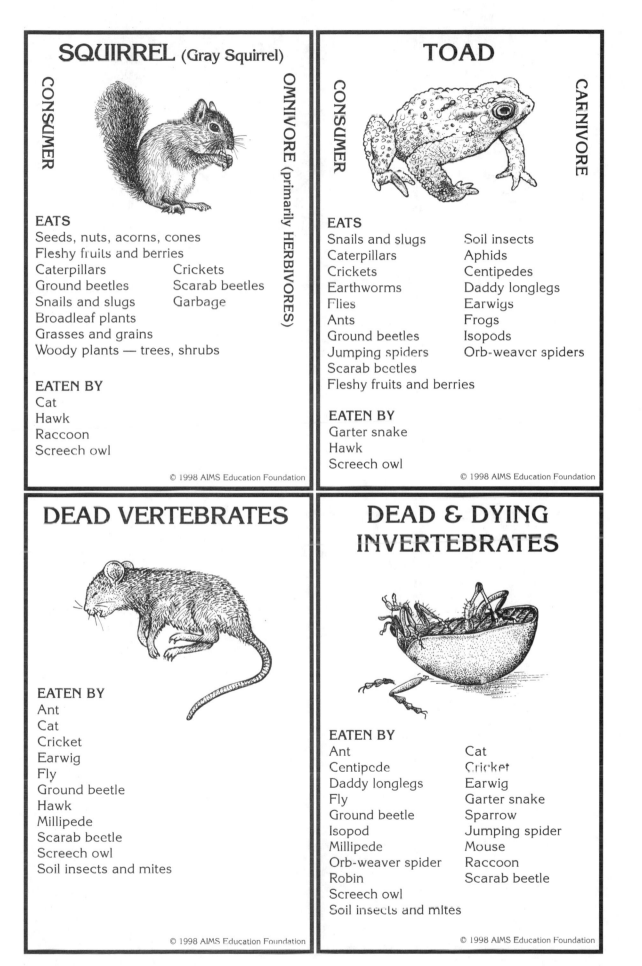

SQUIRREL (Gray Squirrel)

CONSUMER

OMNIVORE (primarily HERBIVORES)

EATS
Seeds, nuts, acorns, cones
Fleshy fruits and berries
Caterpillars   Crickets
Ground beetles   Scarab beetles
Snails and slugs   Garbage
Broadleaf plants
Grasses and grains
Woody plants — trees, shrubs

EATEN BY
Cat
Hawk
Raccoon
Screech owl

© 1998 AIMS Education Foundation

TOAD

CONSUMER

CARNIVORE

EATS
Snails and slugs   Soil insects
Caterpillars   Aphids
Crickets   Centipedes
Earthworms   Daddy longlegs
Flies   Earwigs
Ants   Frogs
Ground beetles   Isopods
Jumping spiders   Orb-weaver spiders
Scarab beetles
Fleshy fruits and berries

EATEN BY
Garter snake
Hawk
Screech owl

© 1998 AIMS Education Foundation

DEAD VERTEBRATES

EATEN BY
Ant
Cat
Cricket
Earwig
Fly
Ground beetle
Hawk
Millipede
Scarab beetle
Screech owl
Soil insects and mites

© 1998 AIMS Education Foundation

DEAD & DYING INVERTEBRATES

EATEN BY
Ant   Cat
Centipede   Cricket
Daddy longlegs   Earwig
Fly   Garter snake
Ground beetle   Sparrow
Isopod   Jumping spider
Millipede   Mouse
Orb-weaver spider   Raccoon
Robin   Scarab beetle
Screech owl
Soil insects and mites

© 1998 AIMS Education Foundation

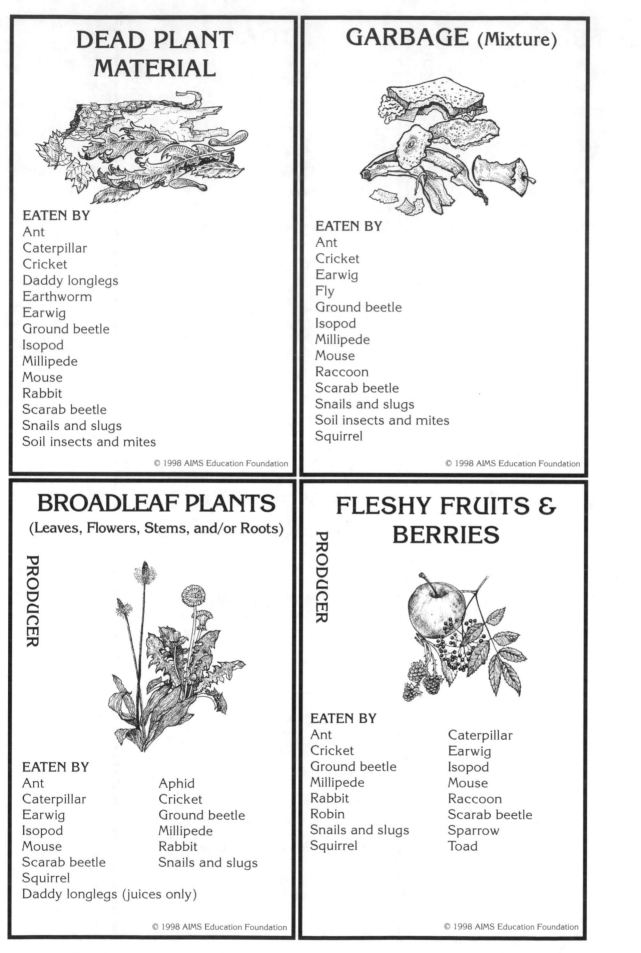

DEAD PLANT MATERIAL

EATEN BY
Ant
Caterpillar
Cricket
Daddy longlegs
Earthworm
Earwig
Ground beetle
Isopod
Millipede
Mouse
Rabbit
Scarab beetle
Snails and slugs
Soil insects and mites

© 1998 AIMS Education Foundation

GARBAGE (Mixture)

EATEN BY
Ant
Cricket
Earwig
Fly
Ground beetle
Isopod
Millipede
Mouse
Raccoon
Scarab beetle
Snails and slugs
Soil insects and mites
Squirrel

© 1998 AIMS Education Foundation

BROADLEAF PLANTS
(Leaves, Flowers, Stems, and/or Roots)

PRODUCER

EATEN BY

Ant	Aphid
Caterpillar	Cricket
Earwig	Ground beetle
Isopod	Millipede
Mouse	Rabbit
Scarab beetle	Snails and slugs
Squirrel	

Daddy longlegs (juices only)

© 1998 AIMS Education Foundation

FLESHY FRUITS & BERRIES

PRODUCER

EATEN BY

Ant	Caterpillar
Cricket	Earwig
Ground beetle	Isopod
Millipede	Mouse
Rabbit	Raccoon
Robin	Scarab beetle
Snails and slugs	Sparrow
Squirrel	Toad

© 1998 AIMS Education Foundation

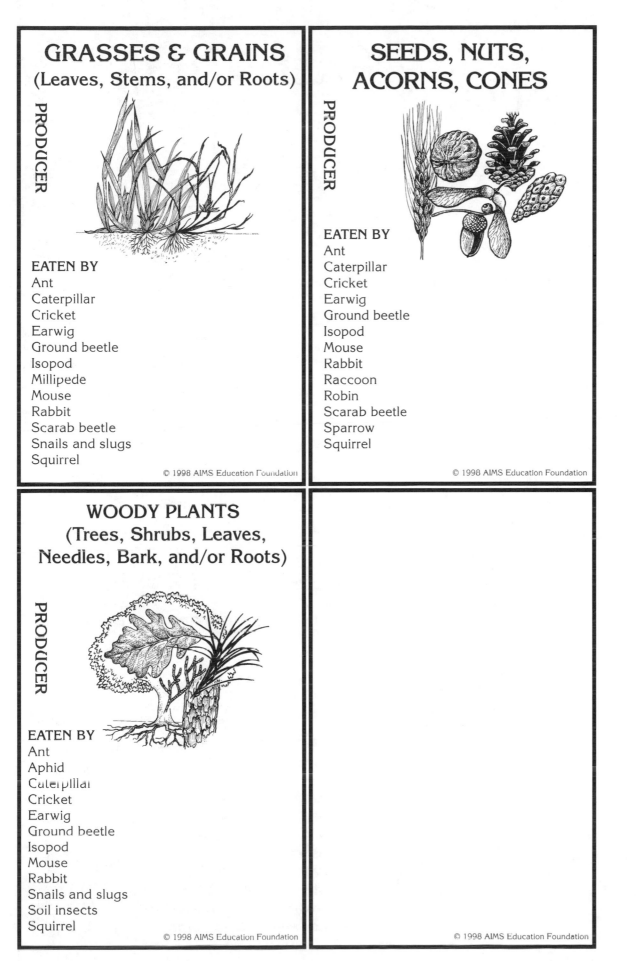

GRASSES & GRAINS
(Leaves, Stems, and/or Roots)

PRODUCER

EATEN BY
Ant
Caterpillar
Cricket
Earwig
Ground beetle
Isopod
Millipede
Mouse
Rabbit
Scarab beetle
Snails and slugs
Squirrel

© 1998 AIMS Education Foundation

SEEDS, NUTS, ACORNS, CONES

PRODUCER

EATEN BY
Ant
Caterpillar
Cricket
Earwig
Ground beetle
Isopod
Mouse
Rabbit
Raccoon
Robin
Scarab beetle
Sparrow
Squirrel

© 1998 AIMS Education Foundation

WOODY PLANTS
(Trees, Shrubs, Leaves, Needles, Bark, and/or Roots)

PRODUCER

EATEN BY
Ant
Aphid
Caterpillar
Cricket
Earwig
Ground beetle
Isopod
Mouse
Rabbit
Snails and slugs
Soil insects
Squirrel

© 1998 AIMS Education Foundation

© 1998 AIMS Education Foundation

Food Chain Song

Words by Suzy Gazlay

Tune: The Green Grass Grew All Around

There was a plant Grew in the ground, Put down some roots, Spread them a-round, And the roots took in wa-ter And the leaves made the food With en-er-gy that came from the sun, from the sun, With en-er-gy that came from the sun.

A tiny bug
With appetite
Munched on that plant
Both day and night,
And it nibbled the leaf,
The leaf from the plant
That made its own food
With energy that came from the sun,
   from the sun,
With energy that came from the sun.

A small green frog
With specks of brown
Spotted that bug
And gulped it down.
Yes, the frog ate the bug
That nibbled the leaf
The leaf from the plant
That made its own food
With energy that came
   from the sun, from the sun,
With energy that came
   from the sun.

Food Chain Song

A hungry snake
Lying in wait
Pounced on that frog:
It tasted great!
Yes, the snake ate the frog
That gobbled the bug
That nibbled the leaf
The leaf from the plant
That made its own food
With energy that came from the sun,
   from the sun,
With energy that came from the sun.

A red-tailed hawk
Was soaring by
It saw the snake,
Dove from the sky
Yes, the hawk ate the snake
That pounced on the frog
That gobbled the bug
That nibbled the leaf
The leaf from the plant
That made its own food
With energy that came from the sun,
   from the sun,
With energy that came from the sun.

The food chain tale
Is never done:
Sun's energy
Moves to each one:
To the hawk from the snake
To the snake from the frog
To the frog from the bug
To the bug from the leaf
That leaf from the plant
That made its own food
With energy that came from the sun,
   from the sun,
With energy that came from the sun.

Pizza Parts and Web Wheels

Topic
Food Chains and Webs

Key Question
From what parts of the food web do the ingredients in a pizza come?

Focus
People generally eat food that comes from all different parts of the food web. Food from every level of the web depends upon plants which use and store energy from sunlight.

Guiding Documents
Project 2061 Benchmarks
- Almost all kinds of animals' food can be traced back to plants.
- All organisms, including the human species, are part of and depend on two main interconnected global food webs. One includes microscopic ocean plants, the animals that feed on them, and finally the animals that feed on those animals. The other web includes land plants, the animals that feed on them, and so forth. The cycles continue indefinitely because organisms decompose after death to return food material to the environment.
- Food provides the fuel and the building material for all organisms. Plants use the energy from light to make sugars from carbon dioxide and water. This food can be used immediately or stored for later use. Organisms that eat plants break down the plant structures to produce the materials and energy they need to survive. Then they are consumed by other organisms.

NRC Standards
- All animals depend on plants. Some animals eat plants for food. Other animals eat animals that eat the plants.
- Populations of organisms can be categorized by the function they serve in an ecosystem. Plants and some micro-organisms are producers — they make their own food. All animals, including humans, are consumers, which obtain food by eating other organisms. Decomposers, primarily bacteria and fungi, are consumers that use waste materials and dead organisms for food. Food webs identify the relationships among producers, consumers, and decomposers in an ecosystem.

- For ecosystems, the major source of energy is sunlight. Energy entering ecosystems as sunlight is converted by producers into stored chemical energy through photosynthesis. It then passes from organism to organism in food webs.

Science
Environmental science
   habitats
   food webs
Life science
   plants
   animals

Integrated Processes
Observing
Classifying
Collecting and recording data
Comparing and contrasting
Applying
Generalizing
Inferring

Materials
For each student:
   web wheel pieces (see *Management 1*)
   paper fastener
   round cracker
   slice of pepperoni
   paper plate or paper towel
   plastic knife or craft stick

For each group of students:
   small cup of pizza sauce or plain tomato sauce
   small cup of shredded cheese

Optional for each group of students:
   a few pieces of green pepper, chopped
   a few sliced olive pieces

Optional for class:
   reference materials

Background Information
(See *The Inside Story: Food Chains, Producers and Consumers ...*, and *Food Webs and Pyramids*.)
   Some animals are omnivores that occupy several different places within the food web. For example, a bear's diet includes berries (plants), honey (product of plant-feeding insects), rodents (herbivores), and fish (herbivores, carnivores, or omnivores). A turtle may eat vegetation, insects, small fish, or frogs.

Most people also are omnivorous consumers who typically eat and receive energy from different locations within the food web. Some individuals or cultures may not eat food from every level, choosing not to consume scavengers, certain meat-eaters, or any kind of animal at all. Some may limit animal products to milk, eggs, and such. These foods still represent a place on the food chain ultimately leading to the consumption of plants by the animals from which they came.

It is important for students to see that food chains are based upon plants, that plants get their energy from the sun, and that this energy is passed along to each consumer on the chain. Deeper understanding of the intricacies of the food web will come with additional experience and information as the students mature.

This activity is designed to heighten the students' awareness of the components of food chains and webs and of their own position as consumers at various levels.

Management

1. If possible, duplicate each wheel of the web on a different color of paper or cardstock. Use yellow for the sun.
2. If there is access to an oven or toaster oven, you may wish to use English muffins instead of crackers and make the pizzas on a larger scale, or actually construct full-size pizzas.
3. For simplicity and the purposes of this activity, it is better not to use mushrooms which are not green plants.
4. Also for simplicity, emphasize the main ingredient of each component. Older students and those with extensive food chain experience may wish to take into account some of the lesser ingredients (animal or vegetable shortening, sugar, spices, etc.).
5. Read the ingredient labels to determine what type of grain was used to make the crackers and whether you have pork-based pepperoni. Adapt the pizza web wheel to reflect these and any additional ingredients you use.
6. It may be helpful to make a demonstration model web wheel from transparencies to use on the overhead projector.

Procedure

1. Ask the students to reflect upon what the word *consumer* now means to them. Guide the discussion to remind them that *consumer* means someone who uses something up.
2. Generate an informal list of different ways humans consume various substances and materials. Help the students differentiate between *consumption* and *waste;* a certain level of consumption is necessary for survival! Be sure the students recognize that they are consumers simply because they eat.
3. Invite the students to think about eating a hamburger and to list the ingredients in a typical burger. Ask them to reflect on what they have learned regarding food chains and extend the list

of each ingredient back to the producer level. Review and clarify the roles of *consumer, producer, carnivore, herbivore, omnivore.*

grass → cow → me

lettuce → me

4. Ask the students where they can find clues to help them know what food chains they become a part of whenever they eat a meal [package ingredients, reference materials]. List and trace the food chains of several familiar foods or meals suggested by the students. Discuss similarities and differences.
5. Explain to the class that they will be looking closely at some food chains of which they are a part. Direct them to assemble the Web Wheel, pointing out that they are represented by the pizza-eating person in the center.
6. Tell the students to write *grass* in a box on the producer level and *cow* in a box at the herbivore level. Demonstrate the use of the wheel by asking them to turn it to show from where hamburger comes, lining up the pointer to *skip* the carnivore level and point to cow, grass, and sun. Explain that they will be analyzing the different ingredients of a pizza, looking for clues to show where each one fits into a food chain.
7. Distribute a cracker to each student. Ask the students to identify its main ingredient [i.e., wheat] and where it came from [wheat plant]. Have them add *wheat* to the producer level and adjust the wheel to show the consumer pointing directly to the wheat. They will need to skip directly to the plant level, which they can do by setting the pizza pointer at the *skip level* notches on the other levels. Explain that most people are omnivores who can consume directly from any of the levels (see *Extensions*).
8. Ask them to spread the cracker with pizza sauce. Again, discuss the source of the sauce [tomatoes, a producer], turning the wheel to the appropriate places and adding information as needed.
9. Similarly, add shredded cheese [milk product from cow, grass] to the pizza; then pepperoni [pork, fed on grain]; then green peppers [plant] and olives [plant] if you wish, adjusting and adding to the web wheel and discussing the food chain each time.

10. As the students enjoy eating the pizza, question them regarding what they have noticed about the food chains of pizza ingredients. Ask for examples of other food chains and work together to fill in missing gaps. (Some research may be necessary.)

Discussion

1. What similarities did you notice each time you traced a food chain? [each one eventually led back to a plant] Would you agree with the statement that all food for all animals (including people) comes from green plants? Defend your answer. Can you think of any food that can't be traced back to a green plant?
2. Could any of these food chains exist without sunlight? Why is the sunlight so important?
3. What are some other ingredients that could go on your pizza? Where would they fit in a food chain? Can you think of anything for your pizza that has a food chain four links or longer?
4. When you finished making your pizza, what kind of leftovers were there? What will happen to these leftovers? What other organisms might end up using them?
5. Could the animals found on your playground be part of any of the food chains connected to your pizza? Explain. How could you find out?
6. Where do you think people fit on the food chain in general? Would you say that people are "top-level consumers"? Explain.

Extensions

1. In addition to eating herbivores such as cows, many people eat omnivores and carnivores too. For example, a chicken could be at either the carnivore or herbivore level because it eats both insects and grain. What other food chains could be added to the web wheel that would include each of the levels?
2. Write new verses of the *Food Chain Song* for different food chains.
3. Try to design a menu in which all the ingredients are from the same level of the food chain.
4. Pick other multiple-ingredient food items and design or adapt a web wheel to show the food chains involved.

Curriculum Correlation

Music
   Sing the song "I Know an Old Lady Who Swallowed a Fly" and discuss whether this represents a food chain.

Literature
   Powell, Consie. *A Bold Carnivore*. Roberts Rinehart Publishers. Niwot, CO. 1995.
   • A different predator, surrounded by some of its prey, is portrayed for each letter of the alphabet.

Home Link

   Trace each of the main parts of your dinner through the food web to its plant source.

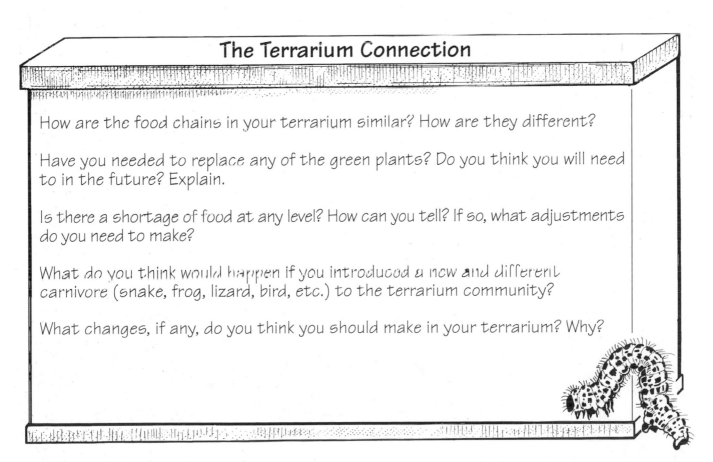

The Terrarium Connection

How are the food chains in your terrarium similar? How are they different?

Have you needed to replace any of the green plants? Do you think you will need to in the future? Explain.

Is there a shortage of food at any level? How can you tell? If so, what adjustments do you need to make?

What do you think would happen if you introduced a new and different carnivore (snake, frog, lizard, bird, etc.) to the terrarium community?

What changes, if any, do you think you should make in your terrarium? Why?

Pizza Parts and Web Wheels

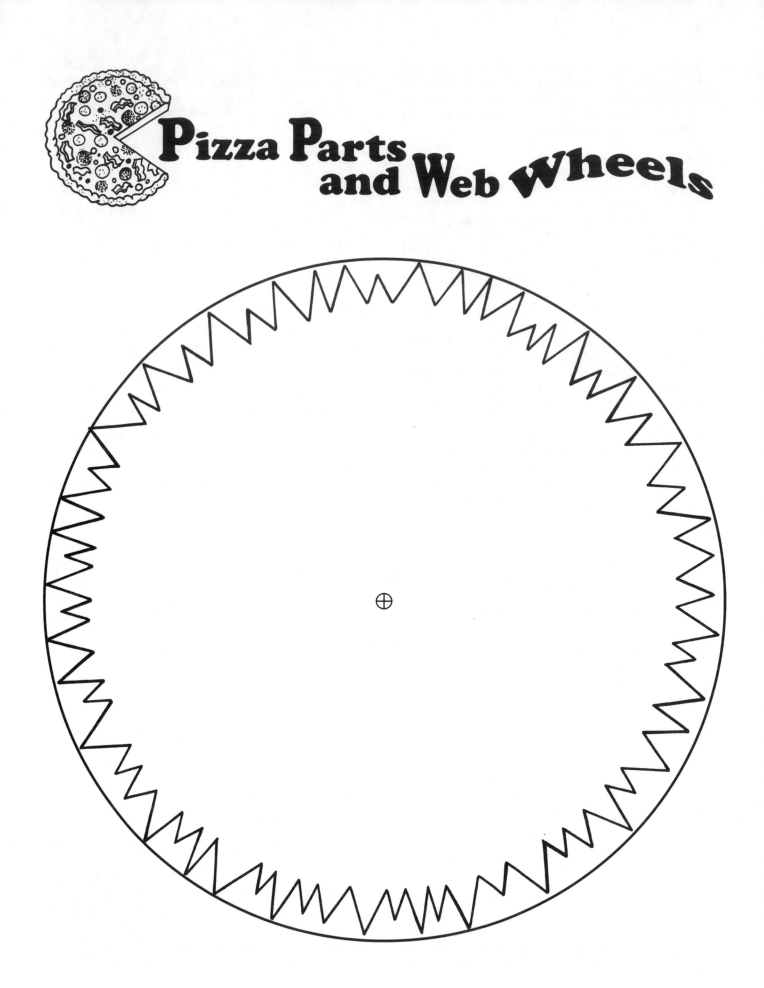

 © 1998 AIMS Education Foundation

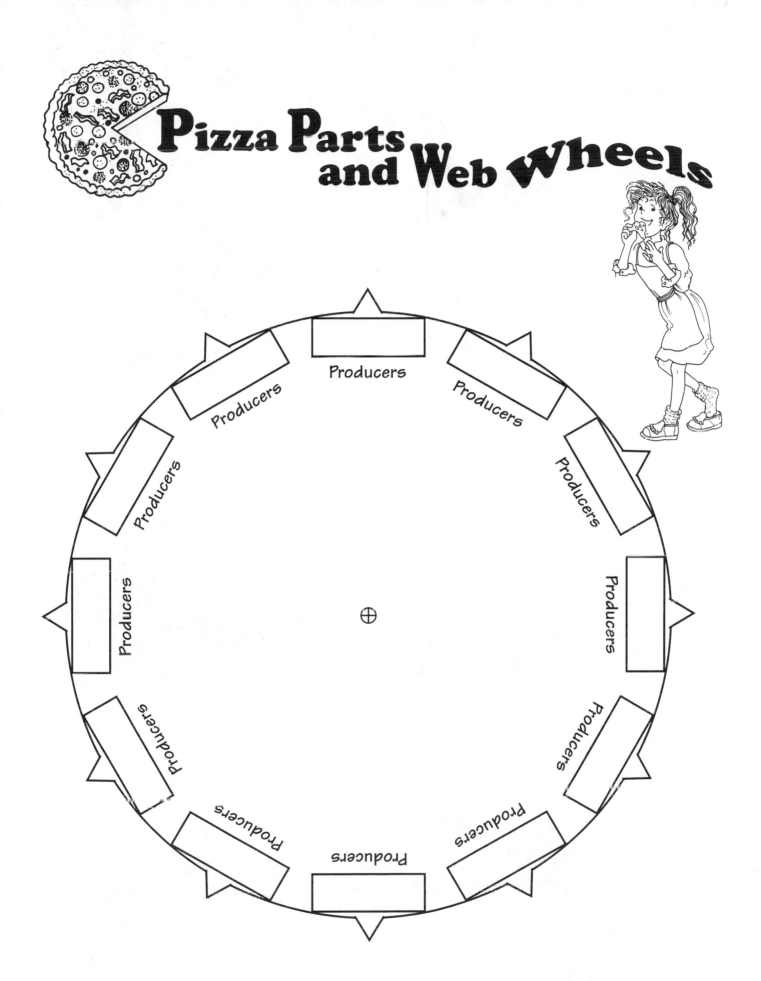

Pizza Parts and Web Wheels

Producers

Producers

Producers

Producers

Producers

Producers

Producers

Producers

Producers

Producers

Producers

Producers

⊕

Pizza Parts and Web Wheels

© 1998 AIMS Education Foundation

Pizza Parts and Web Wheels

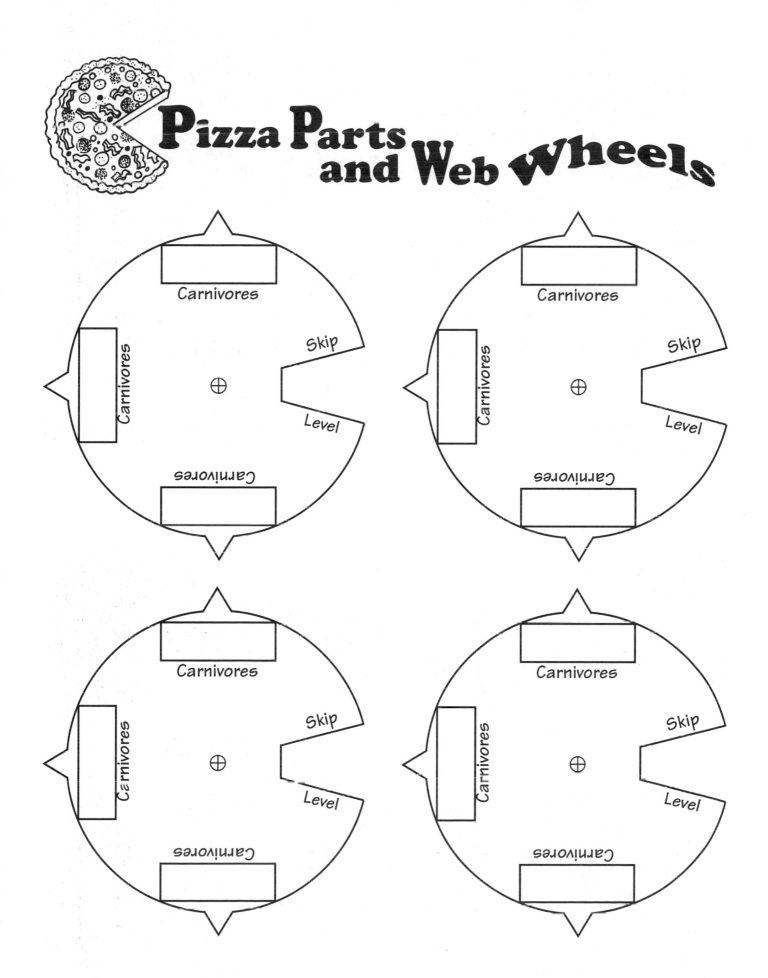

Pizza Parts and Web Wheels

Producing a Producer

Topic
Producers

Key Question
How can I grow a producer that I can eat?

Focus
Green plants are producers. Producers are the basis of the food web. Producers are a significant part of what people eat.

Guiding Documents
Project 2061 Benchmarks
- *Most food comes from farms either directly as crops or as the animals that eat the crops. To grow well, plants need enough warmth, light, and water. ...*
- *Almost all kinds of animals' food can be traced back to plants.*

NRC Standards
- *All animals depend on plants. Some animals eat plants for food. Other animals eat animals that eat the plants.*
- *Populations of organisms can be categorized by the function they serve in an ecosystem. Plants and some micro-organisms are producers — they make their own food. All animals, including humans, are consumers, which obtain food by eating other organisms...*

NCTM Standard
- *Make and use measurements in problems and everyday situations*

Math
Measurement
    length
Averages

Science
Environmental science
    food chains and webs
Life science
    plants

Integrated Processes
Observing
Classifying
Collecting and recording data
Comparing and contrasting
Applying
Generalizing

Materials
For the class:
    household bleach
    disposable gloves

For each group of students:
    one teaspoon alfalfa seed (see *Management 1*)
    Mason jar with ring part of lid (see *Management 2*)
    12 x 12 cm piece of plastic screen (see *Management 3*)
    2-4 slices of bread, whole-grain preferred (see *Management 9*)
    teaspoon measure
    several spoonfuls of margarine
    paper plates
    paper towels
    plastic knife or craft stick
    hand lenses
    long forceps, tweezers, or toaster tongs

Optional for each group:
    box or pan or old towel (see *Management 4*)
    peeled cucumber slices or other plant sandwich ingredients (see *Procedure 8*)
    DiscoveryScope®

Background Information
All people and animals depend on plants to survive. Producers including green plants and certain microscopic ocean organisms are essential because they make their own food, in the process storing energy from the sun. If the producer is eaten, a portion of its stored energy is passed on to the consumer or consumers along the food chain. (Please refer to *The Inside Story: Food Chains; Producers and Consumers ...; Food Webs and Pyramids*.)

In this activity, students grow and eat alfalfa sprouts. In recent years, sprouted alfalfa seeds have gained popularity for human consumption, most often in salads and sandwiches. Alfalfa is also an important crop grown for animal feed, usually in the form of hay, silage, or meal, as well as for grazing. It is a very high source of chlorophyll and is rich in vitamins, minerals, and protein. Alfalfa is valued as a health food and is used in various folk remedies.

Important

Sprouts — as well as any food grown in the classroom to eat — must be handled properly to prevent possible health problems. Plants grown in unsanitary conditions can develop potentially harmful bacteria cultures as they sit in water at room temperature.

Please be sure that the following guidelines are followed:
- Students must always have clean hands (with soap) while handling seeds, sprouts, and equipment.
- Prepare a solution consisting of one part household bleach and nine parts water. Mix a new solution each day it is needed.
- The teacher and students who are using the solution should wear disposable gloves.
- Clean all equipment and surfaces with bleach solution and a clean towel.
- Be sure the bleach solution is used as noted on the student page, both before sprouting the seeds and before eating the sprouts.

Management

1. Alfalfa seed for sprouting can be purchased at a health food store. Radish seeds may be substituted, but they have a spicier taste.
2. Any jar that fits a Mason lid can be used. A 12-16 oz jar is recommended.
3. Plastic screen is the easiest and most sanitary for this setup. Nylon netting may also be used.
4. Jars need to rest at an angle with the lid end down while the seeds are sprouting. Prop them up in a box or along rolled towels placed on a counter or shelf.
5. It usually takes three to five days for the sprouts to grow to eating size. It may take longer if your classroom is cold. Rinsing with lukewarm water (80-90°F) may increase the rate of growth.
6. Start soaking the seeds early Monday morning in order to have the maximum crop to use by Friday. You may wish to soak the seeds Sunday night in order to get a head start. Sprouts left unrinsed over a weekend are liable to dry out or mold.
7. The students should rinse and drain the sprouting seeds at least once a day without touching them.
8. Younger students who are not yet calculating averages should simply measure the sprouts.
9. Choose bread with all-plant ingredients. Use of multi-grain bread, especially with visible grain, seeds or raisins, will add to the discussion.
10. Sandwiches may be made and shared by small groups or partners, as you wish.

Procedure

1. Ask the students to think about plants (fruits, vegetables, nuts, seeds, etc.) they like to eat and list their responses. Have them consider where the plants came from before they reached home, cafeteria, restaurant, or market. Encourage students who have helped grow their own food to share their experiences.
2. Challenge the students to think of foods that are not plants but are made from plants (for example: bread, margarine, fruit drinks, catsup, cookies, crackers, cereals). Discuss what the students may already know about why fruits, vegetables, and foods made from grains and other plant parts are important for us to eat.
3. Remind the students that producers are the only living things that can make their own food. Emphasize that plants use and store energy from the sun, *producing* their own food, and that other living things, like us, get some of that energy by eating (*consuming*) the plant. Encourage the students to use the terms *producer* and *consumer* in their discussion.
4. Tell the students that they will be growing a producer that they will be able to eat in a few days. Distribute the materials and have each group follow the directions on the *Sprouting Seeds* page.
5. Each day have the students rinse and drain the sprouts. Once sprouting begins, direct them to use forceps to pull out three representative sprouts and measure them. If appropriate, have them calculate the average length of the sprouts each day. Have them use a magnifying lens to focus on a single sprout and draw what they see. Discard sprouts that have been removed from the jar.
6. Ask the students to think and talk about the mystery that is unfolding as they watch the seeds sprout and grow. Guide the discussion to help them understand that plants, like all living things, need energy in order to grow. Encourage them to wonder from where that energy is coming [sunlight whose energy was stored in seed from parent plant].
7. Ask the students if they have eaten alfalfa sprouts or seen them used as food or sold in stores as ingredients for sandwiches and salads. Discuss what other ingredients they could use to make a sandwich consisting entirely of producers.
8. On the designated sandwich day, rinse and drain the sprouts as directed. Distribute the ingredients and let the students make All-Producer Sandwiches. As they *consume* the *producers*, have them list all the different plants being eaten. Be sure they include the main ingredients from the bread and margarine packaging. Talk about where each different item originally comes from.

Discussion

1. What are your favorite plants to eat? Do the others in your class agree? What similarities and differences do you see in the favorites mentioned?
2. Think about a typical lunch from a fast food restaurant. Which foods, if any, are made completely from producers? [Note: at many fast food locations, students can ask for a pamphlet listing all the ingredients. They can look to find out such things as whether the fries are fried in vegetable oil or animal-based lard.]
3. If you were planning a whole day's meals to include only producers and foods made from producers, which ones would you choose? Give reasons for your choices.
4. What did you find most surprising or interesting about watching your sprouts grow?

5. Did your sprouts grow at a steady rate or were there certain days that they grew more than others? What reasons can you think of to explain the growth patterns you see?

6. How did the length (or average length) of your sprouts compare to those of your classmates? What might account for the similarities or differences?

7. Since all living things need energy in order to live and grow, where are the alfalfa sprouts getting the energy they need? Where do you get the energy you need?

8. What are some ways that knowing about producers can help you make good choices about foods to buy and eat?

9. What other living things would also enjoy eating the producers you ate today?

Extensions

1. Try sprouting birdseed, millet, mung beans, or other kinds of seeds. A variety of seeds to sprout and eat are available at health food stores. Use a hand lens to compare the different sprouts.

2. Plan, plant, and grow a vegetable garden at school. Enjoy the harvest!

3. Analyze full-page grocery ads from the newspaper to discover how many of the edible items are producers or are made from producers.

4. Plan an entire class feast using only food made from producers.

5. For more activities involving plants and plant growth, see *Primarily Plants* (K-3) and *The Budding Botanist* (3-6), both published by AIMS. Also see the activity, *Plant Food*, in AIMS (Vol. X, No. 7).

Curriculum Correlation

Music (see *Bibliography*)

1. Do the *Plant Parts Food Rap* (*AIMS*, Vol. X, No. 7).

2. Sing "Dirt Made My Lunch" and "Roots, Stems, Leaves, Flowers, Fruits, and Seeds" on the tape *Dirt Made My Lunch* (Banana Slug String Band).

3. For a light-hearted extension, learn the song "Birdseed" on the tape/CD *Almost Grown* by Anne Dodson.

Technology:

Find out more about alfalfa by doing a Web search on the Internet using *alfalfa* as a search word.

Literature

Cole, Henry. *Jack's Garden*. Greenwillow. New York. 1995.

* Based on "This is the House that Jack Built" language pattern; border drawings bring out the elements of the garden habitat at various stages of its development.

Gardiner, John Reynolds. *Top Secret*. Little, Brown, and Company. Boston. 1984.

* A fourth grader's science fair project about finding the secret of photosynthesis takes some interesting turns as he becomes a plant himself. Valid information is woven into an entertaining story.

Home Link

Think about different ways that sprouts could be included in meals at home. Look in cookbooks for recipe ideas and try some of them out. Grow your own sprouts at home for your family to eat.

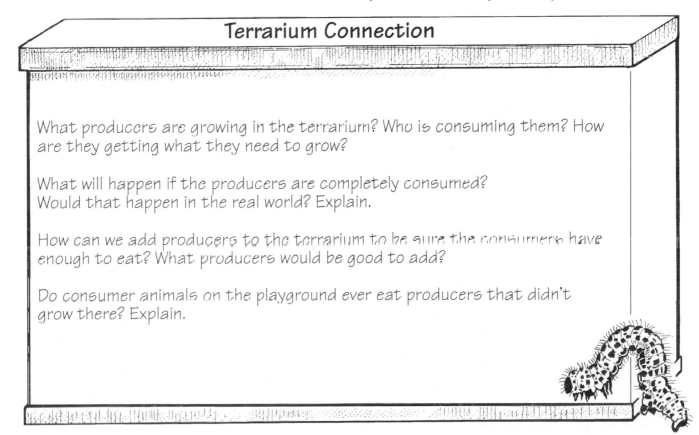

Terrarium Connection

What producers are growing in the terrarium? Who is consuming them? How are they getting what they need to grow?

What will happen if the producers are completely consumed? Would that happen in the real world? Explain.

How can we add producers to the terrarium to be sure the consumers have enough to eat? What producers would be good to add?

Do consumer animals on the playground ever eat producers that didn't grow there? Explain.

Producing a Producer

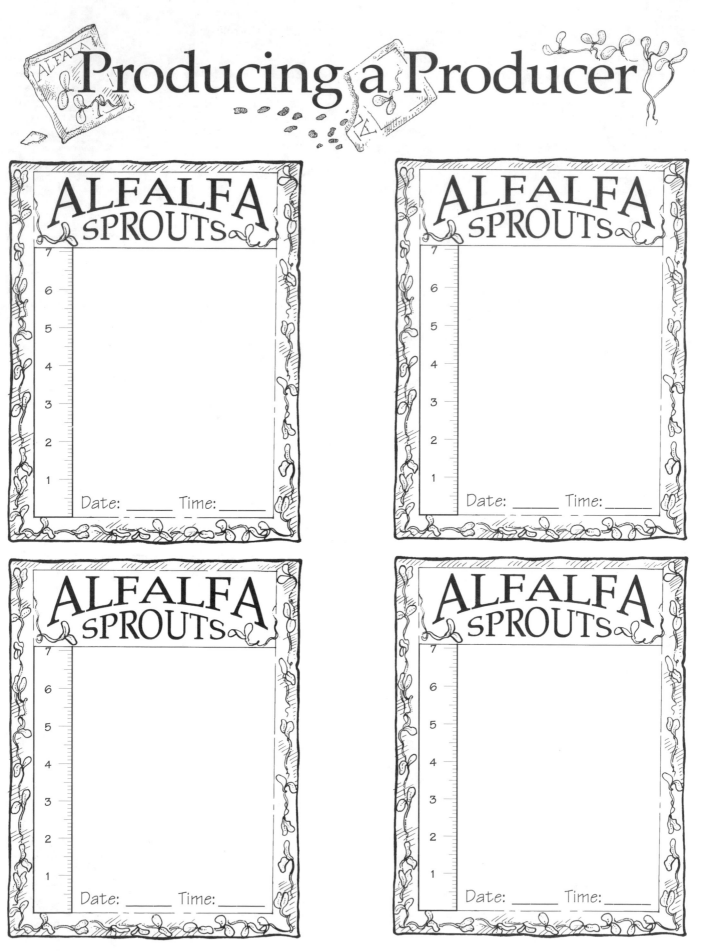

ALFALFA SPROUTS

7
6
5
4
3
2
1

Date: _____ Time: _____

ALFALFA SPROUTS

7
6
5
4
3
2
1

Date: _____ Time: _____

ALFALFA SPROUTS

7
6
5
4
3
2
1

Date: _____ Time: _____

ALFALFA SPROUTS

7
6
5
4
3
2
1

Date: _____ Time: _____

Producing a Producer

Sprouting Seeds

Always wash your hands with soap before handling seeds, sprouts, or equipment.

1. Fill a clean jar 1/4 full of bleach solution. Carefully swish the solution around to wet the sides. Add 1 teaspoonful of seeds to the solution.

2. Cover the jar with a 12 cm X 12 cm piece of screen or net. Hold in place by tightening the ring part of the lid over the screen.

3. After 1 minute, strain out the bleach solution. (Don't remove the lid!). Rinse the seeds under running water for another minute. Fill the jar halfway with clean water and let seeds soak for 3 to 6 hours. Drain again.

4. Tilt the jar at an angle with the screen down. Support it against the side of a container or with a rolled-up towel to keep the angle and prevent it from falling.

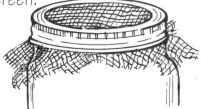

5. Each day, use forceps to carefully remove three sprouts to measure and draw. Replace the lid, fill the jar with water, and gently swirl the water inside the jar. Drain off the water and return the jar to rest at an angle, screen down.

6. When the sprout crop is ready to harvest, rinse thoroughly with bleach solution, drain, rinse again very well with cold water, drain, eat, and enjoy!

Buffet Lunch

Topic
Consumers

Key Questions
How can we find out if some herbivores prefer certain plants and refuse to eat others?

Focus
Some plant-eating animals may eat only certain foods, while others will eat nearly anything that is available.

Guiding Documents
Project 2061 Benchmarks
- *A lot can be learned about plants and animals by observing them closely, but care must be taken to know the needs of living things and how to provide for them in the classroom.*
- *Animals eat plants or other animals for food and may also use plants (or even other animals) for shelter and nesting.*
- *People can often learn about things around them by just observing those things carefully, but sometimes they can learn more by doing something to the things and noting what happens.*

NRC Standards
- *Plan and conduct a simple investigation.*
- *Employ simple equipment and tools to gather data and extend the senses.*
- *Organisms have basic needs. For example, animals need air, water, and food; plants require air, water, nutrients, and light. Organisms can survive only in environments, and distinct environments support the life of different types of organisms.*

NCTM Standard
- *Make and use measurements in problems and everyday situations*

Math
Measurement
   length

Science
Environmental science
   habitats
      food chains and webs
Life science
   plants
   animals

Integrated Processes
Observing
Predicting
Collecting and recording data
Comparing and contrasting
Applying
Generalizing
Inferring

Materials
For each group of students:
   (see directions for *Buffet Box Construction*)
For the class:
   an area for collecting plant and animal specimens
   collecting containers with lids
   paper plate
Optional:
   hand lenses and/or DiscoveryScope®

Background Information
Some consumers are quite selective and depend upon the availability of a certain type of food to survive. For example, koalas and pandas will die if they run out of the bamboo they eat; monarch caterpillars eat only milkweed. Some animals will choose favorite foods among several acceptable possibilities. Some are partial to a certain plant or plants but are able to fall back on other choices if the first preference is not available. Others, like the destructive locust, are far less particular and will eat almost anything green and growing that they find in their path.

Students may wonder if an animal ever gets tired of eating "the same old thing." In their own experience, their enthusiasm for a favorite food may wane if it is the only choice day after day. They may want to know if a "picky eater" critter will accept a more varied diet than one or two items.

How is it possible to tell what a certain animal will eat? This can be a vital question when caring for terrarium animals. For herbivores, a good plan is to be sure to collect specimens of whatever plant the animal was found on or near when it was collected, and to keep that plant in supply. Be aware that the animal may have been feeding on something beside the most obvious plants in the habitat where it was collected. The Buffet Box provides a way to offer choices while not eliminating a plant that is a known food source. It can be adapted to offer as many different choices as the student wishes, and substitutions can be made throughout the investigation.

Keeping critters in the classroom implies taking responsibility for their well-being. Be sure the students monitor closely to see that each creature is eating.

Management

1. Plan ahead with a selected student for the mystery in *Procedure 1*. Choose a sandwich that he or she likes, but one that is not a general favorite among all students, or that contains an unpopular ingredient. Have the student bring the sandwich to school with several bites taken from it. This should be a well-kept secret.
2. Buffet Boxes are particularly well-suited for caterpillars but will also work for other plant-eating animals. If you are using snails, slugs, or other potential cardboard-eaters, keep the Buffet Box under surveillance and return the critters to an escape-proof container overnight. Use only one type of critter in each box.
3. Have the students work in groups of four to six to build the Buffet Box and plan their experiment. You may wish to have an adult make the necessary cuts.
4. The Buffet Box should be set up before the animals are captured. As animals are found, also collect plants from the area and put into water immediately.
5. If suitable critters are not found on your playground, take a collecting field trip around the neighborhood or ask the students to bring some in (along with the plants they were living on). Creatures should be captured carefully so they are not injured in the process. Encourage use of containers with lids or teach the students how to use nets. Check out the collection area ahead of time to avoid bees, wasps, or other problems.
6. Be sure that the animals brought in are planteaters. Some animals found on plants may actually be eating smaller insects living on the plants. While they can be maintained well in a Buffet Box setup, it's a different investigation!
7. If possible, gather small plants (weeds) with the root systems attached. If cuttings are used, cut the stems a second time as they are put into the water. In either case, have the students keep them in water from the time they are collected and maintain the water level in the cups throughout the investigation. Replace plants that wilt or dry out with fresh plants.
8. Animals should be returned to where they were found once the investigation is complete.

Procedure

1. Display the sandwich on a paper plate so that it is evident that several bites have been taken from it. Ask the class to suggest ways of solving the mystery of who has eaten part of this sandwich.
2. Explain that detectives often narrow down the list of suspects by eliminating those who for some reason could not have been responsible. Tell the students that they are all suspects if they have ever been known to eat a sandwich.
3. Take apart the sandwich and make a list of all the components. Then tell them that you are not a suspect because you really don't like to eat ___

and name one of the ingredients. Step to one side of the room and ask anyone else who also prefers not to eat that particular ingredient to join you.
4. Ask if there are any others who would not have eaten the sandwich because of another one of its components. Have them name the ingredient they don't like and ask others who agree to join the group that is standing. Count (including those who were already standing) and record. Continue until only those who would have eaten the sandwich are left seated. Follow through with whatever other clues are needed until the mystery is solved.
5. Look at the list of ingredients and discuss the preferences. Talk about the difference between choosing not to eat a food item because of its taste or appeal and avoiding eating it because it has a bad effect (allergy, etc.). Guide them to understand that for insects and many other animals, food choice is not so much a matter of personal taste but rather of what will meet its particular nutritional needs. Ask the students to think if there is any kind of food that they themselves would never eat under any circumstances and that would do them no good, even though it might be nutritious for other living things. [wood, cardboard, etc.]
6. Ask if any of the students have ever eaten a *buffet* meal. If necessary, explain that in a buffet, lots of different foods are made available so that the diners can choose the things they like to eat and pass by the food items that aren't appealing to them. Point out that in the natural world, animals live in a type of buffet situation. They may have a variety of food possibilities available to them, but some are "picky eaters" and will only eat certain things, while others are willing to sample just about everything.
7. Have each group follow directions to set up a Buffet Box. Direct the students to work together to plan an investigation, determining what type of creature will be living in the box and what kind of plants they think it will eat. If possible, have the students visit the collection site to make observations to help in their planning before they actually collect specimens.
8. Ask the students to make use of their detective skills and recall what evidence they might look for to determine what plants might be food for animals living in a certain area. Encourage them to use the clues they find in choosing which plants to include in the Buffet Box.
9. Students should begin with plants only from the collection area. As the investigation proceeds, encourage them to predict and try other plants that they think the animals might like just as well, giving reasons for the different plants they choose. However, they will need to monitor the box carefully, making sure the animals are eating, and providing them with a constant supply of plants that they will eat. They will also need to add water to the plants daily.

10. Throughout the investigation, have the students keep a careful log of what they observe and their interpretation of what they are finding out, as well as their ideas for refining or expanding the investigation. Ask each group to report their findings to the rest of the class.

Discussion

1. Why do you think some foods are appealing to some people and not to others? Is there a particular food that you really can't stand? Why do you think you react this way to it?
2. What clues did you use to choose the first plants you put in your Buffet Box?
3. In what ways did you find that your critters liked to eat the plants you predicted they would? Did anything about their food choices surprise you? Explain.
4. What evidence did you find to show that your critters ate some plants and not others? What evidence might show that they ate some plants *before* eating others?
5. How were the results of your team's investigation similar to or different from what the other teams found? How can you account for those similarities and differences?
6. What difficulties did you have finding plants that your critter would eat? Explain how you determined what plants to try next.

7. If you continued this study, what would you try to find out next? How would you go about doing it? How could you adapt the Buffet Box to make it work even better for the animal you work with and the experiment you have in mind?

Extension

Continue to work on food-related projects of the students' own choosing. Such studies could include diets of other classroom animals or investigating food preferences of insect eaters. Be sure not to put any animal in a situation where it cannot get food that it will eat.

Curriculum Correlation

Literature

Carle, Eric. *A Very Hungry Caterpillar*. Scholastic, Inc. New York. 1969.
- Delightful picture book for young children tells what a caterpillar ate, including foods not ordinarily on its natural diet!

Cooking

Have the students prepare and share unusual favorite foods, perhaps something from their family traditions. In the sharing process, include a breakdown of the ingredients and where they come from so the students can appreciate the diversity of their own tastes.

Home Link

Ask the students to interview each family member to find their favorite and least favorite foods. Compile the information in a class graph.

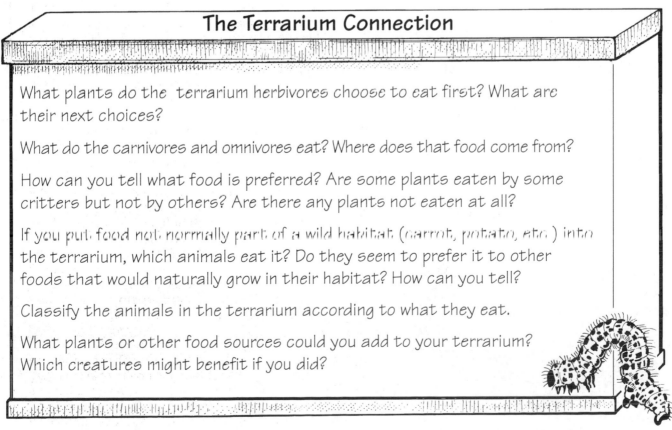

The Terrarium Connection

What plants do the terrarium herbivores choose to eat first? What are their next choices?

What do the carnivores and omnivores eat? Where does that food come from?

How can you tell what food is preferred? Are some plants eaten by some critters but not by others? Are there any plants not eaten at all?

If you put food not normally part of a wild habitat (carrot, potato, etc.) into the terrarium, which animals eat it? Do they seem to prefer it to other foods that would naturally grow in their habitat? How can you tell?

Classify the animals in the terrarium according to what they eat.

What plants or other food sources could you add to your terrarium? Which creatures might benefit if you did?

Invitation to a
Buffet Lunch

Who is invited:

Menu *(describe in words or pictures)*

1   2

3   4

We predict that #_____ will be the favorite item.
Comments and observations:

          © 1998 AIMS Education Foundation

Buffet Box Construction

Materials

Copy paper box or similar box (with or without lid)
4 identical water containers, preferably clear
Utility knife
Scissors
Marking pen
Masking tape
Ruler
Clear plastic wrap
Screen material for top (net, cheesecloth, screen)
Branches with leaves and/or plant samples with roots
Critters invited for lunch
Fast food drink carrier or clay to stabilize the water
    containers, optional

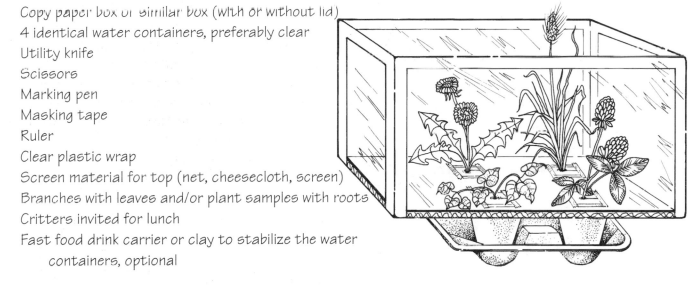

Procedure

1. Measure and mark a 3 cm (1 inch or the width of the ruler) border along the sides and top of each face of the box.
2. Cut out the middle section of each side.
3. Mark the location for each plant specimen in the bottom of the box, spaced evenly. If you are using a carrier to stabilize the water containers, line up the marks to where the cups will be in the carrier.
4. Poke a small hole through the bottom of the box at each location, just wide enough for plant stems to fit through.
5. Cut a length of plastic wrap to fit all the way around the box. Tape one end along the entire length of one of the edges. Continue stretching the plastic wrap around the entire box, taping it securely at the edge where you began.
6. Turn the box bottom-side up, fold tight corners with the plastic wrap, and tape securely at the corners and along all edges.
7. Turn the box right-side up. Stretch the plastic wrap over the top edge and tape securely all the way along the inside so that the windows are as wrinkle-free as possible.

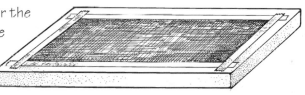

8. If your box has a close-fitting lid, cut a large window out of the lid and tape fine-mesh screen, net, or cheesecloth securely to the inside. Otherwise, use net, cheesecloth, screen, or other porous material to cover the box and tape it down securely. Leave temporary gap to add plants and animals.
9. Poke the roots or bottom of branches of the plants through the holes so that they protrude through the bottom of the box. Fill the cups with water and stabilize them. Set the box on the cups, making sure that the roots or branches are all the way in the water.

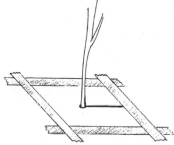

10. Cut a slit and a stem-sized hole in a scrap of paper, slip it around each stem, and tape securely to prevent critters from going through the holes and drowning or escaping. A piece of clay can also be used.
11. Replace the plants as soon as they wilt, dry out, or are consumed.

Lunch is served!

From Leaf to Soil

Piecing Together the Evidence

Topic
Decomposition

Key Question
What does the decomposition process of a leaf look like?

Focus
Leaves are broken down by decomposing organisms and returned to the soil.

Guiding Documents
Project 2061 Benchmarks
- *Change is something that happens to many things.*
- *Animals and plants sometimes cause changes in their surroundings.*
- *Insects and various other organisms depend on dead plant and animal material for food.*
- *Over the whole earth, organisms are growing, dying, and decaying, and new organisms are being produced by the old ones.*

NRC Standard
- *Populations of organisms can be categorized by the function they serve in an ecosystem. Plants and some micro-organisms are producers — they make their own food. All animals, including humans, are consumers, which obtain food by eating other organisms. Decomposers, primarily bacteria and fungi, are consumers that use waste materials and dead organisms for food. Food webs identify the relationships among producers, consumers, and decomposers in an ecosystem.*

Science
Environmental science
    habitats
    decomposition
Life science
    plants
    animals

Integrated Processes
Observing
Classifying
Predicting
Collecting and recording data
Comparing and contrasting
Generalizing
Inferring

Materials
For the class:
    site of dead and decomposing leaves
        (see *Management 1*)
    fresh or recently fallen leaf
    broken down piece of decomposed leaf

For each team of students:
    cup of rich organic soil
    paper towel or piece of newspaper
    toothpicks
    plastic sandwich bags
    hand lens and/or DiscoveryScope®
    12 X 18 inch construction paper
    white glue

Optional:
    paper pre-cut to make books

Background Information
A mystery often involves a chain of events which a good detective needs to piece together. In this activity, the evidence of the chain of events is in the form of dead leaves in various stages of decomposition. What changes happen to these leaves between the time they fall from the tree and when they finally became part of the organic material in the soil?

In the following activity, *Dirt Dwellers*, students will learn more about who or what is consuming the dead leaves. For now, in the course of piecing together the leaf clues, the students will observe certain patterns in the way the leaves disintegrate.

Critters are often apt to nibble first on the more accessible edges of the leaf blade, then continue munching until they reach the center vein. The leaf itself is protected by a natural waxy covering, but any place that cover has been pierced, torn, or otherwise damaged is a prime spot for bacteria, fungus, and other decomposers to move in and spread. The veins are more resistant to decomposition because of their tough cell wall structure. The softer leaf material typically is consumed first, eventually leaving only the fragile skeleton of the leaf that once was. Then that too crumbles and becomes part of the soil.

 © 1998 AIMS Education Foundation

Management

1. Before doing this activity, locate an area where dead leaves have been accumulating for some time and are in various stages of decomposition. If no such site is within reach of the school grounds, a large bag of leaves could be brought in, but it is preferable (and easier) to take the students to the site and let them collect what they need.

2. Walk-on bark or landscaping bark chips that have been on the ground for several years can also be used (adapt the information accordingly). Another reasonable substitute is layers from an unturned compost pile (containing only plant-type compost, i.e., no meat, eggs, or other garbage which can harbor unpleasant odors and potentially harmful bacteria).

3. Students should work in teams of two.

Procedure

1. Remind the students that detectives depend upon good observation skills. They need to recognize even the smallest of clues found in unlikely places.

2. Give each group of students a cup of organic soil and a paper towel or newspaper. Ask them to spread out the sample and examine it, using toothpick probes to separate it into different categories of ingredients. Discuss what they see and know about all the things that are part of good, rich soil. Be sure to include "dead leaves" in the discussion.

3. Show the students a fresh leaf and a piece of decomposed leaf. Remind them that *decomposed* refers to plant or animal material that is no longer living and has been broken down to become part of the soil. Ask the students to think about the different things that might happen to the leaf from the time it falls from the tree or bush until it becomes part of the soil. As detectives, their job is to collect evidence which they will then organize to show what happens to a leaf along the way.

4. Take the students to the collecting site. Have them work with a partner to gather samples of leaves in various stages of decomposition, putting them carefully in a plastic sandwich bag for protection. Younger students should collect at least five samples ranging from freshly fallen to mostly decomposed; older students should be encouraged to collect as wide a range of samples as possible.

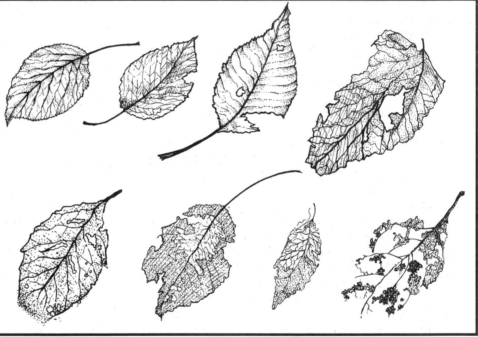

5. Direct the students to look for evidence to help them learn more about what has been happening to the leaves. Encourage them to note any plants, animals, or other signs or traces that could point to "suspects." Close examination of the leaf pile might lead to some interesting clues and theories!

6. Before leaving the area, ask the students to look around and think what physical factors might have affected the leaves on the ground (moisture, wind, amount of light, weather conditions, foot traffic through the area, etc.). Identify the locations where the leaves seem to be most decomposed and discuss possible explanations.

7. Back in class, have the student teams arrange their leaf samples in order from the most complete to the most decomposed. Encourage them to use a hand lens for a closer look, surmising what might have caused the damage and justifying the order they have decided upon. Once they are agreed, have them glue the leaves in place, writing notes or details on the paper around each leaf.

8. Ask the students to share any patterns of decomposition that they notice. Discuss their observations, including any patterns that appear typical and any that seem to be different than the others.

9. Ask each team to use their leaf clues to develop a story of what happens to a particular leaf after it falls from the tree or bush, using a picture book or cartoon panel format. You may wish to read *The Fall of Freddy the Leaf* to get them started.

Discussion

1. What causes of decomposition can you see in your leaf collection? What similarities do you see with some of the other leaf stories? What differences?

76   © 1998 AIMS Education Foundation

2. Which parts of the leaf decompose first? ... last? Is the order of decomposition different for different types of leaves?
3. At what point does it become hard to tell what the leaf originally looked like?
4. Why is it important that leaves decompose? What are some of the benefits? What would happen if the leaves didn't decompose, or if they didn't fall from the tree at all?

Extensions
1. Find out where leaves go after they fall off trees and are raked up and carted off. What are some of the different ways that people dispose of fallen leaves? If you can, track what happens to the leaves from the particular trees where you collected.
2. Figure out some different ways to measure a pile of leaves under a tree.
3. Find and protect an area where decomposers are already at work. Trace and measure a leaf, keep it among the decomposers, and check it every week or two, charting and recording its disintegration.
4. Collect another type of natural decomposing material such as rotting wood. Store it in a clear container and observe, keeping records. Predict how long it will take until it falls apart completely.

5. Illustrate the fallen leaf stories with real leaves or drawings of leaves. Share the stories with younger classes.

Curriculum Correlation
Literature
   Buscaglia, Leo. *The Fall of Freddy the Leaf.* Henry Holt and Co. New York. 1982.
   • A classic book dealing with the cycle of life and death; applies particularly well here to emphasize that the nutrients in living things are recycled to provide for new growth.

Home Link
   Examine leaves that have fallen in your yard or around the neighborhood where you live. How do they compare to the leaves you worked with at school? Are they left on the ground or gathered up? If they are gathered up, what happens to them?

The Terrarium Connection

(If there are not any dead leaves in the terrarium, add several in various stages of decomposition.)

Spend some time watching the small community that is living among the dead leaves in the terrarium.

What different animals can you recognize?

What differences can you see in the leaves from day to day? What evidence can you find that they are changing?

Lightly spray the surface of the leaves and watch to see what happens. How do the critters respond? Do you think that keeping the leaves damp might make a difference in how quickly they decompose? Why do you think so?

Dirt Dwellers

Topic
Decomposers and Consumers

Key Questions
What will you find in the top few centimeters of leaf litter and soil? What do they eat?

Focus
Tiny decomposer animals can be collected and observed with the aid of a microscope or a hand lens.

Guiding Documents
Project 2061 Benchmarks
- *Insects and various other organisms depend on dead plant and animal material for food.*
- *Animals eat plants or other animals for food and may also use plants (or even other animals) for shelter and nesting.*
- *Magnifiers help people see things they could not see without them.*
- *Soil is made partly from weathered rock, partly from plant remains — and also contains many living organisms.*

NRC Standards
- *Populations of organisms can be categorized by the function they serve in an ecosystem. Plants and some micro-organisms are producers — they make their own food. All animals, including humans, are consumers, which obtain food by eating other organisms. Decomposers, primarily bacteria and fungi, are consumers that use waste materials and dead organisms for food. Food webs identify the relationships among producers, consumers, and decomposers in an ecosystem.*
- *Soil consists of weathered rocks, decomposed organic material from dead plants, animals, and bacteria. Soils are often found in layers, with each having a different chemical composition and texture.*

NCTM Standards
- *Describe and represent relationships with tables, graphs, and rules*
- *Systematically collect, organize, and describe data*

Math
Measurement
Counting
Estimating

Science
Environmental science
    habitats
    decomposition

Integrated Processes
Observing
Classifying
Collecting and recording data
Comparing and contrasting
Applying
Generalizing
Inferring

Materials
For Berlese funnel (see Management 9):
    two-liter plastic soda bottle
    1-2 pieces 9x12 inch black construction paper
    6cm x 6cm piece of netting or screen
    strong light source such as a goose-neck lamp
    utilty knife

For the class:
    bucket or large tub
    enough topsoil and leaf litter for each student pair
        to have a cupful
    trowel or large, sturdy spoon
    covered containers
    microscopes or DiscoveryScopes®

For each pair of students:
    hand lens
    newspapers or butcher paper and paper towels
    toothpicks
    cotton swabs
    "holding" container (see Management 3)
    balance
    masses

Optional:
    calculator

Background Information
What happens to the remains of plants and animals fallen to the ground? Gradually they lose shape and form, eventually becoming part of the soil itself. The organisms responsible for this mysterious disappearance are *decomposers*, tiny plants and animals living in the dark, damp habitat of the surface and top few centimeters of the soil.

In previous activities in this section, students learned about their own position in the food web as consumers. In *From Leaf to Soil*, they observed the decomposition process taking place in fallen leaves. Now they have arrived at the "Whodunit?" part of the mystery in which they will meet a different kind of consumer: the decomposers who have been hard at work breaking down and processing the leaves.

Decomposers have the important job of eating and changing dead plant and animal material into very small pieces. As they do so, they leave droppings which are food for other animals or which become an enriching part of the soil. Thus nutrients return to the soil so that it can continue to support plant life.

Leaf litter is an organic mixture consisting mostly of dead leaves. It may also include other plant material and the droppings and remains of animals. When leaf litter piles up, such as under a tree or against a wall, it becomes a habitat in itself, providing for the needs of many different animals. It gives protection from the drying heat of the sun as well as supplying food and water (moisture). Some insects even lay their eggs on dead organic material so that when the young larvae hatch, they will be living right within a waiting food supply. The organisms that visit or dwell in this special habitat typically are most active among the bottom layers, working on the rich material around them. Earthworms, certain types of insect larvae, and other tiny critters in the dirt pull down the bottom layers of decomposing material and continue the process underground.

Not all decomposers are animals. Bacteria and a few kinds of plants that have no chlorophyll and thus can't make their own food (fungi, saprophytes) are also found in leaf litter, especially when it is in a damp, shady area. There will most likely be evidence of bacterial and fungal decomposition in any damp leaf litter sample, but the emphasis in this activity is on decomposer animals.

Decomposition of natural litter is an ongoing process. The ground may always be covered with litter, but the bottom layers are being turned into rich humus even as more layers of new material are added to the top. Think how much would pile up if these critters didn't do their job!

Management

1. If possible, let the students collect the leaf litter so that they will be able to observe the layers of decomposition in progress. Try to collect from an area under a tree or bush that has not been disturbed recently. You should be able to see organic material (leaves, twigs) mixed in with sand or clay as well as some visual evidence of critter life — worms, ants, sowbugs, etc. Do NOT use potting mix because it has been sterilized. If you have trouble finding good topsoil, ask a local gardener or nursery employee. Keep the samples in closed containers to retain moisture.

2. Provide paper towels on top of sheets of newspaper or butcher paper for a relatively easy-to-clean work surface.

3. Each team will need a holding container (plastic cup, petri dish half, margarine dish, jar lid, etc.). If you are using a microscope, use clear plastic holding containers that will fit the stage of the microscope. Flexible plastic cups can easily be cut down to size.

4. If necessary, review the distinguishing characteristics of insects (three body parts, six legs) and spiders (two body parts, eight legs) when the students attempt to classify critters in their sample.

5. A slightly dampened cotton swab is useful for transferring tiny creatures to the holding container. The edge of an index card may also be used.

6. If you or your students have access to "bug boxes" (plastic containers with a built-in magnifier) or DiscoveryScopes®, these will enhance what the students are able to see.

7. Dirt dwellers need to be kept moist or they will die. Line the holding containers with a piece of damp paper towel.

8. At the end of the activity, have the students return their sample to the container. If possible, take the critters and soil back to the original site. As you release them to continue their work of decomposition, you will have a good opportunity to stress the importance of the job these creatures do.

9. Set up the Berlese funnel early in the day. (See *Building a Simple Berlese Funnel.*) It is most effective when the light is on for several hours.

10. Use screen or net with small enough spaces to keep the soil itself from falling through the funnel, but large enough to let the tiny animals get through.  Standard window screen (1-2 mm spaces) or hardware cloth with 1/8" spaces will work well for most types of soil.

Procedure
Part 1

1. Ask the students what they know about what happens to leaves and twigs after they fall from the trees, or to insects and other critters when they die. Discuss how old they think the leaves are in the litter they collected (*From Leaf to Soil*). Ask if they would be able to find leaves that fell a year ago. ... two years ago. ... ten years ago. Encourage them to wonder about where dead leaves go.

2. Guide the discussion to include the possibility that the leaves were eaten. Remind the students that they themselves are consumers, probably omnivores. Ask them if they would think of eating leaf litter. Explain that people don't usually eat dead

tree leaves from the ground, but there are plenty of other consumers who thrive on this kind of food. Point out that the leaves give evidence of being eaten, and ask if anyone has noticed any other clues to the mystery of "Who has been eating the leaves?" Tell them that they will be able to solve this mystery by observing closely and using a hand lens or microscope.

3. Set up the Berlese funnel for later use. Ask the students to be thinking about the purpose of the different parts and what they think might happen to the leaf litter/soil sample.

4. Give each pair of students a large spoonful of the soil/leaf litter, toothpicks for probes, a damp cotton swab, a holding container, and a hand lens. Encourage them to investigate their sample carefully. Demonstrate the use of a damp cotton swab to pick up the smaller critters and put them in a "holding" container lined with a damp paper towel. Point out that these creatures live in a damp habitat and need the moisture in the holding container so they won't dry out and die.

5. Have the students use hand lenses (and microscopes) and draw whatever they see, showing as many details as possible. Encourage them to draw as many critters as they can, each in its own rectangle on the recording page.

6. Have the students compare notes when a team makes a new discovery. Are they finding similar or different critters?

7. Ask the students why they think these dirt dwellers exist. Have them project what would happen in the area where the leaf litter was collected if all these critters disappeared. Guide them to understand that many different tiny animals live in the soil and dead leaves, and that their job is to eat the dead plant and animal material that falls on the ground. Talk about decomposers and the importance of their particular role in the food chain and in the habitat.

Part 2

1. Ask the students what they might expect to find in the container under the Berlese funnel. Encourage them to offer ideas of reasons for each part: Why heat and light? Why moisture in the container? Why black paper? What do they think may have happened to the soil sample and whatever was living in it? Guide them to understand that dirt dwellers' natural environment is dark and damp, which means that they can be expected to move away from the heat and light of the lamp.

2. Give everyone an opportunity to examine the creatures collected from the Berlese funnel under a microscope. Have them draw the organisms they see to add to the data they collected from their own soil samples. Compare the assortment of

creatures from the funnel with those the students found in their soil samples.

3. Ask the students to design a graph or Venn diagram and use their drawings to show the variety of creatures and how many of each species were found.

Discussion

1. What kinds of animals did you find? What are they doing there? How are they alike or different? Describe what you found in such a way that if other groups found similar organisms, they could identify them by your description.

2. In what ways do these creatures seem well-suited to live in the soil? What do you think they eat? Where do you think they get the water they need?

3. What other kinds of things did you find in the sample? What parts of the soil were non-living (never living)? What parts were once living and now are dead and decomposing?

4. Did you find any animals in the Berlese funnel that you did not see in your soil sample? How do you explain this?

5. What do you think happens to animals that live in the soil? What happens to plants when they die?

6. What bigger animals can you think of that also live in the soil, even though you might not have seen them?

7. Why do you think it is important to return the animals to where they were found?

8. What would happen to a habitat if there weren't decomposers? What is important about their particular role?

9. Do you think this sample is a good representation of life found in the soil in the habitat from which it came? Explain. If you took other samples from this habitat, would you expect similar results?

10. Do you think you would find the same types of dirt dwellers in another habitat nearby? Why or why not? What do you think you would find in a similar habitat in some other location?

Extensions

1. Compare the diversity and density of life found in different types of soils and soils from different locations.

2. Use the Berlese funnel to compare population densities of different types of animals from several different locations. Look for variations in such things as type of leaf litter, type of soil, comparative dampness of soil, exposure to direct sunlight, etc.

3. Find the mass of the soil before putting it in the Berlese funnel. Count the number of different creatures found just in this sample, as well as how many individuals of each species and the total

number of animals found. Determine the number of each species and the whole population that might be found in a kilogram of soil from the same site.

4. See *Set Up a Rotting Log Terrarium*.

Curriculum Correlation

Music

1. Sing "Decomposition Ditty."
2. Sing "Decomposition" on *Dirt Made My Lunch* by the Banana Slug String Band.

Literature

Cole, Joanna and Bruce Degen. *The Magic Schoolbus Meets the Rot Squad*. Scholastic, Inc. New York. 1995.

- Decomposition from the inimitable perspective of Mrs. Frizzle and the Magic Schoolbus bunch, focusing on life within a rotting log.

Lavies, Bianca. *Compost Critters*. Dutton Children's Books. New York. 1993.

- Photographic essay showing what is happening in a compost pile. Close-up look at bacteria, mold, and an array of compost critters.

Ring, Elizabeth. *What Rot! Nature's Mighty Recycler*. The Millbrook Press. Brookfield, CT. 1996.

- Focuses on the major decomposers (in addition to rot), including their role in the food chain and within the bigger picture of the habitat. Easy-to-read text; excellent close-up photographs.

Home Link

Look in the yard or planted areas at home, in a nearby park, or in a vacant lot and see if you can find the same critters you found in this activity. Can you find some different ones too? Make drawings of any "new" creatures found and bring them to school to add to the collection of dirt dweller drawings.

The Terrarium Connection

What evidence do you see that decomposers are at work? Are there any large enough to see? Do you think there might be some too small to see? How could you find out?

What do you think happens to leaves or plants that die in the terrarium? What happens to the animal droppings as time goes by?

What eventually happens to food scraps not consumed right away?

Do you have earthworms in your terrarium? What important role do they play in many habitats? Why do you think they are sometimes referred to as "nature's master gardeners"?

Do you see any mold or other kind of fungus? If so, what is it living on? Is there one particular part of the terrarium that mold seems to thrive in? What conditions in the terrarium encourage mold growth?

 © 1998 AIMS Education Foundation

Set Up a Rotting Log Terrarium

- Use a terrarium with a glass cover or a pickle jar with a lid.
- Put a layer of sand or coarse gravel at the bottom.
- Add another layer of potting soil, leaf litter, or humus.
- Find the mass the rotting log or piece of rotting wood and put it in your terrarium. Check the mass once every week or two.
- Mist with water and keep covered. Mist frequently to maintain a moist environment.
- Keep out of direct light.
- Observe and record observations daily.
- When you take the log out to find its mass, note its texture and odor too.
- After observing over time, you may wish to break the wood apart to observe what is happening inside.
- When you are finished, put the remains of the rotting log in a place outdoors where the decomposers will be able to continue their work.

Variations:
- If you live in a place where winters are very cold, set up a terrarium with a rotting log collected during the winter. Watch to learn what creatures use the log to hibernate or seek shelter from the cold.
- Establish a rotting log terrarium for each season of the year and compare what you observe.

Rotting Log Terrarium

What changes do you see? What is going on that causes these changes? What signs of plant and animal life can you find? Where do you see evidence of life even though you may not see the decomposers themselves?

Would you say that a rotting log is a habitat itself? How do you know?

(After you break apart the wood)
Do you see any creatures or evidences of life that you hadn't noticed before? You may be able to find the remains of the tree's cellulose walls. The material will feel like a rope or string.

What creatures or plants have been depending on this rotting log as a habitat? How have each of the needs been met?
Do you think it is accurate to call a rotting log a "dead tree"? Explain.

What will eventually become of this rotting log after you put it back outside?

Building a Simple Berlese Funnel

1. Use a utility knife to cut the neck from a two-liter bottle.

2. Invert the neck portion to make a funnel. Roll a cone of black construction paper to fit inside the funnel.

3. Cut a small piece of screen or netting and tape it so that it covers the small opening of the paper cone. Put the paper cone with screen attached inside the plastic funnel.

4. On a paper towel, trace around the bottom of the holding container; cut out the circle and put it on the inside bottom of the container. Dampen it.

5. Put the holding container inside the bottom portion of the two-liter bottle. Rest the funnel half above it with the spout directed into the holding container. Wrap the entire apparatus with black construction paper and secure.

6. Put about a cup of soil/natural litter combination inside the funnel. Arrange the light source so that it shines directly on the top of the funnel at close range. Wait several hours or until the soil/litter has become brittle and dry.

7. **Caution:** This should be monitored closely so that it does not become a fire hazard.

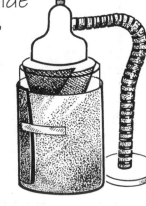

 © 1998 AIMS Education Foundation

Dirt Dwellers

Draw your critters larger-than-life.

84

© 1998 AIMS Education Foundation

Dirt Dwellers

Organize your critters in a graph or Venn diagram.

Decomposition Ditty

Words by Suzy Gazlay

Tune: Did You Ever See a Lassie?

(C₇) F
Have you ev - er stopped to

won - der what would hap - pen if the C

F
gar - bage Al - ways piled up all a -

round us and nev - er went a - way? Quite C (C₇) F

soon we would no - tice we had a real C F C

prob - lem; Then one day we would be

bur - ied: O ter - ri - ble day! C (C₇) F

Have you ever stopped to wonder
Each year when the leaves fall
What would happen if they stayed there
Piled up on the ground?
Each year more would drop till
The world would be covered
Deep enough to lose some people
Who'd never be found!

Did you ever think about all
The stuff in the landfills?
If it stayed the same forever
There'd soon be no room.
But burning our garbage
Can cause air pollution —
Decomposers help the problem
As waste they consume.

It's a good thing we've got earthworms
And millipedes and sowbugs
And bacteria and plants such as
Fungus and mold,
And small mites and insects,
Including their larvae,
Who consume a lot of garbage
And keep it controlled.

Aren't you glad for decomposers,
So quietly munching,
Turning litter into nutrients
So plant life can thrive?
Though many are tiny,
Their work is essential
They help keep the earth in balance
So we all can survive!

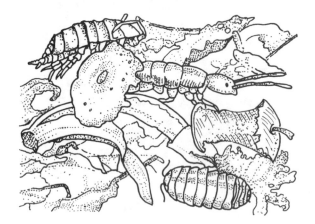

 © 1998 AIMS Education Foundation

Pyramid Pile-Up

Topic
Food Chains, Webs, and Pyramids

Key Question
How can we use a model to show the structure of a food pyramid?

Focus
The class will construct a food pyramid structure to demonstrate the relationships within various food pyramids.

Guiding Documents
Project 2061 Benchmarks
- *Almost all kinds of animals' food can be traced back to plants.*
- *All organisms, including the human species, are part of and depend on two main interconnected global food webs. One includes microscopic ocean plants, the animals that feed on them, and finally the animals that feed on those animals. The other web includes land plants, the animals that feed on them, and so forth. The cycles continue indefinitely because organisms decompose after death to return food material to the environment.*

NRC Standards
- *All animals depend on plants. Some animals eat plants for food. Other animals eat animals that eat the plants.*
- *Populations of organisms can be categorized by the function they serve in an ecosystem. Plants and some micro-organisms are producers — they make their own food. All animals, including humans, are consumers, which obtain food by eating other organisms. Decomposers, primarily bacteria and fungi, are consumers that use waste materials and dead organisms for food. Food webs identify the relationships among producers, consumers, and decomposers in an ecosystem.*

Science
Environmental science
    habitats
        food webs, chains, and pyramids
Life science
    plants
    animals

Integrated Processes
Observing
Classifying
Collecting and recording data
Comparing and contrasting
Applying
Generalizing

Materials
For the class:
    four large cardboard boxes, different sizes
    chart paper or construction paper, yellow and four other colors
    tape
    glue
    encyclopedias, field guides, and other reference materials

For each group:
    drawing and coloring supplies
    yarn
    scissors
    5 X 5 cm paper or cardstock template (see *Management 3*)

Background Information
As food chains describe the food relationships between certain plants and animals, and food webs illustrate the interrelationships between different food chains, food pyramids are a common model designed to show the food relationships within an entire ecosystem.

The shape of the food pyramid model illustrates that it generally takes *much* (either number of individuals or collective mass of the individuals) at the producer level to support *less* at the consumer level, with comparatively *little* at the very top of the consumer level. (Please refer to *The Inside Story: Food Chains; Producers and Consumers ... ;* and *Food Webs and Pyramids* for additional information.)

The food pyramid model in this activity demonstrates not only the mass/number relationships within an ecosystem, but also the multiple relationships of different organisms within the food webs. As the students make the connections throughout the levels, they should begin to see just how interwoven these relationships are. They should keep in mind that most consumers eat a variety of different species. They should be encouraged to show and connect as many different food chain relationships as they can.

Management
1. Before beginning the activity, cover the boxes with paper to mask the writing. Use a different color for each box. Glue the boxes together to form a pyramid stack.

2. Make (or have students make) a cutout from yellow paper representing the sun, large enough to show when the pyramid is placed on top of it.
3. Establish a size limit for the organisms they are making (use the 5 X 5 cm template as a guide; adapt the size if necessary).
4. To avoid duplication, orchestrate which student will make which plant or animal.
5. Encourage students to make use of field guides, Internet, encyclopedias, and other reference materials to learn more about an organism's place in the pyramid. Use the information on the cards from *Life in the Food Chain* and other information the students have gathered as a place to begin.
6. One side of the pyramid structure should be labeled to represent the playground habitat. For younger students, you may choose to have the entire pyramid represent the area they have been studying. For older students, each of the other sides may be a different ecosystem such as a neighboring wild area, the ecosystem that represents your geographic location (grasslands, hardwood forest, etc.), or an area such as the ocean that your class has studied or is particularly interested in learning about. Decide how you want to determine responsibility for researching and constructing each of these areas.
7. It will take time to build and fill in the pyramid. Spread the task over several days as needed, giving students ample time to make the organisms and research the food chain links before discussing the overall results.
8. This activity can be used as an assessment tool. Look for information such as understanding of relationships between producers and consumers, complete and accurate food chains, and use of appropriate vocabulary.

Procedure
Part 1
1. Explain to the students that they will now be putting together all of the clues they have been gathering to make a model showing the variety of food relationships in the playground habitat (or other habitats).
2. Set up the pyramid in a central location, placing it squarely on the sun cutout. Review the concept of food webs and chains from previous activities and ask for different examples. Explain that this is a different way of looking at food chains and webs within the entire ecosystem. Discuss the role of the sun and the significance of each of the levels. Add labels if needed.
3. Ask each group to think of several food chains, two links or longer, involving organisms found on the playground. Be as specific about the identity of each plant and animal as possible: *oak leaf* rather than *leaf*; *robin* rather than *bird*. List these for the class to see. Have each group choose a different food chain from the list. Show them how to use the template to limit size and give them time to draw, color, and cut out the organisms in the chain they chose.

4. Have each group arrange their organisms in food chain order and identify each as producers, herbivores, carnivores, or top-level carnivores (eat other carnivores).
5. Designate the part of the pyramid representing the playground habitat. Ask each group in turn to come and attach their organisms to the appropriate level, explaining their food chain to the rest of the class. If there are duplications of a particular species, glue the individuals next to each other in a group.
6. Discuss the overall display. Give every group a long piece of yarn to connect each of their organisms to show its food chain relationships.
7. Ask the class to look at the connections and see if there are others that can be made. Connect the "new" relationships with pieces of yarn. (For example, two chains might show a robin eating a caterpillar and a snail eating a geranium leaf. Another string could show that the caterpillar could also eat the leaf.)
8. Challenge the groups to think about what other organisms could be added to the pyramid by asking them to recall or research what other foods the different consumers might eat. If that organism is found in or visiting the playground habitat, they should add it to the pyramid with its yarn connections.
9. Encourage the students to look on the playground as well as think about other possible links and add them during the next several days, discussing the growing webs as you go.

Part 2
1. Agree upon ecosystems for the remaining sides of the pyramid. Have the students do the necessary research to display appropriate food webs on each.
2. If any of the ecosystems truly share margins in the natural world (i.e. a forest near your school site; an owl from the forest hunting mice on the playground), it is appropriate to stretch the yarn link from one side to another to show that relationship.
3. As the food pyramid becomes filled in, begin pointing out that *much* (number or mass) is needed to support less at the higher levels. If this is not evident at first, have students add more grass and other producers proportionately, pointing out that more is needed to supply so many.
4. Ask the students to show how they fit in on each side of the pyramid. Have someone put a representative figure at the top level and add appropriate yarn links.

Discussion
1. What similarities and differences do you see on each of the sides of the pyramid? Are there any organisms that appear on every side? If so, what are they? Are there some found only in one ecosystem?
2. At what level(s) does most of the webbing seem to occur? How could you explain this?

3. If you were making a pyramid to show a different ecosystem, how would you expect it to be similar to your pyramid? How would you expect it to be different?
4. What might be some advantages and disadvantages of an organism eating several different things instead of eating just one thing all the time?
5. What are some of the different locations where you might fit into this pyramid? Are your locations always the same as the ones where your classmates see themselves? Explain.

Extensions
1. Set up more pyramids to display information for each of the world's major ecosystems, comparing and contrasting the life forms and relationships.
2. Make menus for herbivores, carnivores, and omnivores showing the food choices available to them at the lower levels of each side of the pyramid.
3. Choose some of the role-playing food web activities from Project Wild or Project Learning Tree.

Curriculum Correlation
Music
1. Revisit the songs learned in previous activities in this section.
2. Compose new versions of "Food Chain Song" or write a rap for each side of the pyramid.

Literature:
George, Jean Craighead. *Who Really Killed Cock Robin?* Harper Trophy. New York. 1991.
• When a robin dies in a New England town known for its clean environmental policies, students unravel the web of contributing factors. Strong point is made for the interconnectedness of the food web. Part of the *Ecological Mystery* series.

Godkin, Celia. *Wolf Island.* W. H. Freeman and Company. New York. 1989.
• Relates what happens to an island population when the wolves leave and the food chain is out of balance, then restored when they return. Makes an important point in a simple, appealing way.

Home Link
Ask your family to join you as you trace the food you eat for dinner back through the food chain all the way to sunlight and green plants.

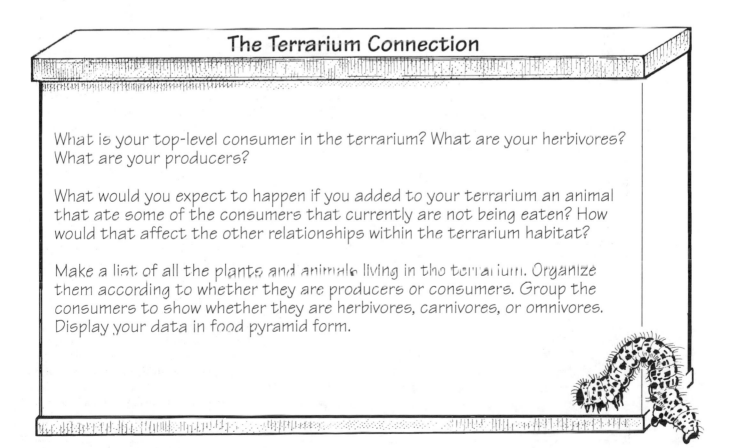

The Terrarium Connection

What is your top-level consumer in the terrarium? What are your herbivores? What are your producers?

What would you expect to happen if you added to your terrarium an animal that ate some of the consumers that currently are not being eaten? How would that affect the other relationships within the terrarium habitat?

Make a list of all the plants and animals living in the terrarium. Organize them according to whether they are producers or consumers. Group the consumers to show whether they are herbivores, carnivores, or omnivores. Display your data in food pyramid form.

The Inside Story
Water...

All living things need water in order to stay alive. Plants and animals use water for many things, including absorbing or digesting food and turning it into energy. In fact, water is spread throughout the cells and body fluids of every organism. Many people are surprised to find out that nearly two-thirds of their body consists of water. Some plants and animals contain even more water than that: think of how much water is part of a watermelon or cactus! If an organism cannot get the water it needs, it will become *dehydrated*. If it stays dehydrated, it will die.

Plants and animals must get the water they need from the habitat in which they live. That water may come from any number of sources, including standing water, ground water, precipitation, and water given off by other living things. Plants take in water through their roots and sometimes through their leaf surfaces. Some animals drink water, some absorb it by living in damp places, and some get what they need from the moisture contained in the plants or animals they eat.

Some plants and animals need a lot of water to survive, and some do quite well with just a little. A willow tree grows best if its roots are in constantly wet soil. A Joshua tree lives only in desert areas where there is very little rain, but it is able to store water for future use. A painted turtle needs to live out its life cycle in or near water and will not survive for long without it; a desert tortoise can survive with very little water.

Each of these has special adaptations enabling it to live in its particular habitat. The willow could not trade places with the Joshua tree, nor could the painted turtle and the tortoise switch homes.

The amount of water in any habitat determines which plants and animals are able to survive and thrive there. This is true for different areas within the habitat as well. On the playground, you may find certain plants and animals living only in the slightly lower areas where runoff from rain or watering collects. If you have sprinklers, you may find some plants and animals living near the sprinkler heads but nowhere else. Other organisms may be found only on higher ground or in dryer areas.

A change in water conditions can cause some populations to move or die. You may have seen ants swarming from a flooded anthill or earthworms crawling onto the sidewalk to escape drowning after a heavy rain. If lack of rainfall or a broken sprinkler result in plants dying, the animals that lived among those plants and depended on them for food, water, and shelter will need to move elsewhere.

Water conditions can be quite different in locations only a few feet or even inches apart: beneath a bush or tree, along the sun-drenched western wall of a building, in the middle of the playing field, at the edge of the blacktop where pieces are beginning to break away, or near a leaking faucet or drainage gutter. Although some plants and animals are able to live in nearly any location on the playground, others will be found only in the places that best suit their needs, including their need for water.

 © 1998 AIMS Education Foundation

Damp Dwellings

Topic
Water in a Habitat

Key Question
Where is the best place on the school grounds to keep a sponge moist?

Focus
Students compare water-conserving conditions in different areas of the playground habitat.

Guiding Documents
Project 2061 Benchmarks
- *For any particular environment, some kinds of plants and animals survive well, some survive less well, and some cannot survive at all.*
- *Plants and animals both need to take in water, and animals need to take in food. In addition, plants need light.*
- *Most living things need water, food, and air.*

NRC Standard
- *Organisms have basic needs. For example, animals need air, water, and food; plants require air, water, nutrients, and light. Organisms can survive only in environments, and distinct environments support the life of different types of organisms.*

NCTM Standards
- *Construct number meanings through real-world experiences and the use of physical materials*
- *Collect, organize, and describe data*

Math
Measurement
    mass
Graphing

Science
Environmental science
    habitats
Life science

Integrated Processes
Observing
Predicting
Collecting and recording data
Comparing and contrasting
Identifying and controlling variables
Generalizing

Materials
For each team or group of students:
    sponge cut in four equal pieces (see *Management 2*)
    container of water
    pipette or eyedropper
    balance
    permanent marking pen (see *Procedure 1*)
    4 sheets of waxed paper
Optional:
    plastic cup or container for each group
    map of playground

Background Information
(Please refer to *The Inside Story: Water.*)

Students may hold the misconception that dehydration occurs only under hot and dry conditions because such conditions are likely to call their attention (thirst) to the fact that they need to replace water they have lost. In fact, dehydration is the result of any situation in which an organism does not take in enough water to replace what has been used up or lost. The normal processes of respiration in animals and transpiration in plants use water; so do such functions as removal of waste. Dehydration can occur as the result of various conditions in the environment, including both heat and cold, causing water loss in the organism and limiting the amount of water available for it to use.

In this activity, the primary loss of water is caused by evaporation, although a small amount may also be lost through handling. A real-world organism with moderate water needs is represented by a small piece of sponge. The different habitat conditions around the school are compared according to how they are able to support the need of the sponge "organism" to retain moisture.

Management
1. Length of time to expose the sponge "organisms" depends on the temperature and humidity conditions. For the most interesting results, let the ones in the driest habitats dry out as much as possible. To determine the best amount of time, it may help to leave a sponge in a dry area the day before the activity and check on it periodically.

92   © 1998 AIMS Education Foundation

2. Sponges which are approximately 10.5 by 7 cm work well. Before beginning the activity, cut each sponge into four equal quarters.

3. For younger learners, designate four specific habitats with as wide a range of drying conditions as possible (i.e., in direct sun, under a bush, on the shaded north side of a building, in an area of filtered sun). Have each group put one sponge "organism" in each location.

4. Sponges should be wrung out so that they contain water but are not dripping. Otherwise, the first observed water loss may actually reflect excess water running out of the sponge. Have the students carry and keep their sponges on a sheet of waxed paper (cut to equal sizes) to minimize water loss through contact with a porous surface or accidental squeezing.

5. Make the size and water content of each sponge as uniform as possible. This can be done by balancing dampened sponges opposite each other on a pan balance and adding water a few drops at a time until the pans are level.

6. If necessary, have the students make a simple sign to leave near each of their sponges explaining that this is part of a science project and please to leave it alone.

7. Ground rules for sponge habitats:
   • All sponges must be placed outdoors.
   • At least four of their six sides must be exposed to the air.
   • Sponges may not be wrapped, buried, or otherwise protected.
   • No water may be added to any sponge during this activity.
   • Student teams should handle only their own sponge and must leave all other sponges untouched.

Procedure

1. Give each student team four quarters of a dry sponge and a permanent marker. Explain to them that the sponges represent living organisms. Have the student teams mark each of their (dry) sponges so they can be distinguished from all others.

2. Give each team a container of water. Tell the students to submerge each sponge in water, wring it out so it is soggy but not dripping, and place it on its own sheet of waxed paper. Direct them to use the balance to adjust the mass of their four sponges to be as similar as possible. Then have them record the beginning mass of each sponge.

3. Tell the class that today's mystery involves finding the best places on the playground for certain organisms (represented by these sponges) to live. Like other organisms, these have specific needs including the right amount of water in their environment. They need to be able to stay damp to survive and thrive. The field detectives' task is to find which areas of the playground have good conditions for them to be able to "live."

4. Go over the ground rules (see *Management 7*) and send the teams out on the school grounds to find four very different habitats for each of their sponges. Have the students record the location of each habitat, giving a brief description of the setting, whether it is in sun or shade, and the type of surface on which the sponge is "living." Direct them to leave each sponge in its habitat and return to class.

5. Ask the teams to sketch and describe each of the habitats they selected. If you have a map of the playground, have them mark each location on the map, or list the choices according to general area: out in the field, along the north fence, near the sandbox, etc. Ask the students to share why they chose some of the locations, as well as their predictions as to whether the sponge will retain moisture or dry out at that particular location. Discuss the students' perceptions of the importance of water to living things, guiding them to understand that all living things must have water to exist.

6. After an appropriate amount of time (see *Management 1*), send the teams out to retrieve their sponges and bring them back to class. Direct the students to note the conditions of the habitat, particularly if the amount of sun or shade has changed.

7. Have the teams record the mass of each sponge and arrange them in order from most damp to least damp. Challenge them to create a graph to display their data.

8. Discuss first within groups and then as a class which conditions caused the sponges to dry out the most and which were the best environments for enabling them to retain water. Generate a class chart to compare the data from each student team. Organize the data to compare different areas of the playground.

9. Talk about the role of water as a necessity of life and an integral part of the structure of all living things. Evaluate each habitat according to the water loss sustained by its sponge "organisms." Guide the students to suggest reasons that the sponges in some habitats lost less water than those in other areas.

10. Ask the students to consider and suggest ways that they avoid excessive water loss as they go about their lives. Work together to identify places to go to keep from losing water when it is hot and dry. Discuss what these places have in common.

Discussion

1. What were some of the reasons you chose each particular place to put your sponges? In which location do you predict your sponge will keep the most water? ... lose the most water?

2. In what ways did each of your sponges change after time spent in its habitat? How do you explain

any changes in each one's mass, the way it feels, its appearance? What has happened to any water that has been lost from any of your sponges?

3. Compare the habitats where the sponge critters retained the most water. What did these habitats have in common? Similarly compare the habitats where they lost the most water.

4. If a "desert sponge" came to your playground, where would be the best place for it to live? What about a "rain forest sponge"? ... a "grasslands sponge"? Explain your thinking.

5. If you could go anywhere on a hot, dry day, where would you go? Why? What do the places suggested have in common with each other?

6. Think about different animals you know about. How do they manage to keep from losing water? Plants can't survive without water either. How does the need for water affect where and how plants grow?

7. How is your sponge similar to real living organisms? How is it different?

Extension

Find and record the mass of each sponge at the beginning of the activity, then determine and graph the amount of water loss at regular intervals throughout the day. Either customary or non-customary units of mass can be used.

Curriculum Correlation

Art

Have the students decorate their sponges to give them more personality.

Creative writing

Form author groups to write a series of sponge adventure stories, each describing a sponge's search for water and other necessities of life in a different environment.

Literature

Cobb, Vicki. *This Place is Dry*. Walker and Company. New York. 1989.

- Description of living in Arizona's Sonoran Desert, detailing the plant and animal adaptations necessary for survival and touching on the history and culture of the area.

Home Link

Ask the students to look for plants and animals in their yards or around their neighborhood, listing them according to whether they are living in soggy, slightly damp, or dry areas. Compare the lists, looking for similarities, differences, and patterns.

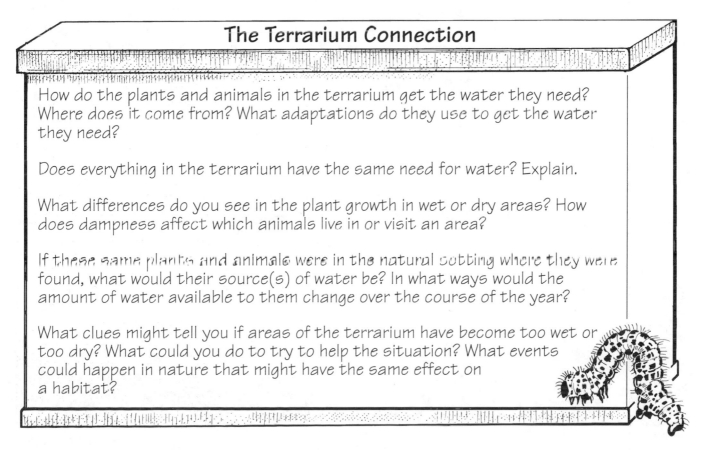

The Terrarium Connection

How do the plants and animals in the terrarium get the water they need? Where does it come from? What adaptations do they use to get the water they need?

Does everything in the terrarium have the same need for water? Explain.

What differences do you see in the plant growth in wet or dry areas? How does dampness affect which animals live in or visit an area?

If these same plants and animals were in the natural setting where they were found, what would their source(s) of water be? In what ways would the amount of water available to them change over the course of the year?

What clues might tell you if areas of the terrarium have become too wet or too dry? What could you do to try to help the situation? What events could happen in nature that might have the same effect on a habitat?

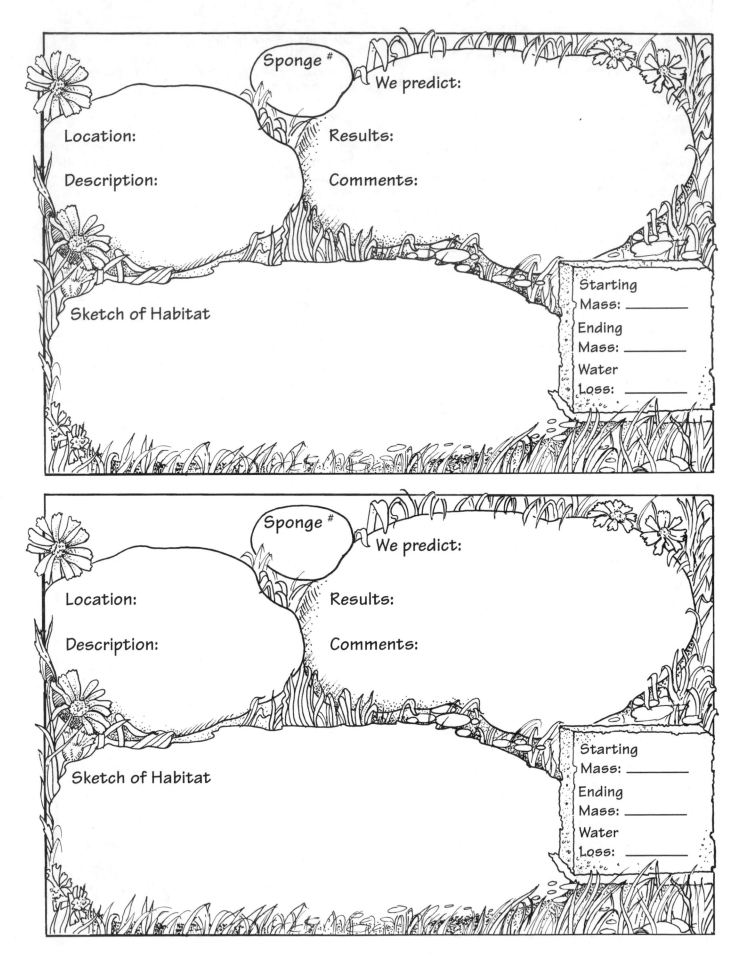

Sponge #

Location:

Description:

We predict:

Results:

Comments:

Sketch of Habitat

Starting
Mass: _____

Ending
Mass: _____

Water
Loss: _____

Sponge #

Location:

Description:

We predict:

Results:

Comments:

Sketch of Habitat

Starting
Mass: _____

Ending
Mass: _____

Water
Loss: _____

© 1998 AIMS Education Foundation

Running on Empty

Topic
Water in Living Things

Key Question
How can organisms replace the water they have lost?

Focus
Students will observe and measure water loss in an exposed damp sponge.

Guiding Documents
Project 2061 Benchmarks
- *For any particular environment, some kinds of plants and animals survive well, some survive less well, and some cannot survive at all.*
- *Plants and animals both need to take in water, and animals need to take in food. In addition, plants need light.*
- *Most living things need water, food, and air.*

NRC Standard
- *Organisms have basic needs. For example, animals need air, water, and food; plants require air, water, nutrients, and light. Organisms can survive only in environments, and distinct environments support the life of different types of organisms.*

NCTM Standards
- *Relate physical materials, pictures, and diagrams to mathematical ideas*
- *Construct number meanings through real-world experiences and the use of physical materials*
- *Collect, organize, and describe data*
- *Construct, read, and interpret displays of data*

Math
Measurement
   mass
   volume
Graphing
Averaging

Science
Environmental science
   habitats
Life science

Integrated Processes
Observing
Predicting
Collecting and recording data
Comparing and contrasting
Identifying and controlling variables
Applying
Generalizing

Materials
For each team or group of students:
   sponge
   graduated cylinder (10 or 50 ml)
   container of water
   pipette or eyedropper
   balance
   masses, customary or non-customary

Background Information
(Please refer to *The Inside Story: Water*)

All living things use water regularly as part of their life processes. Animals lose water every day as wastes move out of their bodies. People and some animals lose water when they perspire. The leaves of a plant give off water in a process called *transpiration*. Big trees, especially those with large leaves, go through large quantities of water each day. A mature maple tree can lose as much as 265 liters (about 70 gallons) of water every hour on a hot summer afternoon.

Water needs to be replaced or the organism will die. If plants cannot take in enough water, they will wilt and soon die. Many animals replenish a part of their water supply by utilizing moisture from the air they are breathing. Some are able to absorb water directly from wet or damp areas of their environment. People and some animals get most of the water they need from consuming liquids and foods.

The human body cannot survive if it loses more than 20% of the water it normally contains. Although people can live as long as two months without food, they can last only a few days — a week at the very most — without water. In normal circumstances, a human needs to take in about 2.4 liters (2.5 quarts) of water every day.

If for reasons of lack of water or severe illness a person is not able to drink or retain the amount of water needed, he or she will begin to suffer from *dehydration*. People who are dehydrated need to drink plenty of fluids. In severe cases, hospitalization is necessary. Without treatment, dehydration will damage the body systems, eventually leading to a painful death.

Management

1. Set up the activity early in the day and do the readings and replenishment later in order to have the longest possible time for evaporation. You may need to begin the activity one day and do the replenishment the next, depending upon the temperature and humidity.
2. For best results, choose the warmest and driest location possible.
3. The same sponges from *Damp Dwellings* can be used again. They should be saturated for this activity but not have excess water running or dripping from them. Once they are placed in the balance, they should not be handled for the duration of the activity.
4. Some graduated cylinders are calibrated so the scale can be read both from top to bottom and from bottom to top, which makes it easier for the students to see how much water they have used to replenish the sponges. If yours are not numbered both ways, duplicate the scale, renumber it from top to bottom (so the numbers are reversed) and tape it next to the scale on the side of each graduated cylinder. An easy way to do this is to put transparent tape right over the scale, trace the markings with a fine point permanent pen, peel off the tape, renumber, and stick it back on next to the scale. If you cover the new scale numbers with more tape or clear contact paper, the writing will last through many washings.
5. If your students are not yet calculating averages, the data concerning the amount of water needing to be replenished could be recorded on a class graph and discussed.

Procedure

1. Give each student team a sponge and a small container of water. Direct them to submerge the sponge in the water and wring it out, leaving it wet, but not dripping, and place it on one pan of a balance. They should then add masses until the pans of the balance are level.
2. The students should check on the balance at regular intervals until the pan of the balance with the sponge is significantly higher than the pan with the masses. The length of time until this occurs will vary depending on the surrounding temperature and level of humidity.
3. Ask your detectives to think about clues they have observed showing that someone is thirsty. Challenge them to think about how they might predict that someone is soon likely be thirsty even before that person starts to show signs. [hot day, active

game, mention of being thirsty, etc.] Discuss what thirst signifies and various ways that people take care of their need for water.

4. Fill a graduated cylinder with water. If the students are not familiar with this scientific measuring device, take time to show them how to read the scale (see *Management 4*). Use a pipette or eyedropper to add water from the cylinder to the sponge, a drop at a time, until the pans of the balance are again level. Determine the amount of water that was needed and record.
5. Find the average number of milliliters needed by the entire class. Guide the students to see the connection between the water they added directly to the sponge and the water plants and animals take in directly.
6. Ask the students to share some of the ways they replenish water their bodies use as they go about their lives.
7. Discuss different ways that plants and animals take care of their need for water. Consider the effect of factors such as surrounding temperature and level of humidity.

Discussion

1. How would the results of this activity compare on a day that was 20° warmer or cooler than today? ... three months from now? ... on a stormy (or dry) day? Explain.
2. Did all of the sponges in the class lose about the same amount of water? How do you account for this?
3. How does your body lose water in the course of a normal day? How do you go about replacing the water your body has lost?
4. What are some of the similarities and differences between the ways that you replenish water and the ways other animals and plants take care of their need for water?
5. Where on the playground might animals be more likely to go to satisfy their need for water? Explain your reasoning. What clues have you noticed? What clues could you look for to find out?
6. What growth patterns on the playground (or other areas) can you find that indicate more (or less) water available for plants? How do you explain what you see?

Extensions

1. How might the outcomes of this activity vary in different conditions of temperature and humidity? Have the students brainstorm, design, and set up a class activity to find out.
2. Some organisms take in some of the water they need by absorbing it directly from their environment. This could be demonstrated by following steps 1-4 of this activity; then placing towels that are wetter

          © 1998 AIMS Education Foundation

than the sponge underneath and around it. Could an organism maintain the water level it needed in this way? Challenge the students to set up a system in which the sponge organism can absorb the amount it needs. Is it possible to replenish the full amount of water lost? Is it possible for the organism to maintain a healthy water level?

3. The mass of one milliliter of water (at 4°C) equals one gram. Have the students measure and record the loss of mass to see this relationship. This could be done by beginning with the wet sponge balanced against gram masses in a pan balance. To determine the mass of water loss, remove masses until the pans are level again, then add up the masses that were removed.

4. Place a fresh plant cutting in a calibrated container of water. Cover the surface of the container with plastic wrap to prevent evaporation. Measure the amount of water consumed by the plant. Compare with similar-sized cuttings from different plants. Encase the entire setup in a plastic bag or enclosed aquarium to observe or collect and measure the water given off by the plant.

Curriculum Correlation

Literature

Robinson, Sandra. *The Rainstick: a Fable.* Falcon Press. Helena, MT. 1994.

- Fable from West Africa about a young boy's quest for the sound of rain in a time of drought. Applies well to reinforce the need for water to sustain life.

Rogasky, Barbara. *The Water of Life.* Holiday House. New York. 1986.

- Beautifully illustrated retelling of the Grimm fairy tale. The water in this story has magical curative powers, but a connection could easily be made to the symbolism of water as essential to life.

Home Link

During a weekend, have the students collect data at home to determine how much water or other liquids (milk, soda, coffee, etc.) their family drinks in a day. Encourage them to bring the data to school to discuss, analyze, and compare, taking into consideration such factors as number and ages of people in the family, size of glasses or cups, time of year, type of liquid, weather conditions, events occurring at the time, etc.

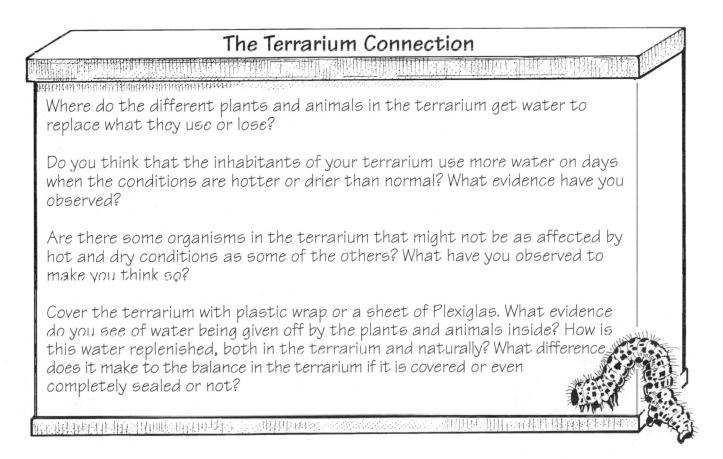

The Terrarium Connection

Where do the different plants and animals in the terrarium get water to replace what they use or lose?

Do you think that the inhabitants of your terrarium use more water on days when the conditions are hotter or drier than normal? What evidence have you observed?

Are there some organisms in the terrarium that might not be as affected by hot and dry conditions as some of the others? What have you observed to make you think so?

Cover the terrarium with plastic wrap or a sheet of Plexiglas. What evidence do you see of water being given off by the plants and animals inside? How is this water replenished, both in the terrarium and naturally? What difference does it make to the balance in the terrarium if it is covered or even completely sealed or not?

Running on Empty

Class average mL needed

_____

Group # _____ Needed

Total # Groups _____

Total # mL Needed _____

Number mL ÷ Number of groups

_____

Our sponge needed

_____ mL

© 1998 A!MS Education Foundation

Here's the Scoop...

The Inside Story
Air...

Air is one necessity of life that many of us tend to take for granted. We don't have to search to find it or work to get it. We usually don't even have to think about breathing it, because our bodies automatically take in air, pull out the oxygen we need, and expel the carbon dioxide waste products we don't need.

Yet all it takes is the experience of not being able to "catch" our breath — perhaps after a hard fall, or strenuous exercise, or being sick with a respiratory illness — for us to realize just how important air is to our lives. For us and for most animals, air is absolutely essential. We can live about a month without food and about a week without water, but we will last only a few minutes without air.

What is air? It is a substance, a mixture of gases, water vapor, and dust that forms a band wrapped around the planet earth. The proportion of gases in air is 78% nitrogen, 21% oxygen, and 1% a combination of other gases. Oxygen is the part of air that we need constantly and use immediately each time we breathe, and without which we would quickly die.

What about fish and other animals that don't live in the air? They use oxygen dissolved in the water around them. There are only a few kinds of organisms — mostly bacteria — that can live without oxygen.

After oxygen is taken in by an organism, it goes out to all the different cells in the body. There it combines with chemicals from the food eaten by that person or animal. The energy produced during this process enables each cell to do its particular job. Carbon dioxide is formed as a part of this process and eventually is returned to the air.

Plants need air too. Their cells use oxygen in a way similar to animal cells. They also use carbon dioxide from the air as part of *photosynthesis*, their food-making process. During this process oxygen is produced and returned to the air. The oxygen in the air we breathe has been made by trees, grass, plants, and algae. Like animals, plants also take in oxygen and give off carbon dioxide, but in much smaller amounts.

Nitrogen — the main ingredient of air — is also essential to life. It is needed for the formation of the cell structure of all living things. Living things can absorb oxygen directly from the air, but they cannot take and use nitrogen gas in the same way. Instead, certain bacteria and algae take nitrogen from the air and change it into a chemical that can be absorbed by plants. Nitrogen is then passed along the food chain and put to use as one organism consumes another. When an organism dies, the nitrogen it its body is returned to the soil where most of it is taken in by plants to become part of another food chain. Some nitrogen, however, is changed back to nitrogen gas by another kind of bacteria and returned to the air.

Compacted Playground

Topic
Soil Compaction

Key Questions
1. What happens to soil when a lot of people walk on it?
2. Why don't plants often grow well in such areas?

Focus
Soil that has been compacted loses its air spaces, reducing its ability to support plant life.

Guiding Documents
Project 2061 Benchmarks
- *Most living things need water, food, and air.*
- *Animals and plants sometimes cause changes in their surroundings.*

NRC Standards
- *Organisms have basic needs. For example, animals need air, water, and food; plants require air, water, nutrients, and light. Organisms can survive only in environments in which their needs can be met. The world has many different environments, and distinct environments support the life of different types of organisms.*
- *Soils have properties of color and texture, capacity to retain water, and ability to support the growth of many kinds of plants, including those in our food supply.*

NCTM Standards
- *Use mathematics in other curriculum areas*
- *Compute with whole numbers, fractions, decimals, integers, and rational numbers*
- *Estimate, make, and use measurements to describe and compare phenomena*

Math
Measurement
   linear
   mass
Graphing
Computing averages

Science
Environmental science
   habitats
Earth science
   soil

Integrated Processes
Observing
Predicting
Collecting and recording data
Comparing and contrasting
Identifying and controlling variables
Applying
Generalizing

Materials
For the class:
   large bucket of loose topsoil
   scoop
   newspapers

For each team of students:
   three flexible plastic cups (see *Management 1*)
   balance
   cardboard mailing or gift wrap tube
   screwdriver (see *Management 1*)
   non-permanent marker
   damp paper towels

Optional:
   calculators
   C or D cells for added mass
   masking or electrical tape

Background Information
Most playgrounds have places where grass doesn't grow well, if at all. Typically these areas indicate heavy use: around a drinking fountain, the pitcher's mound and baselines on the playing field, a shortcut across a corner. Although the bareness may be partially due to wear and tear on the grass, not enough sunlight, or perhaps chemical treatment such as is used to mark base lines, it is also an indication of compacted soil. Under the pressure of the footfalls of hundreds of students over the course of time, the soil in these high-use areas has literally had the air pressed out of it.

The spaces between soil particles are essential to plant growth. Moisture and air are trapped in these spaces, and the plant roots grow down through them. The roots need moisture in order to transfer nutrients to the other parts of the plant. Also, when the air spaces are gone, new plants cannot take root and survive. In some managed park areas, people are being discouraged from walking close to significant trees because the impact of the foot traffic is compacting the soil around the surface roots and causing them to die.

Over time in a natural setting, compacted soil can be remedied by the work of earthworms and other burrowing animals that gradually move in from nearby less compacted areas. On a large scale, plowing or otherwise disturbing and loosening the soil, along with the addition of organic material, will help restore its ability to support plant life.

Management

1. Safety issues:
   - A screwdriver could be dangerous if misused. If this is a concern, you may wish to make *Part 3* a demonstration instead of a small group activity.
   - Use flexible plastic cups that will bend without breaking. If you cannot find these, use paper cups. Brittle plastic cups could be unsafe in this activity.
2. Divide the students into teams of two to four students depending on how many sets of supplies you have available.
3. For ease of cleanup, use newspapers to cover the work area during the first part of this activity.
4. A large screwdriver works best. If it is not going far enough into the ground, add one or two C or D cells, taping them securely to the handle of the screwdriver to increase the mass. Be sure to use the same tool for all areas compared. Either a flat head or a Phillips head screwdriver will work.

5. Younger learners may cut paper strips and glue them to a graph to show the depths of the screwdriver probe rather than measuring in millimeters.
6. If your school has a blacktop playground, this activity can also be done in a neighborhood park.

Procedure

Part 1

1. Take the students to a location where bare or worn areas of grass are clearly visible. Ask them to think of observations that might explain why plants are not growing or are growing less well in these areas. Explain that as detectives they will be looking for possible explanations to solve the mystery behind the missing grass.
2. Back in class, list observations and clues noted. Encourage the students to back up any explanations they offer with supporting evidence.
3. If the discussion has not included the mention of heavy foot traffic, guide it in that direction. Ask the students to think about a time when they have handled something so much that it has actually shrunk in size. [marshmallow, mashing a slice of bread, etc.] Explain that the pressure they have put on that substance has squeezed some of the air out of it, making it smaller. Ask them to think about how this is similar to what happens to soil in a well-traveled area.
4. To give students the idea of what *compaction* means, ask each team to fill two identical cups with equal masses of topsoil. The actual mass does not matter. Have them balance the mass by putting one cup on each side of a balance and moving soil from one cup to the other until they are balanced.

Have the students measure and record the depth of both; also use a marker to show the top line of dirt in each cup.

5. Direct them to set aside one cup, then put the empty cup on top of the other and take turns pushing down with their fist in the empty cup, trying to compact the soil as much as possible.
6. Have them remove the empty cup and check the mass of the two cups again.
7. Ask them to measure and compare the depth of soil in the two cups now and discuss their observations of the soil before, during, and after compaction.

Part 2

1. Tell the students to do the "flatfoot flop" by standing on their tiptoes, then dropping their feet quickly to a flatfoot position. Have them repeat the process several times, then describe how it feels. Ask where they might go to experience both harder and softer landings. Try whatever areas they suggest (carpeting, cement sidewalk, blacktop, grass, sandbox ...) to experience a range of surface hardness.
2. Have each team select five very different locations (only soil or plant growth areas this time; no pavement) where they might expect to find a difference in surface hardness. Be sure that their choices include at least one of the bare spots and an area such as sand or a flower bed that they would expect to be soft. Designate each area A, B, C, D, or E. Have each team record the locations to be tested and predict how they will rank from softest (least compacted) to hardest (most compacted).
4. Send out the teams to test their predictions using the "flatfoot flop" and rank the areas from softest to hardest according to this subjective scale.
5. Optional: Have each team test another team's findings and see if they agree.

Part 3

1. Explain that the students will use a more accurate means of determining soil compactedness by using a screwdriver probe, comparing the depth it will go into the soil under consistent conditions of pressure.
2. Each team will need a screwdriver, a water-based marker, and a cardboard tube to test the same areas previously visited. Encourage the students to control variables as much as possible. They should rest the tube with one end on the ground so that it is perpendicular, if necessary moving aside vegetation as much as possible. Advise them to hold the screwdriver by the end of the handle with their fingertips resting on the end of the tube so that they will drop it without adding any force.

3. When the screwdriver is embedded in the ground, have them carefully pull the tube up and away, then mark ground level on the blade of the screwdriver before they pull it out. They should measure and record the depth in millimeters and wipe off the blade before using it again.
4. Direct the students to take three readings within 15 cm (6 inches) of each other, but not at the exact same spot. They should record this data and then calculate the average for each location.

Discussion

1. In what ways is the compacted soil different from soil with healthy plants? What would need to be done to make it able to support plant life?
2. Were any areas of the playground softer or harder than you expected? What other factors might account for softness or hardness besides soil compaction?
3. Were your results with the probe consistent with the results you found from the "flatfoot flop" method? How do you explain this?
4. What kinds of connections do you see between the area with the most compacted soil and the amount and type of use it gets?
5. If your job were to be sure that grass grows well everywhere on your playground, how would you go about doing it? What changes would you make?

Extensions

1. Continue testing different areas until the whole playground (or a whole section) has been thoroughly tested. Make a map showing areas of most, moderate, and least use based on the results. Analyze what reasons may be behind the evidence found.
2. Dig up two similar-sized chunks of compacted soil. Try not to break them up at all. Put them in separate containers. Add some leaf litter and several earthworms to one. Spray both with equal amounts of water and keep them both moist. Observe the work of earthworms over time compared to what happens to the one left alone.
3. Compare the force needed to drive a 16-penny nail all the way into a 2x4 board, heavily compacted soil, and the asphalt in the parking lot.

Curriculum Correlation

Literature

Kalman, Bobbie and Janine Schaub. *The Air I Breathe*. Crabtree Publishing Company. New York. 1993.

- Solid information about the necessity and importance of air as we use it and share it with others.

Home Link

Ask the students to make a simple map of their backyard, a friend's backyard, or an area of a neighborhood park. Can they predict which areas will have the most compacted soil? Have them use one or both test methods to show which areas have the most and least amount of soil compactedness.

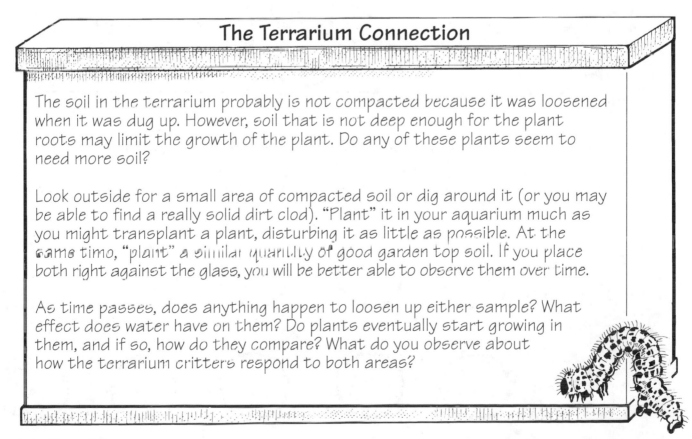

The Terrarium Connection

The soil in the terrarium probably is not compacted because it was loosened when it was dug up. However, soil that is not deep enough for the plant roots may limit the growth of the plant. Do any of these plants seem to need more soil?

Look outside for a small area of compacted soil or dig around it (or you may be able to find a really solid dirt clod). "Plant" it in your aquarium much as you might transplant a plant, disturbing it as little as possible. At the same time, "plant" a similar quantity of good garden top soil. If you place both right against the glass, you will be better able to observe them over time.

As time passes, does anything happen to loosen up either sample? What effect does water have on them? Do plants eventually start growing in them, and if so, how do they compare? What do you observe about how the terrarium critters respond to both areas?

Compacted Playground

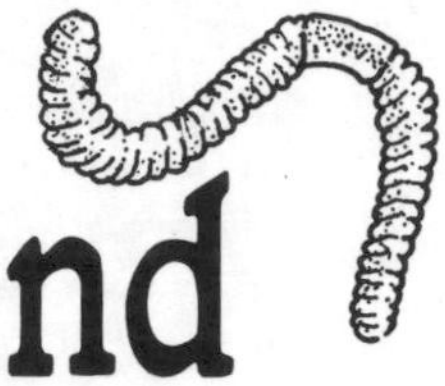

Part 1

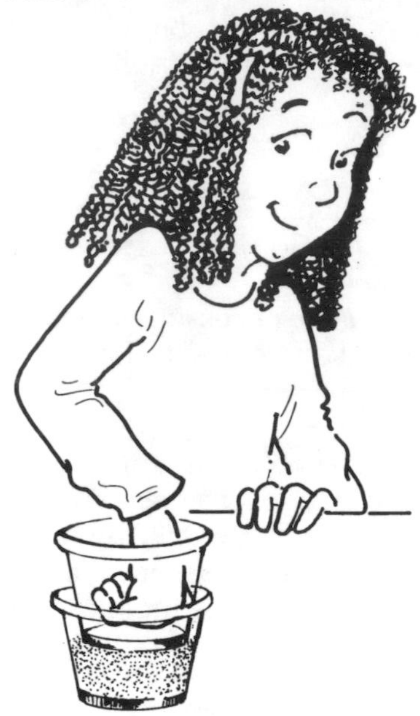

	Compacted	Not Compacted
	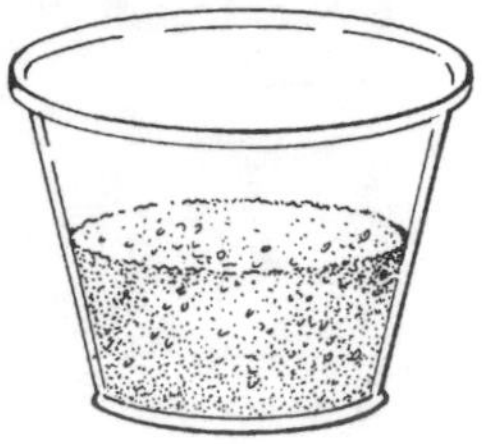	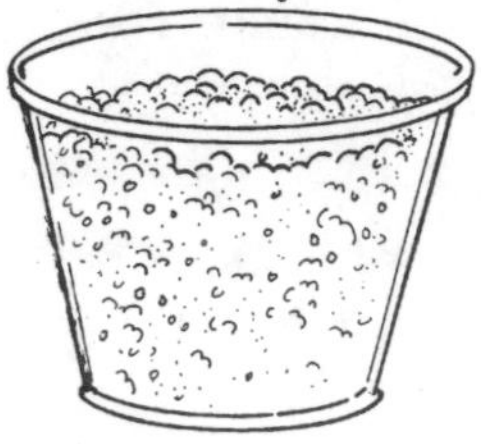
Depth	______	______
Mass	______	______

Observations / Comments / Conclusions

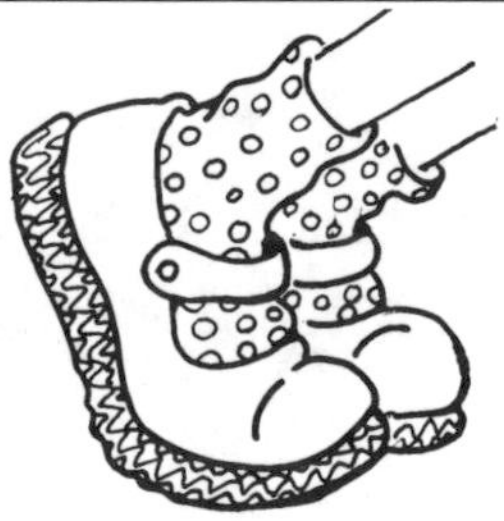

Least Compacted ← 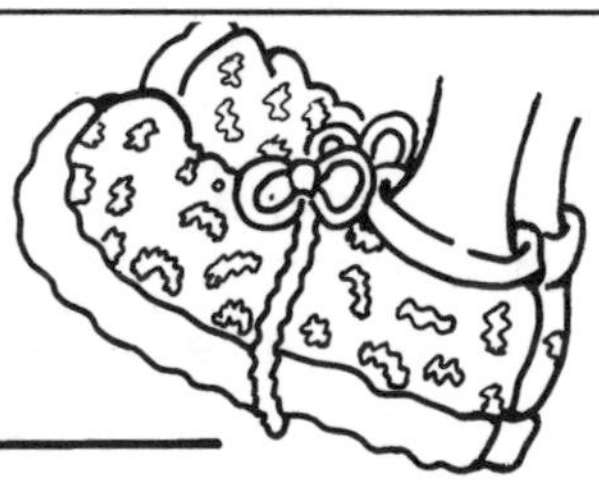 → Most Compacted

Part 2

Predict

Flatfoot Flop results

Part 3

Average probe results

 © 1998 AIMS Education Foundation

Compacted Playground

A Location

Probe results:

Average:

B Location

Probe results:

Average:

C Location

Probe results:

Average:

D Location

Probe results:

Average:

E Location

Probe results:

Average:

105 © 1998 AIMS Education Foundation

A Warrant for Water

Topic
Air and Water in Soil

Key Question
What factors affect how quickly water soaks into soil?

Focus
Students will test water percolation in different areas of the playground habitat and compare water retention in soil samples from these areas.

Guiding Documents
Project 2061 Benchmarks
- *People can often learn about things around them by just observing those things carefully, but sometimes they can learn more by doing something to the things and noting what happens.*
- *Most living things need water, food, and air.*
- *In all environments — freshwater, marine, forest, desert, grassland, mountain, and others — organisms with similar needs may compete with one another for resources, including food, space, water, air, and shelter. In any particular environment, the growth and survival of organisms depend on the physical conditions.*

NRC Standards
- *Organisms have basic needs. For example, animals need air, water, and food; plants require air, water, nutrients, and light. Organisms can survive only in environments in which their needs can be met. The world has many different environments, and distinct environments support the life of different types of organisms.*
- *Soils have properties of color and texture, capacity to retain water, and ability to support the growth of many kinds of plants, including those in our food supply.*
- *Employ simple equipment and tools to gather data and extend the senses.*

NCTM Standards
- *Understand the attributes of length, capacity, weight, mass, area, volume, time, temperature, and angle*
- *Develop the process of measuring and concepts related to units of measurement*
- *Make and use measurements in problems and everyday situations*

Math
Measurement
    length
    time
Estimating
Graphing

Science
Environmental science
    habitats
Earth science
    soil
Life science
    plants
    animals

Integrated Processes
Observing
Classifying
Predicting
Collecting and recording data
Comparing and contrasting
Applying
Generalizing
Inferring

Materials
For each group of students:
    tall can (#10 can, coffee can, etc. with capacity of
        more than 500 mL)
    graduated cylinder (500 or 1000 mL) or 9-oz plastic
        cup (see *Management 2*)
    two-liter bottle of water
    permanent pen
    metric ruler
    trowel or sturdy spoon
    stopwatch or watch with a second hand
    1-3 plastic cups (see *Management 6*)

For the class:
    can opener
    masking tape

Optional:
    piece of wood larger than the circumference of the
        can (see *Management 4*)
    hammer (see *Management 4*)
    cookie sheet(s) or tray(s) (see *Management 7*)

Background Information
The amount of water available in the soil determines whether certain plants can live in an area and how well they will grow. Weather or irrigation may provide sufficient water for healthy plant growth, but if the water isn't retained in the soil long enough for the plants to use it, the plants will die. If the soil holds too much water, the soggy conditions will also limit which plants and animals can live there.

The type of soil in a habitat directly affects how much water is available to the plants growing there. If the soil is mostly clay, or if much of the area is paved, the water will run off and go elsewhere, or just sit in puddles until it evaporates. If the soil is very sandy or full of gravel, the water will quickly run down past the roots of the plants until it reaches a layer of bedrock or clay. The only plants that can do well in one of these situations are those plants that are particularly adapted to that condition. The best soil for most plants contains a sizable amount of organic material. Such soil holds water for future plant use and lets excess water drain off, plus it supplies nutrients for plant growth.

Even if the soil contains organic material, it cannot support plant life well if it is compacted. When water is retained in the soil, it fills the air spaces between the soil particles and clings to the particles themselves. If the soil is compacted, the air spaces between the soil particles are compressed and eventually eliminated. Since these air spaces are the same places where water is stored, the soil's ability to hold water is severely affected as well.

Soil that is of poor quality due to compaction or lack of organic material can be improved by adding compost and plowing or otherwise breaking it up. Earthworms add organic material and create new air spaces as they go about their normal routine.

Management
1. All cans should be the same size or at least have the same diameter. Use a can opener to remove both ends and check for sharp edges. Cover one edge with masking tape to prevent injury (the other end will be in the ground).
2. If graduated cylinders are not available for every group, make your own measuring cups by pouring 500 mL water into plastic cups and marking the top of the water line with a permanent pen or masking tape. You will also need a measure for 150 mL for each group. Consistency is important for comparing results.
3. Use two-liter bottles to transport water to the test sites.
4. If the ground is very hard and the can will not go into it with gentle twisting, place a piece of wood on top of the can and hammer at intervals around the rim to sink it.
5. Chose a demonstration site at which the water will soak in relatively quickly. Monitor the selection of test sites to include both heavily compacted areas (such as baselines or the area around a drinking fountain) and comparatively well-cultivated areas (such as flower beds). Number each site for purposes of graphing and comparing.
6. Older students may choose to test and compare a larger number of sites.
7. If any of the soil samples are damp, *Part 2* may need to be completed over a two-day period to allow the samples time to dry uniformly. Samples may be spread out on a cookie sheet or chart paper to hasten the process.

Procedure
Part 1
1. Ask the students to share what they understand about the importance of air and water in the habitat.

Have them point out different locations of known wet and dry areas on the playground and discuss observations that could account for the varying conditions. If the discussion has not included soil types, remind the class about the different surface areas observed in the activity *Floor Samples* and the compacted area experienced in *Compacted Playground*. Ask the students to consider which of those surfaces they think would retain water and which might not.
2. Encourage them to use clues from the observations they have made so far to suggest reasons why some areas of the playground stay damper and other areas seem to drain or dry out quickly. Refer to *Compacted Playground* and ask them to think about what effect compaction might have on whether water sits on, soaks into, or runs through the soil.
3. Distribute materials to each group. Direct them to measure four centimeters from the untaped end of the can at five or six different locations around the circumference and use the marks as a guide to draw a line all the way around the can. They should also measure and mark a line halfway up the side of a plastic cup, preparing a cup for each site they will be testing.
4. Take the class outside to a predetermined demonstration area. Push or twist a can into the ground so that it is embedded to the four-centimeter mark. Measure 500 mL of water and pour it slowly into the can. Begin timing when the water first touches the ground and stop when the water has completely soaked in.
5. Ask the students to scan the playground and select sites to test that they predict might give a range of different results. Send each group to a different site (or sites) to repeat the test and record their data.
6. When they are through with each test, direct them to take a sample of dirt close to, but not in the wet part of the test site. The sample should be enough to fill the plastic cup to the halfway mark when it is pressed down lightly. This sample should be set aside for *Part 2*.
7. Direct the students to record data from the site(s) they tested as well as several others tested by other groups. Compare and discuss the results, guiding them to understand that water retention in soil depends on both the composition of the soil itself and whether it has air spaces into which the water can soak and fill. Emphasize any connections they can make between whether the soil in an area is compacted (*Compact Playground*) and how quickly water soaks into it.

Part 2
1. When the soil samples in the cups are uniformly dry (see *Management 7*), have the students press each gently to the halfway mark. Any excess soil should be removed rather than packed harder. They should then add 150 mL water, let it sit for two minutes, then pour off any excess water into a graduated cylinder and measure the runoff.

                                        © 1998 AIMS Education Foundation

2. Graph and compare the information. Discuss what might account for any differences they see.
3. Compare the samples with the test results from the playground. Keep in mind that the cup prevents excess water from running through and flowing away, as the water could do in the ground.

Discussion
1. In which areas did you expect the water to soak in quickly? ... slowly? How did your predictions compare with the actual results?
2. How is this test situation similar to natural conditions? How is it different?
3. What does the speed at which water soaks into an area tell you about the air pockets in the soil there? What other factors need to be considered? [composition of soil, water already present]
4. Can soil actually be "full" of water? Explain in your own words what this means.
5. In an area where the soil is already saturated, what happens when more water is added?
6. Compare an area where the water soaked in quickly to an area where it didn't. What factors or circumstances might account for the difference?
7. How does the amount of water held in the soil affect the plants and animals that live there?
8. What differences in dampness and soil compaction might you expect to find in the soil under a tree and a meter away? ... along a wall or fence and a meter or so on either side? Explain your thinking.

Extensions
1. Older students can do several tests in the same area and calculate an average for each location.
2. To simulate desert conditions, test the school sandbox. To compare to rich organic humus, set up and test a container of potting soil.
3. Establish an earthworm colony (see *Terrarium Connection* and *Bibliography Resources*). Observe firsthand the ability of the worms to break up soil and add organic material to it.

Curriculum Correlation
Literature
   Kalman, Bobbie and Janine Schaub. *The Air I Breathe*. Crabtree Publishing Company. New York. 1993.
   • Solid information about the necessity and importance of air as we use it and share it with others.

Home Link
   Have the students list several areas around their home or neighborhood and predict whether the soil would hold water well or not. Challenge them to do one or both tests to find out.

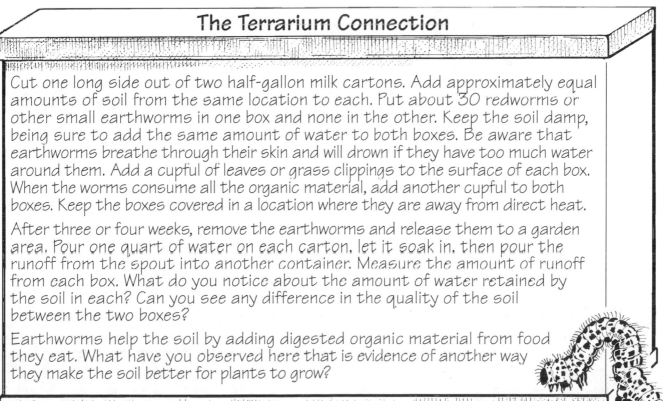

The Terrarium Connection

Cut one long side out of two half-gallon milk cartons. Add approximately equal amounts of soil from the same location to each. Put about 30 redworms or other small earthworms in one box and none in the other. Keep the soil damp, being sure to add the same amount of water to both boxes. Be aware that earthworms breathe through their skin and will drown if they have too much water around them. Add a cupful of leaves or grass clippings to the surface of each box. When the worms consume all the organic material, add another cupful to both boxes. Keep the boxes covered in a location where they are away from direct heat.

After three or four weeks, remove the earthworms and release them to a garden area. Pour one quart of water on each carton, let it soak in, then pour the runoff from the spout into another container. Measure the amount of runoff from each box. What do you notice about the amount of water retained by the soil in each? Can you see any difference in the quality of the soil between the two boxes?

Earthworms help the soil by adding digested organic material from food they eat. What have you observed here that is evidence of another way they make the soil better for plants to grow?

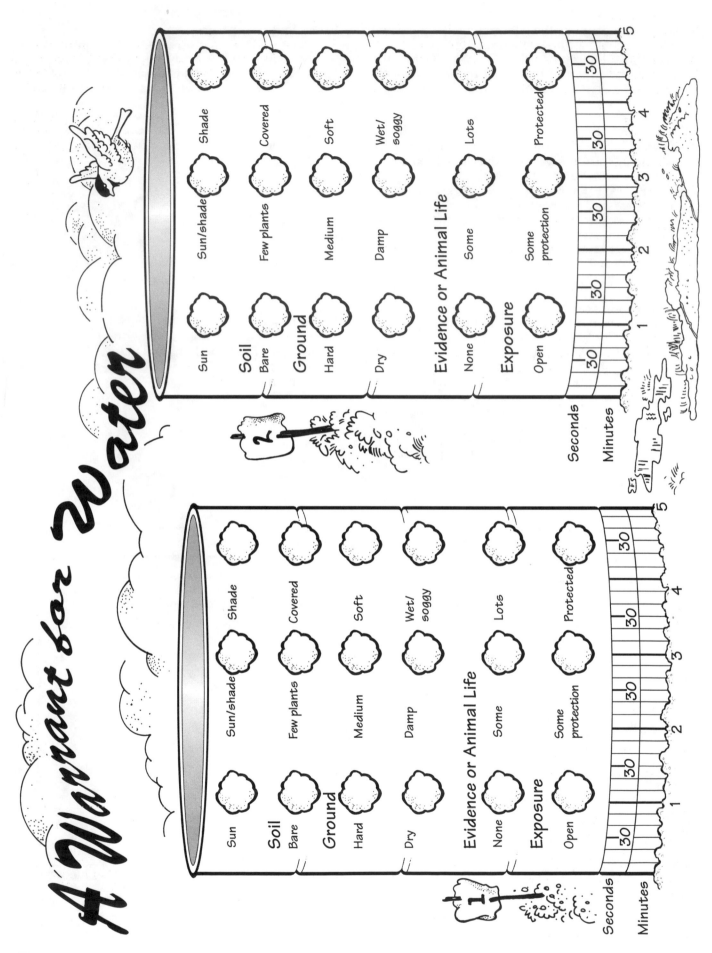

A Warrant for Water

Sun | Sun/shade | Shade

Soil
Bare | Few plants | Covered

Ground
Hard | Medium | Soft

Dry | Damp | Wet/soggy

Evidence or Animal Life
None | Some | Lots

Exposure
Open | Some protection | Protected

Seconds: 30 30 30 30 30 30

Minutes: 1 2 3 4 5

© 1998 AIMS Education Foundation

The Inside Story
Shelter...

Home ... what comes to your mind when you think of that word? Most people want a place where they can be safe and feel protected, be with their family and friends, and rest. Often it is a place to share food and play together. Home is a familiar place to return to each evening when the day's events are done.

It's not so different for most animals. They too need a place where they can be safe, raise their families, and rest. Like people, many need a place where they can be warm and dry when the weather is cold and wet. Although some animals spend much of their lives living or traveling alone, many enjoy the company of others.

When people think of home, they may picture a house or an apartment. In some places people live in tents, caves, grass houses, or some other structure. No matter what they look like, most homes are designed to provide shelter, protecting those who gather there from heat, cold, and weather conditions. They also provide a measure of safety from danger.

For animals, shelter can take a variety of forms. Some build nests, some dig burrows in the ground, others find caves or hollow trees. Many look for shelter in the features of their natural surroundings: beneath a rock, within a pile of leaves, among the roots of a tree. Some animals depend upon other living things: a flea makes its home in an animal's fur. Some organisms like a tree, provide for a whole community: rodents among its roots, beetles beneath its bark, squirrels in its branches, and many more.

Plants need shelter too, although they can't move to get to it. Young seedlings and sprouts may not survive the drying conditions from hours of direct sunlight unless they are sheltered by grasses or low bushes until they are well rooted. Some plants need shelter from the wind. Some must have at least a few hours of shade. Like animals, plants can only live where the conditions are right for them, including their need for shelter.

Design Your Own SHELTER

Topic
Need for Shelter

Key Questions
1. Why do animals and some plants need shelter?
2. What are some of the different kinds of shelters animals use?

Focus
Most animals need a place where they can rest, raise their young, stay warm and dry, and be safe from predators.

Guiding Documents
Project 2061 Benchmarks
- *Animals eat plants or other animals for food and may also use plants (or even other animals) for shelter and nesting.*
- *In all environments — freshwater, marine, forest, desert, grassland, mountain, and others — organisms with similar needs may compete with one another for resources, including food, space, water, air, and shelter. In any particular environment, the growth and survival of organisms depend on the physical conditions.*

NRC Standard
- *An organism's patterns of behavior are related to the nature of that organism's environment, including the kinds and numbers of other organisms present, the availability of food and resources, and the physical characteristics of the environment. When the environment changes, some plants and animals survive and reproduce, and others die or move to new locations.*

Science
Environmental science
    habitats
Life science
    animals

Integrated Processes
Observing
Classifying
Comparing and contrasting
Applying
Generalizing

Materials
For each group of students:
    large plastic garbage bag
    tape
    newspapers
    scissors
(See *Management 4*)

Background Information
Please refer to *The Inside Story: Shelter.*

Management
1. Students should work in teams of two or three to build the shelters.
2. Distribute the task cards so two different teams have the same task.
3. **Safety issue: Any plastic sheeting material can be dangerous if misused. Never allow a student to enclose his or her head in plastic or in any way let it interfere with breathing.**
4. You may wish to provide additional materials for shelter building.
5. Blank task cards are provided for shelter situations suggested by the students.

Procedure
1. Ask the students to talk about their understanding of *shelter* as it applies to their own lives. Guide the discussion to distinguish which elements of shelter are essential [safety, protection from weather, etc.] and which elements add to comfort and may be desirable but are not necessary to life. [fancy house, air conditioning, their own room ...]
2. Remind the students of the clues they found while looking for evidence of life. If necessary, take a walk around the playground to remember or look for more clues. Make a list of all the evidence involving some type of shelter. [nests, burrows, piles of leaves, etc.] Discuss whether these shelters were already part of the environment or if the animal adapted them in some way for its use.
3. Have the students work in small groups to think of all the reasons an animal living on the school playground might need shelter. Compile and discuss the lists.
4. Explain to the students that they will be working with a partner to design a shelter for a particular situation. Distribute the task cards and blank paper for planning. Give the students time to plan what they will build.
5. After the students have built their shelters, give each team the opportunity to show their shelter, explain its purpose, describe the process that went into constructing it, and answer questions from the rest of the class. Compare and contrast the shelters built for similar purposes.

Discussion
1. What were some of the most important things you had to consider as you built your shelter?

2. Where would the best location be for your shelter? Explain your reasoning.
3. What were some of the things all the shelters had in common? What features made some of them unique?
4. If you were going to build another shelter for the same purpose, what would you change? Why?
5. Many plants need shelter too, especially early in their life. What situations can you think of in which a plant might need shelter? [new seedling becoming established, shade from hot sun while still a sprout, protection from strong wind, etc.]

Extension
Encourage each team to design a second shelter, improving upon the model they have built.

Curriculum Correlation
Social Studies
1. Collect or draw pictures of typical shelters from many cultures around the world. List and discuss the similarities and differences. Identify the common needs and purposes of each structure. Relate the style of structure and materials used to the culture, climate, geography, and other factors.
2. Connect this activity specifically to the region(s) or culture(s) you are currently studying.

Literature
Bennett, Paul. *Nature's Secrets: Hibernation.* Thomson Learning. New York. 1994.
• What kinds of shelter do animals use while they hibernate? This book describes where many different animals go to be safe and warm.

Dewey, Jennifer Owings. *Animal Architecture.* Orchard Books. New York. 1991.
• The author describes amazing details and interesting facts about how various animals go about building their homes, depicting the results with detailed pencil drawings. Excellent read-aloud resource.

Hockman, Hilary, editor. *What's Inside? Animal Homes.* Dorling Kindersley. London. 1993.
• Photographs and life-like drawings show the inside and outside of various animal homes. The text describes both the need for that particular type of dwelling and the materials and method used to build it.

MacDonald, Fiona. *Houses: Habitats and Home Life.* Franklin Watts. New York. 1994.
• Here's an interesting social studies correlation showing how people have built shelters throughout history.

Shipman, Wanda. *Animal Architects.* Stackpole Books. Mechanicsburg, PA. 1994.
• This reference for teachers gives detailed information about how different animals use what is in their environment to weave, tunnel, and build shelter. Good material for retelling!

Home Link
What shelter is needed by your pets or pets belonging to people you know? Make a list or draw pictures of different kinds of shelters used by animals you know.

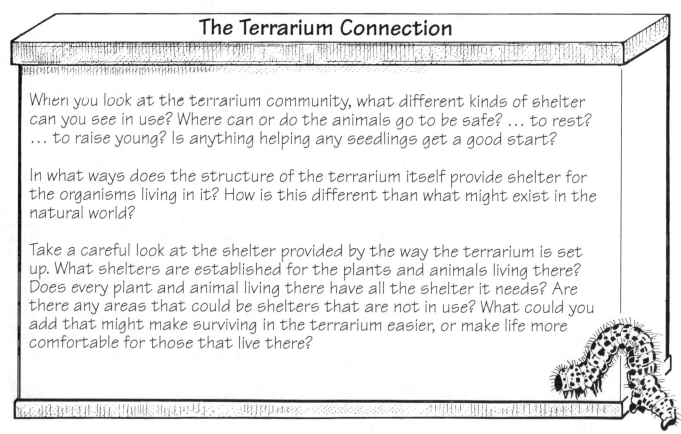

The Terrarium Connection

When you look at the terrarium community, what different kinds of shelter can you see in use? Where can or do the animals go to be safe? ... to rest? ... to raise young? Is anything helping any seedlings get a good start?

In what ways does the structure of the terrarium itself provide shelter for the organisms living in it? How is this different than what might exist in the natural world?

Take a careful look at the shelter provided by the way the terrarium is set up. What shelters are established for the plants and animals living there? Does every plant and animal living there have all the shelter it needs? Are there any areas that could be shelters that are not in use? What could you add that might make surviving in the terrarium easier, or make life more comfortable for those that live there?

You are a small mammal living in the forest. You need a place where you can be protected from a large predator who lives nearby, but you must be able to get in and out quickly for food and water.

You are a mammal living in a grassy field. You need a warm, safe place to raise your litter of babies.

You are an animal who lives in an area where it rains frequently. You need a shelter that will keep you dry, both from the rain above and the puddles or even flood water on the ground.

You are an animal who lives where it is very cold in the winter. You need a shelter where you can be warm and undisturbed as you sleep through the winter.

You are an animal who lives where it is warm most of the time. You need fresh, cooling air in your shelter, but you still need to be safe from your enemies.

You are a small fish living in a tidepool. You need a place to be safe from the larger fish who swim through the tidepool whenever the tide is high.

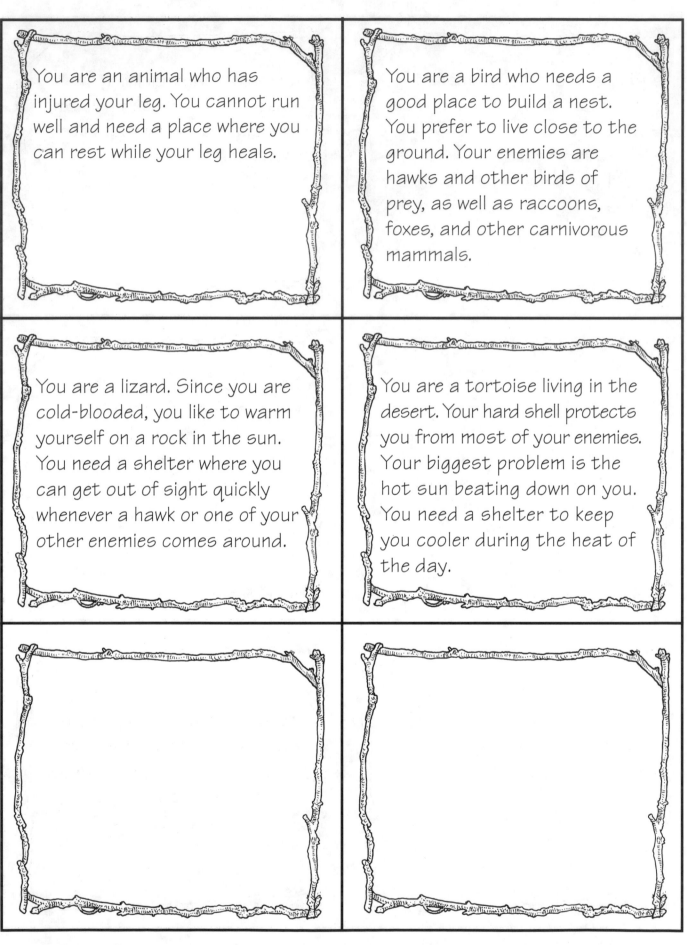

You are an animal who has injured your leg. You cannot run well and need a place where you can rest while your leg heals.

You are a bird who needs a good place to build a nest. You prefer to live close to the ground. Your enemies are hawks and other birds of prey, as well as raccoons, foxes, and other carnivorous mammals.

You are a lizard. Since you are cold-blooded, you like to warm yourself on a rock in the sun. You need a shelter where you can get out of sight quickly whenever a hawk or one of your other enemies comes around.

You are a tortoise living in the desert. Your hard shell protects you from most of your enemies. Your biggest problem is the hot sun beating down on you. You need a shelter to keep you cooler during the heat of the day.

The Inside Story Space...

Do you ever feel too crowded? Have you ever told people around you that you need more room? Perhaps you share a room with a brother or sister and sometimes wish that you had more space to yourself. Maybe your classroom seems crowded, or the cafeteria, or the playground. You may not be comfortable having a lot of people around you when you are in line or in a crowded room. It may bother you if one other person is simply standing too close to you.

Most people are usually not comfortable with being in a crowded situation for long. Our need for space has a lot to do with feeling safe. It also reminds us of our other basic survival needs: food, water, air, and shelter. In situations where there are many people and limited food or water, people push and shove to get what they need to survive. When it gets too warm and stuffy in a crowded room, we are reminded of our need for fresh air to breathe. Shelter implies a place where we can safely rest, but this may not be possible in a small place with too many people.

Plants and animals also need space. Seeds sprouting too close together compete with each other for available water and nutrients in the soil. When this happens, the strongest plants survive and the weakest ones die. Farmers and gardeners understand this, so they plan for the right number of healthy plants in the space available, spreading out seeds as they are planted and thinning out plants that are too close together.

Often animals establish a territory in order to have enough food and water for themselves and their young. Large animals may need quite a lot of space to hunt or graze. Their family's survival depends upon their area, so they will fight to keep others from consuming the food and water in the territory they have claimed. Smaller animals generally need less space, but their space likewise must be sufficient to provide food and water for themselves and their offspring. Even the tiniest habitat, such as a leaf or small piece of rotting wood, can only provide for the needs of a limited number of inhabitants.

Social animals, such as ants and bees, thrive in crowded living conditions with members of their own group. However, each of these colonies needs space around it to ensure enough food and water for all members of the colony.

If a population of animals gets too large and overcrowded, or if changing conditions cause less food or water to be available, many of the inhabitants will fight, leave, or die. Eventually a new balance will be reached between the space available and the number of animals able to live there successfully.

115 © 1998 AIMS Education Foundation

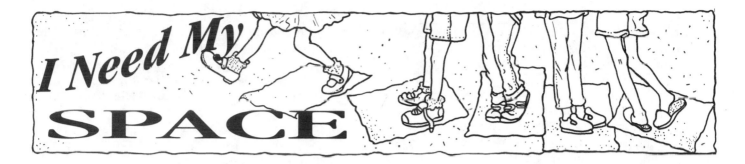

Topic
Need for Space in a Habitat

Key Question
What happens if an organism doesn't have enough space to live?

Focus
Students will experience the need for space shared by all living things.

Guiding Documents
Project 2061 Benchmarks
- *Changes in an organism's habitat are sometimes beneficial to it and sometimes harmful.*
- *In all environments — freshwater, marine, forest, desert, grassland, mountain, and others — organisms with similar needs may compete with one another for resources, including food, space, water, air, and shelter. In any particular environment, the growth and survival of organisms depend on the physical conditions.*

NRC Standards
- *Organisms have basic needs, which for animals are air, water, and food. Plants require air, water, and light. Organisms can only survive in environments in which they can meet their needs. The world has many different environments, and distinct environments support the life of different types of organisms.*
- *An organism's patterns of behavior are related to the nature of that organism's environment, including the kinds and numbers of other organisms present, the availability of food and resources, and the physical characteristics of the environment. When the environment changes, some plants and animals survive and reproduce, and others die or move to new locations.*

NCTM Standards
- *Develop spatial sense*
- *Understand the attributes of length, capacity, weight, mass, area, volume, time, temperature, and angle*
- *Make and use measurements in problems and everyday situations*

Math
Measurement
  area

Science
Environmental science
  habitats
Life science
  plants
  animals

Integrated Processes
Observing
Comparing and contrasting
Applying
Generalizing

Materials
For each student:
  one full-sized (two-page) sheet of newspaper

Optional:
  traffic cones, chairs, yarn, or chalk to mark off area

Background Information
  Please refer to *The Inside Story: Space*

Management
1. Use two-page sheets of a standard newspaper measuring approximately 56 cm by 68 cm.
2. Delineate an area with the following measurements according to your class size:
   20-24 students   3.5 meters by 4.0 meters
   25-29 students   4.0 meters by 4.0 meters
   30-34 students   4.0 meters by 4.5 meters
   35+   students   4.0 meters by 5.0 meters
3. Stake out the boundaries of the space with traffic cones, yarn, chairs, or chalk on pavement so they are visible and clear to the students. A basketball court works well: use the lines already painted to show two sides of the area.
4. Choose the student page best suited to the level of your class. Encourage the students to work together to cut out the representative grids so that they will have one rectangle for each person present in the class.

Procedure

> Open ended: Students who have had experience with scaling can use grid paper and determine their own scale rather than using the student page.

1. Ask the students to think about how much space they need to be comfortable and happy. Discuss how little space they think they could actually live in.

2. Give each of the students a two-page wide sheet of newspaper and explain that this represents the minimum amount of space that they as unidentified organisms need to live, survive, and grow.

3. Take them to the area of the activity and have them stand around the edges. Explain that this is the habitat in which they are going to be living. If their newspaper "habitat" overlaps that of anyone else, both of them will be weakened and most likely will not survive.

4. Select two students and send them into the habitat area. They can put their newspaper "space" wherever they want within the boundaries and stand on it to stake out their territory. Once it is put down, it cannot be moved during the rest of the activity.

5. Explain that the environment is healthy and population is thriving, so it doubles. Ask the students to determine how many individuals it would take to double the population and send that number of students in to establish their "space." Encourage comments and observations from both the "organisms" and the observers.

6. Ask the students again to determine the number needed to double the population and send that number in to establish their space. Encourage everyone to discuss their observations. Have the population double once more. Ask the students to identify areas that are comparatively densely or sparsely populated. Discuss the factors that could affect density in a natural habitat. [location of water or food, better soil, or especially good growing conditions]

7. Send in the remaining students one or two at a time so everyone can watch where they establish themselves. Ask them to explain the reason(s) they chose their location. Ideally not everyone will fit without some overlap of newspapers. The newest members of the population will need to find someplace in the habitat to stand, even if there isn't enough space.

8. With all student organisms in place, discuss the situation in the habitat. Encourage the students to point out the more and less densely populated areas. Determine which organisms will most likely not survive and which others (very close but not quite overlapping) might be at most risk if a contagious disease, fire, or high wind came through. Explain that this is also true in a natural

habitat; plants and animals that are able to locate in the best conditions with enough space around them are the ones that will most likely grow up healthy and survive.

9. Ask the students to consider if there might be a better way to arrange themselves so that more organisms could survive and be healthy. Encourage their responses until someone suggests putting the organisms in rows; then have them pick up their papers and re-establish themselves in rows and columns. Discuss the amount of space used and how much, if any, is left over.

10. Back in the classroom, have the students try out various arrangements of living space on the appropriate student sheet, gluing down the arrangement that they think seems to be the best.

Discussion

1. Is the amount of space you have at home too much, too little, or just enough? Explain your answer.

2. Discuss the difference between "wants" and "needs." How much space do you want to be happy and comfortable? How much space do you think you really need to be able to live? Is there a difference? Explain.

3. How do you know when you are feeling crowded? Describe your feelings when you are in a crowd.

4. How did you decide where to establish yourself in this "habitat"? How difficult was it to find a spot? How did you feel when others came in after you?

5. Were there any areas where the survival rate might be better than in other places? How do you explain this?

6. When you were all arranged in rows, how did it feel compared to the other (random) way? Which way might be a better way for more organisms to survive if they lived arranged like this? Give reasons for your answer.

7. Which is more like the way things grow in nature, the first (random) way or the second (rows) way?

8. Crops on farms are usually grown in neat rows. Do you think this is a good idea? Justify your answer.

9. Why do you think it is important to pull the weeds in a flower or vegetable garden? What do weeds have in common with the flowers or vegetables?

Extensions

1. Look around the school grounds and see if you can find an area densely populated with very young plants. If possible, protect that area from being weeded or mowed and watch what happens to the plants over a period of time.

2. Set up an experiment in which you plant radish or other fast growing seeds in identical small flower pots or paper cups. Plant one seed in the first cup,

two in the second, four in the third, eight in the fourth, and so on, continuing to double until you have seeds spaced 1 cm. Give them the same amounts of water and exposure to sunlight and compare the plants as they sprout and mature.

3. Divide the classroom in half by running a string down the middle of the room. For an hour or two, carry out your normal schedule, but keep all the students in only half of the room. Discuss the students' reaction to this experience.

Curriculum Correlation
Literature

St. Exupery, Antoine. *The Little Prince.* Harcourt, Brace, and World. New York. 1943

- In the first seven chapters of this classic fable, the prince reflects upon his difficulties in finding space for himself and the flower he loves on the very tiny planet on which he lives.

Home Link

Make a map of your bedroom at home. If you share the room, show which areas belong to whom. Make a second map showing how the room would be shared if you added two more people to the same room. Try to arrange it so that everyone has a fair share of the space and is able to reach and use what they need.

The Terrarium Connection

Would you say that every living thing in the terrarium has enough space? How would you define "enough"? Explain your answers.

If you have an overcrowded situation in a terrarium, observe the behavior of the animals and the growth patterns of both plants and animals. Can you see any signs of stress or change brought on by overcrowded conditions?

Observe the plants and animals over time to determine how their needs for space change throughout their life cycles.

What correlation do you see between the size of an organism and its need for space? Do the more active or faster-growing organisms need more space than some of their slower neighbors? How could you find out?

In a crowded terrarium situation, what determines which organisms survive? If this community were out in the natural world, what factors would help keep it from getting overcrowded?

I Need My SPACE

Draw the arrangement that worked best.

I Need My SPACE

Cut out 30 pieces of paper measuring 2 x 4 cm. How many can you place in the area below so that none overlap?

Glue down the arrangement that worked best.

I Need My SPACE

Cut out these pieces. Use them to determine the best arrangement of living space.

121

© 1998 AIMS Education Foundation

It's Bean a Great Place to Live

Topic
Need for Space in a Habitat

Key Question
What different arrangements of animals can there be in a habitat giving each one the space it needs?

Focus
Every living thing needs a certain amount of space in which to live and find the food, water, and shelter it needs to survive.

Guiding Documents
Project 2061 Benchmarks
- *Most living things need water, food, and air.*
- *Plants and animals both need to take in water, and animals need to take in food. In addition, plants need light.*
- *In all environments — freshwater, marine, forest, desert, grassland, mountain, and others — organisms with similar needs may compete with one another for resources, including food, space, water, air, and shelter. In any particular environment, the growth and survival of organisms depend on the physical conditions.*

NRC Standard
- *Organisms have basic needs, which for animals are air, water, and food. Plants require air, water, and light. Organisms can only survive in environments in which they can meet their needs. The world has many different environments, and distinct environments support the life of different types of organisms.*

Math
Counting

Science
Environmental science
  habitats
Life science
  plants
  animals

Integrated Processes
Observing
Comparing and contrasting
Applying
Generalizing
Inferring

Materials
For each pair of students:
  assortment of six different kinds of beans (see *Management 1*)
  crayons or colored pencils (see *Management 2* and *Procedure 6*)
  4 different colors crochet thread or thin yarn, about 30 cm long (for *Part 2* only, see *Management 4*)
  scissors
  glue

Background Information
Please refer to *The Inside Story: Space.*

Management
1. Use six easily distinguishable types of beans, avoiding duplication of color, or use small lima beans, white beans, or pinto beans which have been spray painted different colors.
2. On the *Habitat Map* page, students will need to color lightly so the symbols on the map can still be seen.
3. If students are unfamiliar with legend markings on a map, additional time may be needed to help them understand the *Habitat Map.*
4. For younger students, *Part 1* will probably be sufficient. Teachers of older students should follow procedures for *Part 1* and *Part 2*. However, they should use the *Bean Habitat Clues, Part 2* page instead of the *Bean Habitat Clues, Part 1.*
5. It may be helpful for students to glue down the beans on their pages.

Procedure
Part 1
1. Discuss why every living thing needs space to live, including how plants and animals use the space they live in.
2. Give each team a *Habitat Map*. Explain that the symbols in each of the spaces are clues telling what conditions are found there — shade, water, dry, dead leaves, grass, rocks. Remind the students that each of these conditions is good for some living things but not for others. Clarify that several different conditions may occur in one location, such as leaves in the shade and grass in the sun.

3. Have the students pick out a sample of each different kind of bean and glue it in place on the *Bean Habitat Clues, Part 1* page. (Older students will use *Bean Habitat Clues, Part 2*.) They should also choose a different color to represent each bean and color in the appropriate box.

4. Remind the students that many animals live right in or near the food they eat. Ask for examples they have seen on the playground [isopods in dead leaves, earthworms in the soil, aphids on plants]. Explain that in this activity each type of bean represents a certain kind of animal that lives in specific conditions. Some "bean" animals don't need much space, but others require more room.

5. Challenge the student teams to work out an arrangement of bean animals on the *Habitat Map*, following the clues and placing the animals in such a way that each has the space it needs. When an animal requires multiple spaces, each of those spaces must share a common side. Point out that many different — and correct — arrangements are possible, and that students will sometimes have to choose to place one bean animal instead of another.

6. Younger students may find it helpful to color or outline the spaces as they make decisions, gluing the bean to the *Habitat Map* at that time. However, this will limit making adjustments as they finish placing bean animals. If possible, students should wait to color their maps until they are satisfied with the arrangement of the bean animals.

7. Once each team has completed its map, have them count each type of bean they placed and record. Discuss which arrangement enables the habitat to support the greatest number of animals, as well as some of the trade-offs in which choosing more of one type of animal meant placing less of another.

Part 2 (Continuation for older students)

1. Point out that habitats include roving predators whose need for space may be quite large and even extend beyond a particular smaller habitat. Ask the students to recall evidence or actual observation of predatory animals which include the playground as part of their territory (cats, birds of prey, raccoons, etc.). These hunting animals require a significant amount of space in order to find enough animals to eat.

2. Supply each team with four different colors of string. Challenge them to follow the bottom portion of *Bean Habitat Clues, Part 2*, making string loops and arranging them so that the predator whose territory a loop represents will have enough food inside the loop. The loops cannot overlap. Again, choices of arrangements will need to be made.

3. Ask each team to glue down the string loops and complete their activity page showing what each color and string loop represents. Display the maps

and have the students compare the arrangements. Discuss the similarities and differences.

Discussion

1. What connections can you make between how much space an animal needs, its size, and the amount of food it eats?

2. What reasons can you think of that might explain why an animal might need more space in one location than it would if it were living somewhere else? [sparse plant growth, less available food, competition, etc.]

3. In what ways was your map similar to others in the class? In what ways was it different? What were some of the reasons for similarities and differences?

4. If you were to make another *Habitat Map,* what changes would you include? Why?

Extensions

1. Laminate several additional *Habitat Maps* and make them available with beans and overhead marking pens in a learning center. Encourage students to try other arrangements and see if they can increase the number of bean animals that can live in the habitat.

2. Create a habitat map of the playground to show where different animals have space to live. Make a legend to show existing conditions. Assign a color to each of the different animals commonly found living there and color in the area where they are found. Look for high density and scattered populations. Use string loops to show where various predators have been observed.

3. Challenge students individually or collaboratively to design their own habitat map scenario for others to work out.

Curriculum Correlation
Social Studies
Compare this type of mapping to other maps you are using.

Literature
Cherry, Lynne. *Flute's Journey: The Life of a Wood Thrush.* Harcourt Brace & Company. San Diego. 1997.
• A migratory wood thrush competes to survive in space increasingly limited by habitat lost to development and clearing of land.

Home Link
Pick five or six common animals living in a small area at your home or in a neighborhood park. Make a habitat map showing where you have observed each one's space to live.

The Terrarium Connection

Are one or two types of plants or animals doing particularly well? Are they reproducing? Did any do well for a while and then die?

If so, you probably have competition going on in the terrarium. As in the natural world, these plants and animals are competing for the food, water, air, shelter, and space they need. The stronger ones will take over and the weaker ones will die. When some reproduce, their offspring will compete too — even with their own parents!

In the wild, when animals get too crowded they will either move away, fight, or die. In a terrarium, they can't leave, so some will naturally die either by fighting or by lacking what they need.

What can you do to help make the enclosed habitat of a terrarium even more like the natural world? What might you do if a particular plant or animal population seems to be taking over?

It's Bean a Great Place to Live
Habitat Map

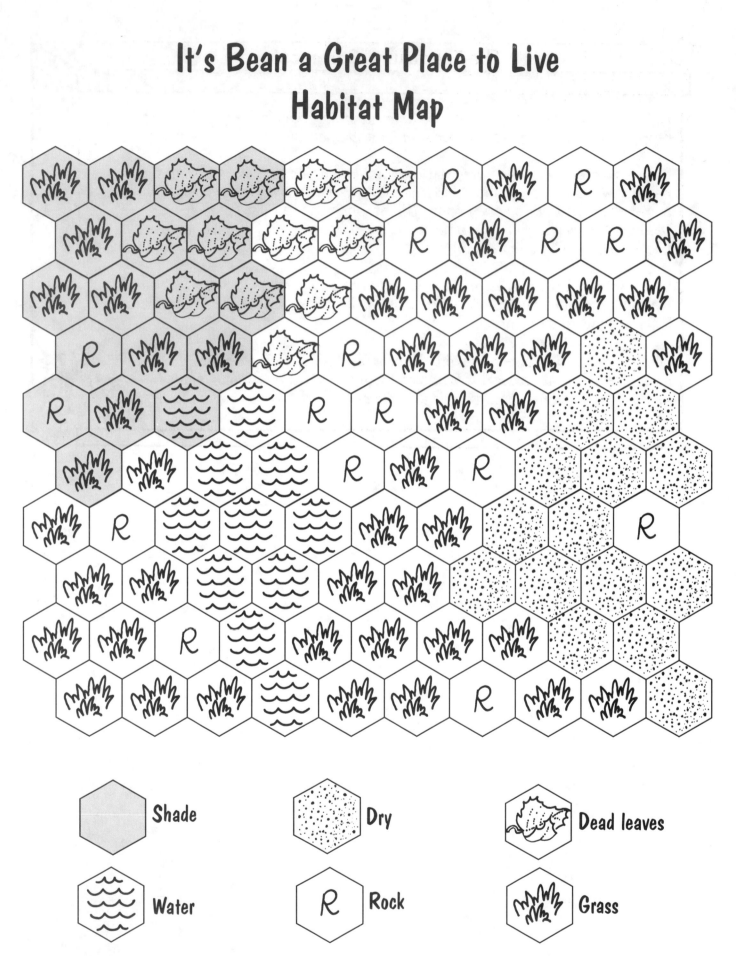

Shade

Dry

Dead leaves

Water

R Rock

Grass

It's Bean a Great Place to Live

Number used

Bean Habitat Clues Part 1

_____ **A** lives in dead leaves
needs one space
(◯ Bean ☐ Color)

_____ **B** lives in dry areas
needs five spaces
(◯ Bean ☐ Color)

_____ **C** eats grass
needs three spaces
(◯ Bean ☐ Color)

_____ **D** lives under rocks
needs one space
(◯ Bean ☐ Color)

_____ **E** must live in water
needs two spaces
(◯ Bean ☐ Color)

_____ **F** lives only in shade
can live in leaves, grass, or under rocks
needs two spaces
(◯ Bean ☐ Color)

 © 1998 AIMS Education Foundation

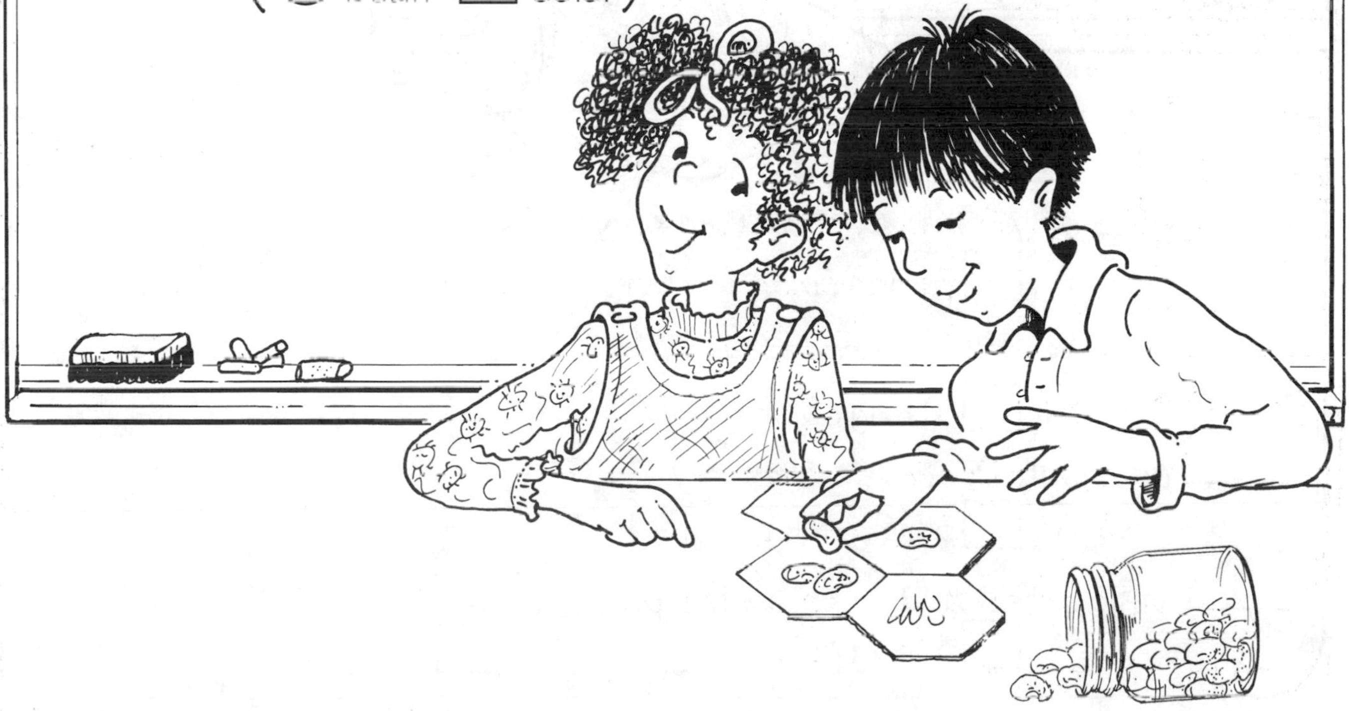

It's Bean a Great Place to Live

Bean Habitat Clues Part 2

Number used

_____ **A** lives in dead leaves
needs one space
(◯ Bean ☐ Color)

_____ **B** lives in dry areas
needs five spaces
(◯ Bean ☐ Color)

_____ **C** eats grass
needs three spaces
(◯ Bean ☐ Color)

_____ **D** lives under rocks
needs one space
(◯ Bean ☐ Color)

_____ **E** must live in water
needs two spaces
(◯ Bean ☐ Color)

_____ **F** lives only in shade
can live in leaves,
grass, or under rocks
needs two spaces
(◯ Bean ☐ Color)

_____ eats only A and C; needs ten prey
☐ String color

_____ eats everything; needs five prey
☐ String color

_____ eats only E; needs three prey
☐ String color

_____ eats only D and A; needs five prey
☐ String color

© 1998 AIMS Education Foundation

Tree Houses

Topic
A Tree as a Habitat

Key Question
What organisms live in a tree, and how does the tree provide for their needs?

Focus
A tree provides shelter and food for many different organisms.

Guiding Documents
Project 2061 Benchmarks
- *Animals eat plants or other animals for food and may also use plants (or even other animals) for shelter and nesting.*
- *Organisms interact with one another in various ways besides providing food. Many plants depend on animals for carrying their pollen to other plants or for dispersing their seeds.*

NRC Standard
- *Organisms have basic needs. For example, animals need air, water, and food; plants require air, water, nutrients, and light. Organisms can survive only in environments, and distinct environments support the life of different types of organisms.*

NCTM Standards
- *Develop and apply strategies to solve a wide variety of problems*
- *Recognize and apply deductive and inductive reasoning*
- *Apply mathematical thinking and modeling to solve problems that arise such as art, music, psychology, science, and business*

Math
Logic

Science
Environmental science
    habitats
Life science
    plants
    animals

Integrated Processes
Observing
Predicting
Collecting and recording data
Comparing and contrasting
Applying
Generalizing

Materials
For each group of students:
    hand lenses and/or DiscoveryScopes®
    clipboard or lapboard
    counters for the logic puzzles
    chart or butcher paper, optional
    binoculars, optional

Background Information
   A single tree may provide an entire habitat for a host of living things, from the tiny organisms dwelling in its leaves, bark, leaf litter, and roots to the larger animals nesting on its branches or living in its hollow interior. Other plants may thrive nearby or even live right on a tree because of the specific conditions determined by its presence. Entire food chains exist entirely within the tree's structure. Decomposers and herbivores come to dine on the living and fallen leaves or bark. Other animals come to feed on them and are in turn preyed upon by larger predators. Many different organisms can find all they need — food, water, air, shelter, space — in and around a single tree.
   Often a tree is an essential part of a larger habitat. A bird that pauses from flight to perch on a branch is using the tree for temporary shelter as a place to rest. So is a toad that digs into the damp soil at the base of the tree in the heat of the day and then moves on to another location during the night. The organisms we observe on a tree as they look for food and shelter may come from thousands of miles away or live their entire life cycle within the tree. All are part of the tree's complex and diverse community of life.

Management
1. Divide the class into three groups of "level" experts: those who study what is going on close to the ground, those who look to see what is happening in the zone from ground level to eye level, and those who will find out what is happening in the area above them.
2. Form teams containing at least two specialists from each group. Send each team to survey a different tree. If you are limited to one tree, you may need to have the teams take turns making their observations.
3. For best results, take a close look at nearby trees and choose the one(s) you are going to observe before involving the students. Generally speaking,

the older and larger the tree, the more variety of inhabitants you will find.

4. Be sure that the students persist in looking closely at all parts of the tree, including dead leaves around the base, as well as in the earth near and among the roots. Not all evidence of organisms living in the tree may be obvious at first glance. If possible, use binoculars to examine the upper reaches of the tree.

5. It may be difficult for students to find and recognize plants growing in or on the tree. Look for tiny plants in cracks and parasites such as mistletoe. Use a hand lens to search out moss, lichen, or fungus, especially in damp, shaded areas.

6. If the classroom does not have any plants in containers besides the terrariums, you may want to bring one in just to broaden the discussion.

7. Prior experience with solving logic problems is recommended (see *Curriculum Correlation — Math*).

Procedure

1. Ask the students for examples of how the classroom environment provides what is needed for different organisms living there: people, plants, insects (both in the terrariums and living free), classroom pets, and so on. Have them identify the evidence that tells them how the classroom is meeting these needs. Emphasize that the success of each organism depends on whether the habitat, natural or artificial, can meet each of those needs.

2. Ask the students to think of some other examples of habitats, especially small ones, that provide in different ways for a variety of plants and animals.

3. Take the class outside for a careful examination of a tree or trees. Direct the "level" experts to work together to observe every piece of evidence they can find to discover what is going on in the zone they are responsible for. Encourage them to record what they see using descriptions and/or drawings.

4. Bring each team together to record their data and compile a list of what they observed. Discuss what each organism was gaining by being in or near the tree. [short-term or long-term shelter, food, etc.]

5. Compile a list of which different life forms were found at each of the levels. You may wish to draw a large tree on chart paper and have the students draw or describe what they found showing where it was located. See *Extension 3*.

6. Give the teams the opportunity to visit all the trees to see organisms found by other teams and to recheck their tree to see if they can find some of the organisms they may have missed.

7. Challenge the students to solve the logic puzzles using whatever problem-solving strategies work for them.

Discussion

1. Were there any areas of the tree that seemed more populated than other areas? What might explain this?

2. Do you think the organisms living in the tree are helping it or hurting it in any way? What clues help you determine this?

3. Are any of your needs not provided for in the classroom? What about the other living things there? If not, how (or where) are those needs met? Does the tree supply everything needed by every plant or animal you saw in or around it? If not, how do those organisms get what else they need?

4. Were there some animals you believe are living in the tree or visiting it, although you didn't actually see them? What clues could you find to prove they were there?

5. Which of the creatures you observed do you think will live in the tree for their whole lives? Which do you think may be just stopping by? Are there any that you suspect are regular visitors? What makes you think so?

6. Are there any organisms that were found in one or more trees, but not in all? What could be some reasons for this?

7. Who or what do you think will be living in this tree or visiting it in a month? ... 3 months? ... 6 months? ... a year?

8. What else would you like to know about who lives in this tree or uses it? How could you find out?

Extensions

1. Continue observation of the same tree(s) throughout the year, keeping a chart or log of the various forms of life noted seeking food and shelter there.

2. Observe the organisms found living in or around a dead tree and/or a rotting log or large piece of wood and compare.

3. Chart the data collected as a three-ring Venn diagram with a ring for each of the zones observed.

4. Plant a tree!

Curriculum Correlation

Literature

Bash, Barbara. *Desert Giant: The World of the Saguaro Cactus*. Sierra Club. San Francisco. 1989.

- The towering plant providing food and shelter for diverse animals is a saguaro cactus rather than a tree. Watercolor illustrations add a special touch to the informative text.

Cherry, Lynne. *The Great Kapok Tree*. Harcourt Brace Jovanovich. San Diego. 1990.

- Birds, animals, insects, and a child explain the importance of a large tree in the rain forest to the man who is about to cut it down.

Guiberson, Brenda. *Cactus Hotel*. Henry Holt and Company. New York. 1991.

- Beautifully illustrated chronicle of 200 years of life of a saguaro cactus, a primary source of food, water, and shelter for the creatures who live in the Sonoran Desert.

 © 1998 AIMS Education Foundation

Reed-Jones, Carol. *The Tree in the Ancient Forest.* Dawn Publications. Nevada City, California. 1995.

- Repetitive poem relates the interdependence of a 300-year-old tree and the plants and animals that live around it. Potential foundation for retelling using plants and animals from any habitat.

Romanova, Natalia. *Once There Was a Tree.* Dial Books. New York. 1985.

- A simple, thought-provoking narrative about some of the different living things that use the stump of a tree. To whom does it belong?

Thornhill, Jan. *A Tree in a Forest.* Simon & Schuster. New York. 1991.

- For more than 200 years, a maple tree is the center of its special world in the middle of the forest. We watch its history unfold and, as time passes, observe its changing interaction with the other plants and animals of its habitat.

Creative Writing

Write a story or picture book about all the different plants or animals using your tree. Students may want to use one of the suggested literature books as a reference.

Math

For additional experience with logic puzzles, see the AIMS publication *Primarily Bears.*

Home Link

Encourage students to plant a tree at home or participate in a local tree planting project and report back to the class.

The Terrarium Connection

As a tree provides food and shelter for all sorts of different plants and animals, is there anything living and growing in the terrarium that is also providing food and/or shelter for something else?

What evidence can you find that any of the plants or animals there are being used to meet the needs of another plant or animal?

What could you add to the terrarium that might help feed and shelter any of the creatures living there?

 © 1998 AIMS Education Foundation

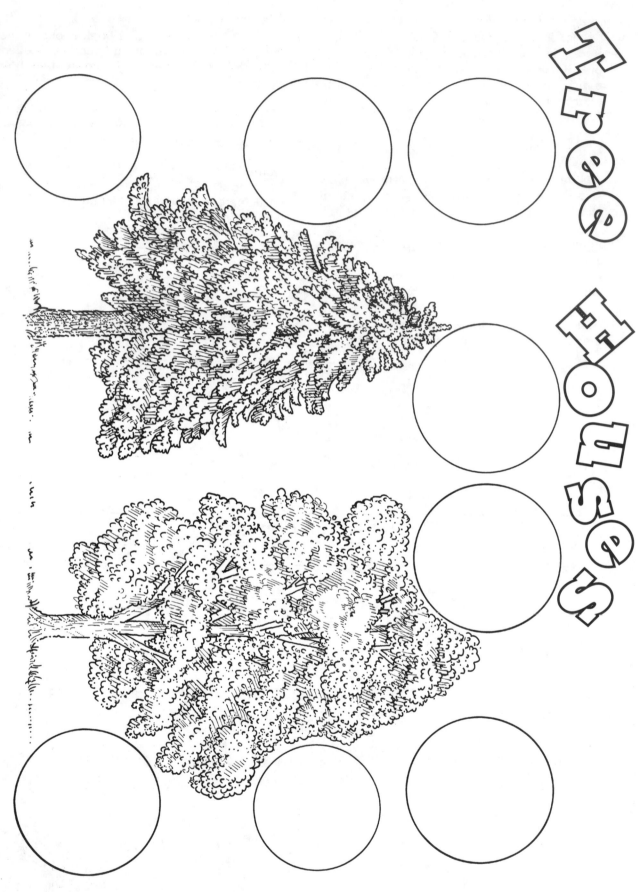

Tree Houses

In each circle, draw a different animal or plant observed living on the tree you examined. Choose the tree on this page most like yours and draw a line from the circle to the place on the tree where it was found.

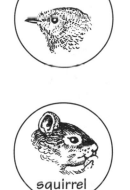
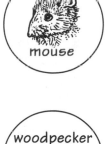

Over the years, woodpeckers have pecked six holes through the bark and into the trunk of this tree. Now other birds and animals have taken them over, sometimes remodeling them to fit. One woodpecker still lives here with its family. The other holes now belong to an owl, some chickadees, a family of mice, a raccoon, and some squirrels. Figure out who lives where.

- No birds live immediately above or below other birds.
- The top and bottom homes belong to a creature living alone.
- The owl picked a home as high as possible.
- The woodpecker kept its favorite spot right above the raccoon.
- The squirrels live higher in the tree than the mice do.

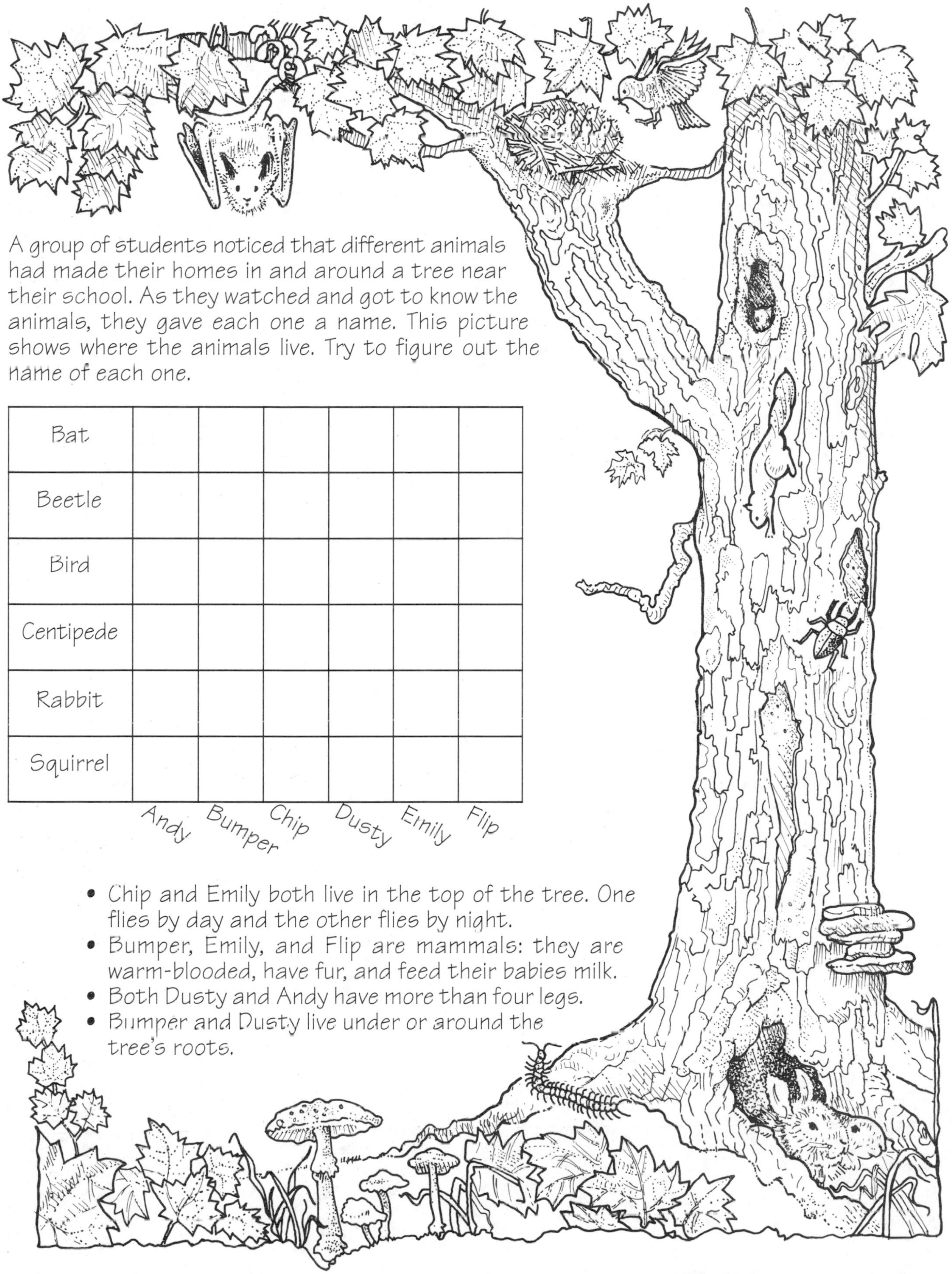

A group of students noticed that different animals had made their homes in and around a tree near their school. As they watched and got to know the animals, they gave each one a name. This picture shows where the animals live. Try to figure out the name of each one.

	Andy	Bumper	Chip	Dusty	Emily	Flip
Bat						
Beetle						
Bird						
Centipede						
Rabbit						
Squirrel						

- Chip and Emily both live in the top of the tree. One flies by day and the other flies by night.
- Bumper, Emily, and Flip are mammals: they are warm-blooded, have fur, and feed their babies milk.
- Both Dusty and Andy have more than four legs.
- Bumper and Dusty live under or around the tree's roots.

              © 1998 AIMS Education Foundation

This tree branch is providing food and shelter for six different kinds of insects. Follow the clues to arrange them in order.

The caterpillar and aphid are not at either end or next to each other.

The leaf-mining fly is directly between the aphid and the leaf insect.

The treehopper is somewhere to the left of but not next to the leaf-mining fly.

The treehopper and the aphid are the two in the middle.

The gall wasp is the first one on the left.

treehopper

caterpillar

aphid

gall wasp

leaf insect

leaf-mining fly

© 1998 AIMS Education Foundation

Design-a-Habitat

Use what you have learned about habitats as you design a board game or card game. You will bring your game to school to play with your classmates. Here are your guidelines:

- You may use the playground habitat or another habitat of your choice for your theme.
- The design, decoration, theme, questions, and means of earning points all should reflect your habitat theme.
- Use what you know about your habitat — relationships, food chains, needs and lives of the plants and animals that live there, and so forth — as you create your game.
  - Write out all the directions so that other students can understand what they need to know to play the game, even if you are not there to explain.
  - You may use ideas from other games you know, but the design, board, cards, markers, questions, and anything else you use must be made or drawn by you.
  - Have fun with this project!

     © 1998 AIMS Education Foundation

Investigating Other Habitats

Now that you have learned about your playground habitat, what's the next step?

Visit a different habitat! Look for another place to investigate — perhaps a nearby national, state, or local park or open-space region, or even a park or vacant lot in your neighborhood.

What should you do when you get there?

- Use your senses to get to know your new habitat. What clues can you find by looking, listening, smelling, touching?
- Compare each location with the playground habitat you have learned about. What evidence of life do you see? What is similar or different about the food chains, availability of water, types of shelter, and space available? What predator-prey relationships do you see? Do you see the same types of plants and animals?
- Visit your new habitat at different times of the day and year, or in different weather. What changes do you notice over time?
- Record temperature (soil and air), wind, rainfall over time.
- Spread out an old white sheet or other light-colored material on the ground under and close to a bush. Shake the branches over the material. Observe the critters that fall on the sheet.
- If collecting is permitted, set up a terrarium with plants and animals from the new habitat. Be responsible for the care, feeding, and well-being of any critters you collect. When you are through observing them, return them to where you found them.
- If collecting is permitted, start a plant collection from the habitat. Press your specimens between sheets of newspaper under a stack of books until dry, then mount on blank paper.
- Collect, analyze, and compare samples of soils from different parts of the habitat.
- Look for patterns: Are there certain plants and animals that always occur together? Is there a connection between certain organisms and the dampness of the ground or the amount of sunlight in a particular place?
- Choose an animal and spend ten minutes observing it, following wherever it goes. Work with a friend to keep track of it, taking notes. Make a list of questions about it. Find out how it walks, eats, moves, and rests. How fast or slow can it move? How is it adapted to live in this place? Observe its eyes, mouth, legs, and the way it is put together. Use reference books or the Internet to learn all you can about it. Find out what other animals are its friends, neighbors, and enemies. Draw pictures of what the world looks like from its perspective. Imitate it. Write and illustrate a story about it to share with younger students.
- Create a field guide for the area, listing and drawing the different plants and animals you observe. Keep adding to it.

136   © 1998 AIMS Education Foundation

Helpful Hints for Habitat Trips

Things to take on a habitat trip:

- journal or notebook — when carefully kept with notes, observations, and sketches, this is a naturalist's most valuable tool!
- hand lenses — you may wish to drill and put on laces or strings to wear — every student should have one!
- bucket or other container
- trowel or garden fork

Optional:

- small shovel or spade
- camera
- tape recorder
- compass (wear on string with hand lens)
- field microscope
- white sheet or light-colored material
- insect net
- collecting/ observation containers

 © 1998 AIMS Education Foundation

General Guidelines for Setting Up a Terrarium or Aquarium

Containers

- All sorts of containers will work: glass or plastic aquariums, plastic boxes, large jars, kitchen storage containers, tubs, or anything that can hold a reasonable amount of water or moist soil and be enclosed securely enough to prevent escapes. (See *Easy-to-Make Equipment*.)
- Used containers are fine. Check for leaks if an aquatic or particularly soggy terrarium is planned. Repair with aquarium sealant from a pet store.
- If the container is glass, heavy, or flexible, put it on a board or piece of plywood so that it can be moved easily and safely if necessary.
- Everything used should be biologically clean. This means that all tools and containers used for both setup and maintenance should be washed well first (scrub, but don't use soap), then rinsed very thoroughly. Don't use chemicals.
- Keep a secure lid on the terrarium. (See *Easy-to-Make Equipment for directions*.)
- If the container has clear sides, wrap a strip of black paper around the outside as high as the surface of the soil. Dirt-dwelling critters will then be more likely to burrow close to the sides where the students can observe them.

Water

- A local pet store should know if the water in your area is safe to use for fish or other creatures. Bottled spring water or healthy, non-polluted pond water may be preferable to tap water.
- Don't use distilled water. Distilling removes the natural salts needed by most organisms.
- If tap water is used either to set up or replenish a terrarium, let it sit in an open non-metal container for at least 24 hours to get rid of chemicals or copper it may contain.
- Keep any water supplies, as well as the terrarium itself, at room temperature. Don't put it in the direct sun or near a heat source.
- Land-dwelling animals need a water source. Use a shallow plastic dish or jar lid with either a piece of clean sponge or a layer of gravel barely covered with water (to prevent drowning). Monitor to see which the animals prefer and adjust accordingly.
- Watch closely for signs of drying out. Add "rain" in the form of spray from a mist bottle whenever it is needed.

Foundation

- Put a 3 – 4 cm layer of washed gravel on the bottom (drainage system). Optional: cover the gravel layer with 0.5 cm of aquarium charcoal for a filter.
- If the soil is fine, cover the gravel/charcoal layer with pieces cut from nylon stockings to prevent the soil from filling in the spaces between the gravel pieces.
- Include a depression where water or dampness can be retained longer than at the surface.
- Set up the physical environment first: water, soil, sand, rocks, climbing sticks, or whatever non-living (or no longer living) elements are to be included. Let It sit for several days to settle.

Adding Plants and Animals

- Balancing a terrarium involves making mistakes and learning from them. Not everything put in a terrarium is necessarily going to thrive or even survive. When something dies, analyze whether this was in the natural course of things or whether the balance in this small ecosystem is not where it should be, and make adjustments accordingly.
- Trial and error is a valid way to discover how best to provide water and other needs for the organisms in a particular terrarium.
- A true habitat involves predator-prey relationships. If some of the animals require live food, or if the food supply in the terrarium becomes exhausted, additional food will need to be provided.
- Start small, get it balanced, add cautiously.
- When digging up small plants, include as much of the root system as possible and keep them damp while transporting them. Put them in the terrarium and give them a chance to get established. Give them room to grow and spread. Determine how much water they will need and how often they will need it.
- Add a few creatures and see how they do. Then add more creatures as seems appropriate, keeping in mind that this is a very small habitat. Overcrowding inevitably leads to a disaster.

Dismantling

When it is time to dismantle a terrarium, return all animals to the area where they were collected under conditions in which they can survive. If this is not possible, release them in a similar area where other animals of the same type are observed.

Never release an animal into an area where it is not native. Many areas have laws dealing with this issue. The alternatives include:

- keep and care for it
- share with other classes who will care for it
- give it to someone who is qualified to care for it
- transport it to an area where other animals of the same type live
- destroy it humanely

 © 1998 AIMS Education Foundation

Easy-to-Make Equipment

Housing — Terrariums
Plastic or Glass
Many plastic or glass containers can quickly and easily be turned into suitable terrariums as long as they can be completely enclosed so as not to allow inhabitants to escape. Often all that is needed is a secure vented lid (see *Terrarium Covers* below).

Clear-sided containers make the best terrariums for classroom viewing. Basic five-, ten-, and fifteen-gallon aquariums can be purchased at pet stores or through catalogs. Also check the classified ads in your newspaper. Gallon jars ("pickle jars") also make good terrariums. Other possibilities include plastic storage containers, plastic shoeboxes, dishpans, and so forth.

Screen Cages
A terrarium housing larger flying insects, such as butterflies or ladybird beetles, can be made from a piece of aluminum screen and two round containers at least 3-4 cm deep, such as cake pans or potted plant saucers. Form a cylinder with the screen, measuring so that it will just fit inside the round containers. Fasten the seam with hot glue or sew it with wire, taking care that no gaps occur.

Stand the cylinder on end in one of the round containers and secure it with plaster of Paris or hot glue. When it has hardened, add soil or sod. Use the other round container for a lid. Potted plants or cuttings with aphids or other food supplies can be added as needed. If the cuttings are in water, seal the openings of their containers so that terrarium inhabitants don't fall in and drown. As in other terrariums, a dampened piece of sponge or cotton ball is a good source of moisture.

Note: Insects tend to be less active when the surrounding temperature is cool. Keep this in mind when opening the container.

For many more excellent ideas for large and small terrariums, see *Caring for Insect Livestock: An Insect Rearing Manual* by Gary Dunn (see *Bibliography — Resources*).

Box Terrariums
Shoeboxes, milk cartons, and other boxes may be set up like the Buffet Box (see *Buffet Lunch*), using plastic wrap and screen to cover openings. Do not use this type of terrarium as permanent housing for crickets, snails, or any other animal that eats paper or cardboard.

Terrarium Covers
For Aquariums
Choose gray or silver plastic or fiberglass screening to allow more light into the terrarium.
1. Measure a piece of lightweight flexible screening
    - 5-cm wider than the width of the aquarium
    - 5-cm longer than the length of the aquarium
2. Cut 5-centimeter wide strips of heavy cardboard (corrugated is fine)
    - 2 strips 5-cm longer than the width of the aquarium
    - 2 strips 5-cm longer than the length of the aquarium
3. Spread the screen out on a work surface. Place the cardboard strips on the screen to form a rectangle with the inside corners not quite touching. The cardboard should cover about 5 cm of screen on each side. Use the grid on the screen to guide you as you line up the strips.

4. Staple the strips of cardboard to the screen at roughly 5-cm intervals. When all strips are in place, check the fit on the aquarium. You should be able to put on and take off the cover easily, but there should not be much space between the cardboard and the rim of the aquarium.
5. Use a hot glue gun to secure the screen to the inside of the cardboard. Be careful — hot glue runs easily through the spaces in the screen. If needed, apply pressure with a piece of scrap cardboard.
6. Line up the 5-cm width of each cardboard strip and tape securely together to form the corners of the lid. A triangular pouch of screen will form on the inside of each corner.
7. Again, check the fit of the lid on the aquarium. Adjust if necessary by retaping the corners.
8. Flatten the pouch in each corner against one of the adjacent sides and tape it along the edge so it lies flat.

For Gallon Jars

1. Measure a square of lightweight flexible screening about 5-cm wider than the diameter of the mouth of the jar. (Measurements can be approximate.)
2. Cut 2.5-cm wide strips of manila folder or tagboard 3-cm longer than the circumference of the mouth of the jar.
3. Wrap one of the tagboard strips around the mouth of the jar and secure it with a hot glue gun. Check the fit on the jar. You should be able to put on and take off the cover easily, but there should not be much space between the cardboard and the glass. Trim it to be flush with the top of the glass rim.
4. Work with the tagboard ring on the jar to give it stability. Center the square of screen across the top of the ring. Put a dot of hot glue on the outside of the ring and tack down the screen. Repeat directly across the ring. Tack twice again halfway between the first two spots, each time gently pulling the screen tight.
5. Run a line of hot glue out from each tack spot to secure the screen. As the excess screen begins to protrude, make a flat "hospital corner" and glue it down. Trim excess screen from the bottom of the ring.
6. Tack the middle of the second tagboard strip to the screen, placing it so that the bottom edge barely rests on the shoulder of the jar. Continue gluing all the way around until the second strip covers the first strip and the screen.
7. Trim any excess tagboard from the top of the ring.

Plastic Boxes with Covers

If you are using a plastic shoe box or similar container with a lid and want it to be a permanent terrarium, cut out most of the plastic in the center of the lid and use a glue gun or model cement to secure a piece of screen to cover the hole. Be sure that the glue line is uninterrupted all the way around the screen so that nothing will be able to escape. Do not use white glue. An option is to poke vent holes in the lid with a heated nail or ice pick, or use a drill.

Water Sources for Terrariums

Pill Bottle Fountain

Cut a "plug" from a cellulose sponge to fit snugly in the opening of a clean plastic pill bottle, film canister, or other vial. Use hot glue to attach a piece of popsicle stick beneath the opening to prevent rolling. Fill the container with fresh water; clean and refill as needed.

Rocky Wading Pond

Put large gravel (about 1 cm) in a plastic jar lid. Add water to the top of the gravel so critters can get water without falling in and drowning.

Sponge Pond

Put a piece of clean cellulose sponge in a plastic jar lid. Keep the sponge damp, replenishing often. Clean as needed.

 © 1998 AIMS Education Foundation

Collecting Devices and Strategies
Holding Jar
A jar or small plastic container may be used for transporting critters from the place of capture to the terrarium. The container should have vents in the lid and a few dampened leaves inside. It should never be left in direct sunlight, and the captives should be released into the terrarium as soon as possible. Caution students to be very careful whenever they use any equipment, especially glass.

Beating the Bushes
Put a piece of white chart paper, butcher paper, poster board, or fabric under a bush. Shake the branches or tap them with a stick. You will be able to see and gather the insects that fall from the bush.

Butterfly Net
A simple butterfly net can be made from a rectangle of light fabric or strong netting sewn together on three sides and hemmed on the fourth side. To make a cone-shaped net, sew on two sides of a triangle and hem the third side. Stretch a wire coat hanger to make a circle. Use wire cutters to remove the hook. Untwist the wire with pliers, run it through the hem, and twist it back together again. Securely tape the twisted part of the hanger to a broomstick or similar pole.

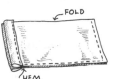

Use the net to sweep back and forth across areas of tall grass or bushes. The sweeping motion will take insects and spiders to the "toe" of the net. Transfer the captives to a terrarium or holding jar.

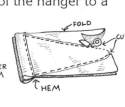

Caution: Be careful of bees, wasp, and other stinging insects.

Pitfall Trap
A pitfall trap consists of an open container buried in the ground so that the top of the container is level with the ground. Often some type of bait is used. Various critters wander along and fall in, but can't escape. The container should have slick sides. Jars, cans, plastic containers and cups, and buckets all work well. If you use a shallow container such as a margarine tub, cut a hole in the lid leaving a ring. This ring provides a lip that will keep insects from escaping. Spread petroleum jelly (like Vaseline®) around the inside edge of the container to discourage escapes.

Shield the pitfall with a piece of wood, cardboard, or an old plate held up with small rocks at least three centimeters above the ground. This prevents rain or other water from collecting in the container, as well as protecting the "catch" from birds or other predators. If you create barriers of cardboard, wood, or plastic jammed into the ground at right angles to the trap, insects will run into the barrier, follow it, and fall into the trap. Try placing a barrier between two pitfalls!

Put a few pieces of loose newspaper or some dead leaves in the bottom of the "pit" to provide some shelter and security for the captives.

It is important to follow these guidelines:
- The trap must be checked often, preferably several times a day. Many animals will die if left in the trap for more than a few hours.
- You may catch a small mammal. Never handle a small animal with bare hands! Gently use a sturdy stick to assist the animal in escaping or wear adequate protective gloves to release it away from the students.
- When you finish using a pitfall trap, dig it up and fill in the hole.

It is helpful to put a piece of damp sponge in the bottom of the container to provide moisture and prevent drowning. Experiment with using different types of food for bait, or no food at all.

Potato Trap

Slice a potato lengthwise, hollow out both halves, and cut a V-shaped notch in each end. Put the halves back together and place it in a damp, cool area where critters are likely to be found. Cover it with dead leaves. Isopods, centipedes, and various insects should start gathering inside the potato within a day or two.

Soda Bottle Trap

Cut off the top 13-15 cm of an empty two-liter soda bottle (at the "shoulder," 1-2 cm below the point at which the sides of the bottle start curving inward). Turn the top of the bottle around to point to the interior of the bottle. Leave it resting on its side in various locations. Experiment with using different kinds of bait. This device works like a lobster trap or crab pot.

Other soft plastic bottle will work too. Adapt the measurements as needed.

Shelter Board Trap

Leave some old pieces of wood, cardboard, or even newspaper lying around in different locations. Various organisms will use them for shelter and move in beneath them.

Sugar Bait

Combine fermented, mashed fruit such as apples and bananas with molasses or thick syrup. Heat and mix well. Apply the mixture to tree trunks or fence posts with an old paint brush. Another strategy is to dip a clean rag into the mixture and hang it from a branch or tree trunk. Use a jar to capture insects attracted to the bait. Always be cautious about collecting when bees and wasps are present.

Nighttime Observation and Collecting

Many insects are more active by night than by day, so the students do not often get the opportunity to see them in action. An evening observation may turn up critters whose "evidence" is normally seen only in daylight.

Many invertebrates are attracted to light; others shun it. Animals that visit sugar-bait areas at night are not usually the same ones that come by day.

Recording

Lapboards

A simple and inexpensive way to make lapboards is to buy a sheet of masonite and have it cut into 9-by-12-inch or 10-by-12-inch pieces. Most building supply stores will cut it for a price; the woodshop classes at your local secondary school will probably do it for free. Use clothespins or large binder clips to attach papers to the board. Some masonite comes with a special surface laminate on one side and is very easy to wipe clean. A standard 4-by-8-foot sheet of masonite will make 40 9-by-12-inch or 32 10-by-12-inch boards.

Who's Who in the Habitat ...

WANTED

Beetles

Collection Strategies
- Look under rocks, logs, debris especially in grassy areas or near water.
- Some beetles fly, some don't. Flightless beetles can be cornered and captured by picking them up. Use a net to collect those that fly.
- When possible, collect soil and natural surface litter from the collection area.

Container Preference
Glass or plastic with ventilated lid

Setup
Use 2–3 cm of small gravel, covered with 3–5 cm clean sand or dirt. Make it deeper at one corner for burrowing. Add a flat rock, chunk of bark, or small piece of wood for beetles to hide under. Keep another corner constantly damp as a source of water. Growing plants aren't necessary; they will be uprooted and possibly eaten.

Food
Diet depends on the type of beetle. Carnivores: flies, worms, crickets, mealworms. Scavengers: small pieces of cooked chicken or raw hamburger, soft fruits or vegetables, dead insects, dog kibble. Herbivores: grass seed, small bird seed, rabbit/guinea pig alfalfa pellets.

Maintenance
Add water to the damp corner every day.

Possible Problems and Solutions
Water: If the damp corner is allowed to dry out, the beetles will die.
Diet: Monitor closely to be sure beetles are eating, providing a variety of food until you learn what they will eat.

Background Information
There are more varieties of insects than any other animal, and there are more kinds of beetles than any other insect! So far, scientists have identified about 500,000 different species of beetles. All beetles have four life cycle stages: egg, larva (worm-like grub), pupa, and adult. In a balanced terrarium situation, the beetles may reproduce so that each stage of the life cycle can be observed (the eggs may be microscopic).

Beetles found on school playgrounds are likely to be ground beetles or scarab beetles, but there are many possibilities. A good field guide or help from a local entomologist or wildlife center may help identify the beetles and determine what they eat. Mealworms, the larvae of darkling beetles, are available in pet stores. Easy to raise in the classroom, they thrive in 4-5 cm of oats, cornmeal, or bran, plus potato, zucchini, apple, or other firm fruit or vegetable as a source of moisture.

 © 1998 AIMS Education Foundation

Who's Who in the Habitat ...

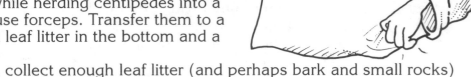

WANTED

Centipedes

Collection Strategies
- Carefully move rocks, logs, flower pots.
- Do not pick up by hand. Some species, particularly in tropical regions or the western United States, can inflict a painful and possibly harmful bite.
- Wear gloves while herding centipedes into a container, or use forceps. Transfer them to a container with leaf litter in the bottom and a ventilated lid.
- At same time, collect enough leaf litter (and perhaps bark and small rocks) from the site to use in the new habitat.

Container Preference
Glass or plastic with ventilated lid

Setup
Use 2–3 cm rich forest soil, potting soil, or peat moss; add decaying wood and leaf litter. Keep moist, not soggy, at all times. Provide a chunk of bark large enough for them to hide under.

Food
Live food: Sow bugs or other isopods; mealworms; cricket nymphs; some beetles and spiders, earthworms
In a balanced setup, isopods will eat leaf litter, reproduce, and provide a constant food supply for the centipedes.

Maintenance
Keep a piece of potato in the terrarium for the sowbugs; keep soil damp all the time; take out rotting food; mist with water daily.

Possible Problems and Solutions
Do not crowd with other centipedes as they prey on each other. They can be kept with millipedes which secrete an irritating substance that keeps centipedes away.

Background Information
The name *centipede* means "100 feet," but they actually have anywhere from 15 to 175 pairs of legs. Their long body has many segments, but unlike millipedes, each body segment has its own pair of legs. Centipedes eat earthworms and insects, using the hooked fangs on their first segment to inject venom into their prey. They are nocturnal and prefer staying out of sight in underground burrows or beneath dead leaves, rocks, and logs. Amazingly speedy, they are usually seen only as they make a mad dash for cover, sometimes slipping through cracks and into spaces that seem far too small for them. Female centipedes roll their sticky eggs along the ground to pick up bits of soil for camouflage. Some centipede mothers even guard their young until they can take care of themselves.

Who's Who in the Habitat ...

WANTED

Crickets

Collection Strategies
- Chase down with a net or a container and index card in an area where you can hear them chirping.
- Be sure you enjoy the sound of chirping before you decide to house crickets in your classroom!

Container Preference
Glass or sturdy plastic with ventilated lid.
Need a larger container (10-gallon aquarium or larger) for breeding. Provide a screen cover for the container.

Setup
Put clean sand (no salt) 2–5 cm deep in bottom of container. Put large, clean gravel in a dish and cover with water so the crickets can drink without falling in and drowning. Provide dry grass, dead leaves, toilet paper tubes or egg carton pieces piled up for crickets to hide in. (Very important to prevent territorial battles.)

Food
Dry dog food, poultry laying mash, apple, carrot, potato, celery, lettuce, rolled oats
Very young crickets need soft food like bananas or crushed dry dog food.

Maintenance
Remove molding food and droppings; keep habitat dry and warm (27–32° C or 80–85° F). Crickets will survive at lower temperatures but will not do as well or grow as fast.

Possible Problems and Solutions
Use only glass, plastic, and strong screen. Crickets will chew through paper products. Keep temperature as constant as possible. Don't let habitat get wet or moldy. Overcrowded crickets will attack each other.

Background Information
Crickets have three life stages: eggs, wingless nymphs which look much like small adults, and adults. They have long hind legs for jumping, wings which are too short to enable them to fly, antennae which are often longer than their body, and two tail-like structures called *cerci* at the end of their abdomen. The familiar cricket song is produced by the male rubbing his wings together. Each wing has a *file,* a thick vein with cross ridges, and a *scraper* with a sharp edge. A cricket chirps by rubbing the scraper of one wing across the file of the other. Male and female crickets hear the songs with hearing organs located on their front legs and use the songs to find each other.

Who's Who in the Habitat ...

Earthworms can be easily and successfully raised in the classroom. They will consume garbage, turn shredded newspaper into rich compost, and provide opportunities for many effective lessons on life cycles, animal behavior, and recycling. For complete information on setting up an earthworm community, please refer to the resource books listed in the *Bibliography*. The following guidelines are intended for keeping earthworms in terrariums along with other critters.

Collection Strategies
- Avoid the temptation to collect a lot of worms. A few small worms will do best in a multi-critter terrarium situation.
- Fill a bucket with soil from the same area where you found the worms.

Container Preference
Plastic or glass

Setup
Layer the bottom with 2–3 cm of gravel to prevent problems with pooled water. Add 6–10 cm of good organic garden soil from the area where the worms were collected. Add a layer of grass clippings, dead leaves, etc. Wrap black paper around the outside of the container to the top of the dirt line.

Food
Grass, dead leaves, scraps of fruits or vegetables, broken egg shells

Maintenance
Keep the soil moist at all times. The container needs to be kept away from direct sunlight or any source of extreme heat or cold.

Possible Problems and Solutions
Meat and dairy products are not suitable foods and will result in odor and bacteria problems. Do not use potting soil or earth that is so rich in organic material that it holds water for a long period of time.

Background Information
Earthworms are the master gardeners, the great recyclers. They generally live 7.5 to 45 cm below the surface where they eat their way through the soil, consuming plant and animal material. Their burrows enable more air and water to get into the soil. They also mix together the different layers of soil, enriching it with their waste material (castings) so that it can better support plant life.

There are more than 3000 known types of earthworms ranging in length from one millimeter to three meters. They are found in moist, warm soil in most parts of the world.

Who's Who in the Habitat ...

WANTED

Earwigs

Collection Strategies
- Look under rocks, logs, flower pots, bricks near buildings.
- Pick them up (their pincers are usually too small to hurt you) and put them in a jar.
- Use a pit-fall trap (see *Easy-to-Make Equipment*).

Container Preference
Use glass or plastic with ventilated lid. Lid needs to be secure with small vents or fine-mesh netting to prevent escape.

Setup
Put 2–3 cm gravel on bottom; add 5 cm damp soil, piling it deeper at one end. Add small stones, plants, and a flat rock or piece of wood. Keep the lower end constantly moist.

Food
Leaves, bran cereal with molasses, apples, pulpy fruits, cooked chicken, raw hamburger, dog food, aphids and some other insects (dead or alive), mealworms

Maintenance
Keep moist; spray frequently; remove rotting food.

Possible Problems and Solutions
Keep damp but not soggy; be sure they have a good place to hide.

Background Information
Earwigs get their name from the mistaken belief that they crawl into the ears of sleeping people. These insects are nocturnal scavengers who eat leaves and other vegetation, especially the softer green parts, leaving the harder "skeleton" of veins and stems behind. They will sometimes eat other small invertebrates, alive or dead. They use their pincers only to defend themselves and prefer running to flying. A female earwig does not leave her eggs like other insects do. She lays them in a protected spot and guards them, often keeping her body wrapped around them. She moves them around and licks them frequently to keep them clean and moist. When they hatch, she continues to take care of her young until they are nearly full grown.

Who's Who in the Habitat ...

WANTED

Isopods
(Sowbugs,
Pillbugs,
Roly-polies,
or Wood Lice)

Collection Strategies
- Look under rocks, logs, boards, bricks, flower pots, or in cracks in cement. If there is leaf litter around, collect it to put in their new home.
- Put down cardboard pieces in a damp spot. Leave it overnight, then look under it.
- Hollow out a potato half and put it face down. The sowbugs will probably gather under it.
- Make a potato trap (see *Easy-to-Make Equipment*).

Container Preference
Use glass or plastic with ventilated lid.

Setup
Use 2–3 cm good garden or forest soil or potting soil; add decaying bark and leaf litter; perhaps rest a piece of cardboard on a few pebbles to provide a dark sheltered area.

Food
Dead leaves; rotting wood; raw potato, carrot, zucchini; lettuce; soft, ripe fruit; unsweetened dry cereal

Maintenance
Remove rotting food and replace with fresh as needed; sprinkle or spray soil to keep it constantly damp but not soggy. In a balanced situation they will reproduce fairly quickly.

Possible Problems and Solutions
Keep container damp, but not soggy. Remove moldy food. Observe closely to be sure they are eating.

Background Information
Isopods are related to lobsters and crayfish and are among the few examples of land-dwelling crustaceans. They must live in damp places since they breathe through gill-like structures. Isopods are not insects, but like insects they are members of a larger group called *arthropods* and have the characteristic hard outer body covering and jointed legs. They also have two pairs of antennae which may have special humidity receptors. They generally eat decaying vegetation. Female sowbugs protect their eggs by carrying them in a special pouch under the abdomen. The young are able to take care of themselves as soon as they are born. Pillbugs, also called "roly-polies," roll up when disturbed, but sow bugs do not.

Who's Who in the Habitat ...

WANTED

Ladybugs

Collection Strategies
- Look for them around plants, especially where there are aphids. Avoid picking them up with fingers as they are easily damaged.
- Try brushing them into your hand or allowing them to crawl onto you.
- Ladybugs may also be ordered from biological supply sources and many garden centers.

Container Preference
Use glass or clear plastic with ventilated lid or screened container; should be large enough to allow for free flight. (See "Screen Cages" in *Easy-to-Make Equipment*)

Setup
Include an aphid-covered plant or branch. If a branch is used, put it in a container of water and cover the opening of the container with foil so the ladybugs don't fall in and drown. Add a wet cotton ball for water. Mist with water to provide droplets for drinking.

Food
Live aphids — one ladybug can eat 100 aphids a day! Put an infested plant in the terrarium. Good sources are roses and weeds. Some ladybugs eat whiteflies, mealybugs, or scale insects.

Maintenance
Replace aphid-covered plant whenever needed, changing the water in its container.

Possible Problems and Solutions
Ladybugs are escape artists. Check the container thoroughly for gaps or cracks. Keep them supplied with a constant source of aphid-infested plant material.

Background Information
Ladybugs are also known as ladybird beetles. One common species, native to Australia, was imported to the United States in the late 1800s to save the citrus crop in California which was being threatened by scale insects. Ladybugs have continued to be one of our most helpful insect predators. Both larva and adults eat aphids and other small insect pests. Other animals don't like to eat ladybugs because they have a very bitter taste.

There are about 5000 different kinds of ladybugs. They come in a variety of colors including red, orange, yellow, and black. Their spots come in different patterns too, or they may have no spots at all. Although most kinds are helpful, there are a couple of types that damage plants.

Who's Who in the Habitat ...

WANTED

Millipedes

Collection Strategies
- Look under rocks, logs, and flower pots, moving them slowly and quietly.
- Use a plastic spoon or index card to lift and transfer millipedes to a container with leaf litter in bottom and lid with holes punched.
- Collect leaf litter and other plant debris from the site to use in the new habitat.

Container Preference
Use glass or plastic with ventilated lid.

Setup
Use 2–3 cm of earth from site or potting soil as close as possible to the same type as where the millipedes were found; also gather lots of bark and leaf litter from the same area. Peat moss may also be used. Since millipedes are plant eaters, they can share a small space successfully as long as food is supplied.

Food
Plant material from area where found; dead leaves, cacti, pine needles; carrot, apple, or potato slices; lettuce, celery, grapes, bananas; most fruits except citrus

Maintenance
Sprinkle or mist soil daily to keep it damp but not saturated.

Possible Problems and Solutions
Millipedes will die very quickly if their environment dries out.

Background Information
Millipedes have long bodies with many segments but, unlike centipedes, most segments have two pairs of legs. Although their name literally means "1000 feet," most have around 50 pairs of legs. One species has 376 pairs of legs! They range in length from a fraction of an inch to a foot long. Each time a millipede molts, it adds three or more segments to its length. Some females lay their eggs in nests and stay with the eggs until they hatch. Many millipedes have an unusual defense system. Each segment has a pair of glands, one on each side. If the millipede is disturbed, the glands give off a foul-smelling liquid which effectively keeps it from being eaten.

Who's Who in the Habitat ...

WANTED

Snails and Slugs

Collection Strategies
- Look in damp places, especially at night or in the early morning.
- Water an area well to encourage them to come out, or collect after a rain.
- Look under and around flower pots, stones, walls, cement edges, fences, etc.

Container Preference
Use glass or plastic (they will eat through cardboard); secure ventilated covering. If vents are large, put loose-weave fabric across the top before securing the lid.

Setup
Use 2-4 cm moist soil for burrowing, branches to climb on, damp sponge for constant moisture.

Food
Fresh and dead leaves; fresh fruits and vegetables, oats, lettuce
Rabbit pellets are easy and don't rot as quickly.
Snails need calcium for their shells. Roll oats or rabbit pellets in calcium carbonate before adding them to the terrarium. The amount of calcium carbonate that sticks to the food should be sufficient to maintain healthy shells. Crushed egg shells may also be used. Snails may go several days without eating.

Maintenance
Replace food if it begins to mold. Keep terrarium cool and damp at all times, away from direct sunlight or source of heat.

Possible Problems and Solutions
If the terrarium is too dry, snails will crawl into their shells and stay for a long time. Try misting them. It is natural for them to estivate at least periodically.
Insufficient calcium in their diet can result in thin fragile shells (see *Food*). Slugs can get mites if the terrarium is not kept clean. To treat, roll slugs on paper towel to clean off. A few types of snails will prey on other snails.

Background Information
Snails and slugs are part of a group of animals called mollusks, many of whom live in the ocean. Their relatives include clams, oysters, squids, and octopuses. Snails have a thin, one-piece spiral shell, but slugs have only a small internal shell or none at all. They produce and travel on a "slime trail" which protects them from sharp or rough areas in their path. Their eyes are on stalks and can distinguish light from dark. Most use a *radula*, a sandpaper-like tongue with hundreds of tiny teeth, to scrape algae or green plants, but a few types are predatory. They have well-developed muscle systems and are amazingly strong and well coordinated. Slugs can get through tiny openings, stretching as much as eleven times their normal length.

Who's Who in the Habitat ...

WANTED

Spiders

Collection Strategies
- Look around buildings, on bushes, in corners, in open areas. Follow webs to find orb-weavers; look up on fence posts, walls, or table tops for jumping spiders.
- Be aware of local venomous spiders and avoid. When in doubt, don't handle.
- Use stick, leaf, or card to gently coax into a container. Observe area; provide similar materials for building and similar food supply in the new habitat.

Container Preference
Use glass or clear plastic with secure, screened lid.

Setup
Orb-weavers: No soil; provide twigs or small branches for web building
Jumping spiders, burrowing spiders, ground dwellers: 4-5 cm damp soil, natural debris, small twigs, sphagnum moss

Food
Spiders eat only living things. Leave an outside light on at night to attract flying insects. Catch them and put in the terrarium for the spider to catch. Try flies, fruitflies, sowbugs, crickets, mealworms, and other insects.

Maintenance
Mist occasionally with a spray bottle; use a damp sponge or moss for humidity.

Possible Problems and Solutions
May need to keep separate, since spiders may prey on each other. Keep wet cotton in a shallow dish to increase humidity. Avoid bacteria or mold; remove dead insects and change the cotton frequently.

Background Information
There are 70,000 different known species of spiders. All have two main body parts (cephalothorax and abdomen), four pairs of legs, a pair of *pedipalps* for grabbing prey, and a pair of *chelicerae*, which end in fangs. Spiders have four to six special glands called *spinnerets* , each of which produces a different type of silk for such purposes as webs, egg sacs, protective coverings, and draglines.

Spiders are carnivores, usually preying on insects. They eat the body fluids of their victims, sucking them out and leaving behind the hard outside coverings.

Only about 10% of spiders weave geometric webs. An orb-weaver can tell by vibrations when an insect is caught in its web. Others chase or pounce upon their victims. A jumping spider uses silk to attach itself to the surface before it leaps. If it misses, it just hauls itself back up the thread and is ready to try again.

Troubleshooting

It is inevitable that some organisms in the terrarium will not survive. Some will fall prey to others above them in a food chain. Some may lose in a territorial struggle. Some may succumb to illness or old age. These events occur in every habitat. However, in the housing of any captive animals there is a responsibility for seeing that their needs are met and that they are able to survive comfortably within the natural order of things.

Resolving problems concerning a terrarium habitat provides an excellent opportunity to apply thinking skills and understanding of basic ecological principles. The following common problems offer suggestions for solutions to try. Encourage students to develop their own strategies for these and any other situations that may be encountered.

Ants

If there are ants normally in or around your classroom, you may need to protect your terrariums from invasion. Ants will carry off specimens and eggs as well as food not intended for them.

A good line of defense is water. Try raising the terrarium above surface level by standing it on baby food jars, film canisters, empty spools, blocks, or even mounds of clay. Center each leg in a small pie tin, margarine tub, or similar container. Keep at least 3 cm (1 inch) of water in each container so that the ants cannot get to the aquarium without crossing a "moat."

Keep in mind that if insect repellent is sprayed in the classroom, it will likely affect the critters in the terrariums too.

Flies, Gnats, Bees, and Wasps

Food and decaying plant material in the terrarium may attract insects you'd prefer not to encourage. A tight-fitting screened lid will keep them out. If they persist, consider flypaper strips or easy-to-make traps rather than chemicals.

Mosquitoes

Pond water may contain mosquito larvae. Fortunately mosquito larvae are a preferred food for several different species. If no natural predator is living in your terrarium, consider adding one. Since any species added changes the habitat, this can become part of the learning experience.

 © 1998 AIMS Education Foundation

Mold

Decaying plant material may be a normal part of the habitat, or it may cause problems. It may also be an indication that the terrarium environment is too humid. In general, if food material is actively growing mold, it should be removed.

Escapees and Unwanted Visitors

If the inhabitants of the terrarium are escaping, or if uninvited, small flying insects are coming in, check all openings. Use a hot glue gun or silicone bathtub caulking to cover open vents with a piece of screen. To make a loose-fitting cover more secure, add layers of felt or other fabric (or a cardboard strip) either to the inside of the cover or to the outside of the terrarium where they meet. For climbing or crawling escape artists, thinly apply a 3 cm band of petroleum jelly (Vaseline®) around the inside of the terrarium near the top.

If escapes continue, you might need a container with taller or slicker sides for the particular organisms you are housing.

Uneaten food may attract other insects to the terrarium. Try to provide only as much food as will be consumed fairly quickly, feeding more often but with less food at a time. Remove leftover food promptly if it becomes a problem.

Drying Out

A terrarium habitat in a heated classroom can dry out very rapidly. Unless it is a desert terrarium, it should be misted often enough to keep a dampness level similar to the natural conditions outside. If it gets too dry, mist more frequently or use a pipette to increase water content in the soil. The lower soil levels should be maintained to have more moisture than the surface. Add water gradually to avoid flooding. If drying out is a continual problem, lay a sheet of clear plastic wrap on top of the terrarium cover. If the plastic is fastened down, add holes for ventilation.

Temperature Extremes

The normal fluctuation of classroom temperatures can demand more tolerance than the terrarium dwellers would normally need outside. Keep the terrarium away from heat and air conditioning vents, direct sunlight, doorways, and other hot and cold spots in the room. The temperature inside the terrarium can be somewhat stabilized by covering it with plastic wrap.

Dying Plants

If the plants are not thriving or are dying before being eaten, it may be the result of too much water, not enough water, or inadequate light levels. Try replanting them in different spots in the terrarium, closer to or farther away from the damp areas. If insufficient light seems to be the problem, try moving the terrarium to a southern exposure window, use a plant light, or simply replace the plants as needed.

Bibliography

Baines, Chris. *Old Bool.* Crocodile Books, USA (Interlink Publishing Group, Inc.) New York. 1989.

Bash, Barbara. *Desert Giant: The World of the Saguaro Cactus.* Sierra Club. San Francisco. 1989.

Bennett, Paul. *Nature's Secrets: Hibernation.* Thomson Learning. New York. 1994.

Bourgeois, Paulette. *The Amazing Dirt Book.* Addison Wesley Publishing Company, Inc. Reading, MA. 1990.

Buscaglia, Leo. *The Fall of Freddy the Leaf.* Henry Holt and Co. New York. 1982.

Carle, Eric. *A Very Hungry Caterpillar.* Scholastic, Inc. New York. 1969.

Cherry, Lynne. *Flute's Journey: The Life of a Wood Thrush.* Harcourt Brace & Company. San Diego. 1997.

Cherry, Lynne. *The Great Kapok Tree.* Harcourt Brace Jovanovich. San Diego. 1990.

Cobb, Vicki. *This Place is Dry.* Walker and Company. New York. 1989.

Cole, Henry. *Jack's Garden.* Greenwillow. New York. 1995.

Cole, Joanna and Bruce Degen. *The Magic Schoolbus Meets the Rot Squad.* Scholastic, Inc. New York. 1995.

Dendy, Linda. *Tracks, Scats, and Signs.* NorthWord Press, Inc. Minocqua, WI. 1995.

Dewey, Jennifer Owings. *Animal Architecture.* Orchard Books. New York. 1991.

Dunrea, Olivier. *Deep Down Underground.* Aladdin Books (Macmillan). New York. 1993.

Fitzsimmons, Cecilia. *Nature's Hidden Worlds: Animal Habitats.* Raintree Steck-Vaughn Publishers. Austin, TX. 1996.

Gaffney, Michael. *Secret Forests.* Golden Books (Western Publishing Company, Inc.). New York. 1994.

Gardiner, John Reynolds. *Top Secret.* Little, Brown, and Company. Boston. 1984.

George, Jean Craighead. *Who Really Killed Cock Robin?* Harper Trophy. New York. 1991.

Godkin, Celia. *Wolf Island.* W. H. Freeman and Company. New York. 1989.

Guiberson, Brenda. *Cactus Hotel.* Henry Holt and Company. New York. 1991.

Hockman, Hilary, editor. *What's Inside? Animal Homes*. Dorling Kindersley. London. 1993.

James, Betsy. *Mary Ann*. Dutton Children's Books. New York. 1994.

Johnson, Kipchak. *Worm's Eye View*. The Millbrook Press. Brookfield, CT. 1991.

Kalman, Bobbie and Janine Schaub. *The Air I Breathe*. Crabtree Publishing Company. New York. 1993.

Kitchen, Bert. *When Hunger Calls*. Candlewick Press. Cambridge, MA. 1994.

Lauber, Patricia. *Seeds Pop Stick Glide*. Crown Publishers. New York. 1981.

Lauber, Patricia. *Who Eats What?* HarperCollins. New York. 1995.

Lavies, Bianca. *Compost Critters*. Dutton Children's Books. New York. 1993.

MacDonald, Fiona. *Houses: Habitats and Home Life*. Franklin Watts. New York. 1994.

Merrill, Jean. *The Girl Who Loved Caterpillars*. Philomel. New York. 1992.

Overbeck, Cynthia. *How Seeds Travel*. Lerner Publications. Minneapolis. 1982.

Powell, Consie. *A Bold Carnivore*. Roberts Rinehart Publishers. Niwot, CO. 1995.

Reed-Jones, Carol. *The Tree in the Ancient Forest*. Dawn Publications. Nevada City, CA. 1995.

Ring, Elizabeth. *What Rot! Nature's Mighty Recycler*. The Millbrook Press. Brookfield, CT. 1996.

Robertson, Kayo. *Signs along the River*. Roberts Rinehart, Inc. Niwot, CO. 1986.

Robinson, Sandra. *The Rainstick: a Fable*. Falcon Press. Helena, MT. 1994.

Rogasky, Barbara. *The Water of Life*. Holiday House. New York. 1986.

Romanova, Natalia. *Once There Was a Tree*. Dial Books. New York. 1985.

Shipman, Wanda. *Animal Architects*. Stackpole Books. Mechanicsburg, PA. 1994.

Silver, Donald M. *One Small Square: Backyard*. W. H. Freeman & Co. New York. 1993.

St. Exupery, Antoine. *The Little Prince*. Harcourt, Brace, and World. New York. 1943.

Stock, Catherine. *Where Are You Going, Manyoni?* Morrow Junior Books. New York. 1993.

Thornhill, Jan. *A Tree in a Forest*. Simon & Schuster. New York. 1991.

Young, Caroline. *The Big Bug Search*. Usborne Publishing Ltd. London. 1996.

Resources

Appelhof, Mary. *Worms Eat My Garbage*. Flower Press, 10332 Shaver Road, Kalamazoo, MI 49002. 1982.

Audubon Society Field Guides. (identification by topic);
Audubon Society Nature Guides. (identification by ecological area). National Audubon Society. Alfred A. Knopf. New York.

Burnett, Robin. *The Pillbug Project*. National Science Teachers Association. Washington, DC. 1992.

Dunn, Gary A. *A Beginner's Guide to Observing and Collecting Insects*. Young Entomologists' Society, Inc. Lansing, MI. 1994.

Dunn, Gary A. *Caring for Insect Livestock: An Insect Rearing Manual*. Young Entomologists' Society, Inc. Lansing, MI. 1993.

Dunn, Gary A. *The Insect Identification Guide*. Young Entomologists' Society, Inc. Lansing, MI. 1994.

Hickman, Pamela M. *Bug Wise*. Addison Wesley. Reading, MA. 1990.

Hoffman, Jane. *Exploring Earthworms With Me*. Backyard Scientist, P.O. Box 16966, Irvine, CA 92713. 1994.

Holley, Dennis. *Animals Alive! An Ecological Guide to Animal Activities*. Roberts Rinehart Publishers. Niwot, CO. 1994. (care, feeding, housing)

Kalman, Bobbie and Janine Schaub. *Squirmy Wormy Composters*. Crabtree Publishing. New York. 1992.

Kneidel, Sally. *Pet Bugs: A Kid's Guide to Catching and Keeping Touchable Insects*. John Wiley & Sons, Inc. New York. 1994.

Levi, Herbert. *Spiders and Their Kin*. Golden Press. New York. 1987.

Rights, Mollie. *Beastly Neighbors*. Little, Brown and Company. Boston. 1981.

Zim, Herbert S. and Clarence Cottam. *Insects: A Guide to Familiar American Insects*. Golden Press. New York. 1987.

Series

Individual books about specific animals or plants available as part of a series:

Animal Habitats. Belitha Press. London.
Backyard Buddies. Michael Elsohn Ross. Carolrhoda Books, Inc. Minneapolis.
Discovering Nature. The Bookwright Press. New York.
Eyewitness Books. Alfred A Knopf. New York.
First Facts . Silver Press. New York.
Keeping Minibeasts: Franklin Watts. New York.
Lerner Natural Science. Lerner Publications. Minneapolis.
Look Closer . Dorling Kindersley, Inc. New York.
Nature Watch Books. Carolrhoda Books, Inc. Minneapolis.
Stopwatch Books. Silver Burdett Press. Englewood Cliffs, NJ.
The Fascinating World of ... Barron's. Hauppauge, NY.

Resources especially for the teacher:

Lang, Susan. *Nature in Your Backyard*. Millbrook Press. Brookfield, CT. 1995.

Montgomery, Sy. *Nature's Everyday Mysteries (1993); Seasons of the Wild (1995)*. The Curious Naturalist Series. Chapters Publishing Ltd. Shelburne, VT.

Recordings

Almost Grown. Anne Dodson. Beech Hill Music, P.O. Box 14, Camden, Maine 04843. (207) 236-9576. Email: beechhil@midcoast.com http://www.midcoast.com/~beechhil/ADodson/recordings.htm

Dirt Made My Lunch. The Banana Slug String Band. P.O. Box 2262, Santa Cruz, CA 95063. (408) 476-5776 (phone and FAX).
http://www.bananaslugstringband.com/

Singing Songs of Science. AIMS Education Foundation. P.O. Box 8120, Fresno, CA 93747. (888) 733-2467.
http://www.aimsedu.org/ (product catalog)

Web Sites

Bugwatch
http://bugwatch.com/index.html
Featuring "Bugs you want in your computer"; designed for teachers and students; provides information and photographs of common insects.

Gordon's Entomological Home Page
http://www.ex.ac.uk/~gjlramel/welcome.html
Designed for kids; unusual and interesting facts; great place to ask expert entomologists questions about insects.

Minibeast World of Insects and Spiders
http://www.tesser.com/minibeast/
Varied resources for teachers and students including Young Entomologist Society.

University of Kentucky Entomology Youth Facts
http://www.uky.edu/Agriculture/Entomology/ythfacts/entyouth.htm
Kid-friendly, lot of information; fun ideas and activities involving insects.

Entomology Sites - Texas A & M University
http://entowww.tamu.edu/entoweb/
A good place to start when looking for links to follow.

Entomology - Penn State
http://www.ento.psu.edu/
Includes a well-organized insect gallery of photographs.

Michigan Entomological Society Entomology Notes
http://insects.ummz.lsa.umich.edu/MES/notes/entnote17.html
Good and growing reference site.

Young Entomologists' Society (Y.E.S.)

1915 Peggy Place
Lansing, MI 48910-2553
(517) 887-0499

http://insects.ummz.lsa.umich.edu/YES/YESinfo.html

Source of bimonthly newsletters and quarterly journals; activity ideas and guides; handbook guides for collecting, identifying, and rearing insects; bibliographies; "buggy" store; and more. Students and adults can become members.

Materials

Classroom Supplies
    pencils, crayons (or markers)
    marking pens: fine-point, permanent and washable
    tape: masking and transparent
    rulers (metric), scissors, stapler
    glue, paper clips, paper fasteners

Equipment
    balance and masses
    terrarium(s), assorted (see *Easy-to-Make Equipment*)
    graduated cylinders: 10 or 50 ml; 500 or 1000 ml (or 9 oz cup)
    hand lenses
    thermometers
    pipettes or eyedroppers
    stopwatch or watch with a second hand
    spray bottle(s)
    strong light source such as a goose-neck lamp
    measuring spoons
    can opener

Recommended
    DiscoveryScopes®
    Brock Magiscopes® or other microscopes

Optional
    bucket or small tub and trowel or sturdy spoon
    C or D cells (can be expired)
    calculators
    clipboards or lapboards (see *Easy-to-Make Equipment*)
    hammer, screwdrivers
    paring knife and utility knife (teacher use)
    plywood to fit under glass terrarium
    tarp
    watering can

Materials
    chart or butcher paper
    construction paper: white (12 x 18), black, yellow, assorted colors
      (may use butcher paper for colors)
    copy paper (white, yellow, at least three other colors)
    card stock
    copy paper boxes or similar cardboard carton, 1 per group
    four large cardboard boxes, different sizes
    cardboard mailing or gift wrap tubes
    newspapers
    small containers with lids (i.e. soft margarine tubs)
    two-liter plastic soda bottles
    tall cans (#10 can, coffee can, etc. with capacity of more than 500 ml)
    string (strong)
    thread
    yarn, assorted, at least 4 different colors
    alfalfa seed to sprout
    bleach
    assortment of six different kinds of small beans

Materials

bread, whole-grain preferred, 2-4 slices per group
margarine
pizza sauce or plain tomato sauce
round crackers
shredded cheese
sliced pepperoni
clean gravel
golf tees or large nails
small flower pots or containers with drainage holes
plastic screening, 12 cm x 12 cm per group
cups or containers, plastic or paper: 1 to 5 oz; 8 oz or larger
cups, flexible plastic: 8 or 9 oz
mason jars with ring part of lid, one per group
cotton swabs
new sponge, one per group
toothpicks
large plastic garbage bags
paper bags (lunch size), plates, towels
plastic knives or craft sticks
plastic sandwich bags
clear plastic wrap
waxed paper

Optional
3 x 5 cards
clay
traffic cones (4)
boxes, pans, or old towels
cookie sheet(s) or tray(s)
fast food drink carriers
screen material for covers (see *Easy-to-Make Equipment*)
scrap cardboard, heavy
piece of wood, one foot square or larger
green pepper, chopped
peeled cucumber slices
potatoes (baking size)
sliced olive pieces
pleated coffee filters

© 1998 AIMS Education Foundation

The AIMS Program

AIMS is the acronym for "Activities Integrating Mathematics and Science." Such integration enriches learning and makes It meaningful and holistic. AIMS began as a project of Fresno Pacific University to integrate the study of mathematics and science in grades K-9, but has since expanded to include language arts, social studies, and other disciplines.

AIMS is a continuing program of the non-profit AIMS Education Foundation. It had its inception in a National Science Foundation funded program whose purpose was to explore the effectiveness of integrating mathematics and science. The project directors in cooperation with 80 elementary classroom teachers devoted two years to a thorough field-testing of the results and implications of integration.

The approach met with such positive results that the decision was made to launch a program to create instructional materials incorporating this concept. Despite the fact that thoughtful educators have long recommended an integrative approach, very little appropriate material was available in 1981 when the project began. A series of writing projects have ensued and today the AIMS Education Foundation is committed to continue the creation of new integrated activities on a permanent basis.

The AIMS program is funded through the sale of this developing series of books and proceeds from the Foundation's endowment. All net income from program and products flows into a trust fund administered by the AIMS Education Foundation. Use of these funds is restricted to support of research, development, and publication of new materials. Writers donate all their rights to the Foundation to support its on-going program. No royalties are paid to the writers.

The rationale for integration lies in the fact that science, mathematics, language arts, social studies, etc., are integrally interwoven in the real world from which it follows that they should be similarly treated in the classroom where we are preparing students to live in that world. Teachers who use the AIMS program give enthusiastic endorsement to the effectiveness of this approach.

Science encompasses the art of questioning, investigating, hypothesizing, discovering, and communicating. Mathematics is a language that provides clarity, objectivity, and understanding. The language arts provide us powerful tools of communication. Many of the major contemporary societal issues stem from advancements in science and must be studied in the context of the social sciences. Therefore, it is timely that all of us take seriously a more holistic mode of educating our students. This goal motivates all who are associated with the AIMS Program. We invite you to join us in this effort.

Meaningful integration of knowledge is a major recommendation coming from the nation's professional science and mathematics associations. The American Association for the Advancement of Science in *Science for All Americans* strongly recommends the integration of mathematics, science, and technology. The National Council of Teachers of Mathematics places strong emphasis on applications of mathematics such as are found in science investigations. AIMS is fully aligned with these recommendations.

Extensive field testing of AIMS investigations confirms these beneficial results.

1. Mathematics becomes more meaningful, hence more useful, when it is applied to situations that interest students.
2. The extent to which science is studied and understood is increased, with a significant economy of time, when mathematics and science are integrated.
3. There is improved quality of learning and retention, supporting the thesis that learning which is meaningful and relevant is more effective.
4. Motivation and involvement are increased dramatically as students investigate real-world situations and participate actively in the process.
   We invite you to become part of this classroom teacher movement by using an integrated approach to learning and sharing any suggestions you may have. The AIMS Program welcomes you!

© 2002 AIMS Education Foundation

AIMS Education Foundation Programs

A Day with AIMS®

Intensive one-day workshops are offered to introduce educators to the philosophy and rationale of AIMS. Participants will discuss the methodology of AIMS and the strategies by which AIMS principles may be incorporated into curriculum. Each participant will take part in a variety of hands-on AIMS investigations to gain an understanding of such aspects as the scientific/mathematical content, classroom management, and connections with other curricular areas. *A Day with AIMS®* workshops may be offered anywhere in the United States. Necessary supplies and take-home materials are usually included in the enrollment fee.

A Week with AIMS®

Throughout the nation, AIMS offers many one-week workshops each year, usually in the summer. Each workshop lasts five days and includes at least 30 hours of AIMS hands-on instruction. Participants are grouped according to the grade level(s) in which they are interested. Instructors are members of the AIMS Instructional Leadership Network. Supplies for the activities and a generous supply of take-home materials are included in the enrollment fee. Sites are selected on the basis of applications submitted by educational organizations. If chosen to host a workshop, the host agency agrees to provide specified facilities and cooperate in the promotion of the workshop. The AIMS Education Foundation supplies workshop materials as well as the travel, housing, and meals for instructors.

AIMS One-Week Perspectives Workshops

Each summer, Fresno Pacific University offers AIMS one-week workshops on its campus in Fresno, California. AIMS Program Directors and highly qualified members of the AIMS National Leadership Network serve as instructors.

The AIMS Instructional Leadership Program

This is an AIMS staff-development program seeking to prepare facilitators for leadership roles in science/math education in their home districts or regions. Upon successful completion of the program, trained facilitators may become members of the AIMS Instructional Leadership Network, qualified to conduct AIMS workshops, teach AIMS in-service courses for college credit, and serve as AIMS consultants. Intensive training is provided in mathematics, science, process and thinking skills, workshop management, and other relevant topics.

College Credit and Grants

Those who participate in workshops may often qualify for college credit. If the workshop takes place on the campus of Fresno Pacific University, that institution may grant appropriate credit. If the workshop takes place off-campus, arrangements can sometimes be made for credit to be granted by another institution. In addition, the applicant's home school district is often willing to grant in-service or professional-development credit. Many educators who participate in AIMS workshops are recipients of various types of educational grants, either local or national. Nationally known foundations and funding agencies have long recognized the value of AIMS mathematics and science workshops to educators. The AIMS Education Foundation encourages educators interested in attending or hosting workshops to explore the pos-sibilities suggested above. Although the Foundation strongly supports such interest, it reminds applicants that they have the primary responsibility for fulfilling *current* requirements.

For current information regarding the programs described above, please complete the following:

Information Request

Please send current information on the items checked:

____ *Basic Information Packet* on AIMS materials   ____ *A Week with AIMS®* workshops
____ *AIMS Instructional Leadership Program*   ____ Hosting information for *A Day with AIMS®* workshops
____ *AIMS One-Week Perspectives* workshops   ____ Hosting information for *A Week with AIMS®* workshops

Name _____   Phone _____

Address _____
       Street   City   State   Zip

© 2002 AIMS Education Foundation

We invite you to subscribe to *AIMS*®!

Each issue of *AIMS*® contains a variety of material useful to educators at all grade levels. Feature articles of lasting value deal with topics such as mathematical or science concepts, curriculum, assessment, the teaching of process skills, and historical background. Several of the latest AIMS math/science investigations are always included, along with their reproducible activity sheets. As needs direct and space allows, various issues contain news of current developments, such as workshop schedules, activities of the AIMS Instructional Leadership Network, and announcements of upcoming publications.

AIMS® is published monthly, August through May. Subscriptions are on an annual basis only. A subscription entered at any time will begin with the next issue, but will also include the previous issues of that volume. Readers have preferred this arrangement because articles and activities within an annual volume are often interrelated.

Please note that an *AIMS*® subscription automatically includes duplication rights for one school site for all issues included in the subscription. Many schools build cost-effective library resources with their subscriptions.

YES! I am interested in subscribing to *AIMS*®.

Name _____ Home Phone _____

Address _____ City, State, Zip _____

Please send the following volumes (subject to availability):

_____	Volume	VII	(1992-93)	$15.00	_____ Volume XII	(1997-98)	$30.00
_____	Volume	VIII	(1993-94)	$15.00	_____ Volume XIII	(1998-99)	$30.00
_____	Volume	IX	(1994-95)	$15.00	_____ Volume XIV	(1999-00)	$30.00
_____	Volume	X	(1995-96)	$15.00	_____ Volume XV	(2000-01)	$30.00
_____	Volume	XI	(1996-97)	$30.00	_____ Volume XVI	(2001-02)	$30.00

_____**Limited offer: Volumes XVI & XVII (2001-2003) $55.00**
(Note: Prices may change without notice)

Check your method of payment:

☐ Check enclosed in the amount of $_____

☐ Purchase order attached (Please include the P.O.#, the authorizing signature, and position of the authorizing person.)

☐ Credit Card ☐ Visa ☐ MasterCard   Amount $ _____

Card # _____   Expiration Date _____ _____

Signature_____   Today's Date _____

Make checks payable to **AIMS Education Foundation.**
Mail to *AIMS*® Magazine, P.O. Box 8120, Fresno, CA 93747-8120.
Phone (559) 255-4094 or (888) 733-2467 FAX (559) 255-6396
AIMS Homepage: http://www.AIMSedu.org/

© 2002 AIMS Education Foundation

AIMS Program Publications

Actions with Fractions 4-9
Bats Incredible! 2-4
Brick Layers 4-9
Brick Layers II 4-9
Cycles of Knowing and Growing 1-3
Crazy about Cotton Book 3-7
Critters K-6
Down to Earth 5-9
Electrical Connections 4-9
Exploring Environments Book K-6
Fabulous Fractions 3-6
Fall into Math and Science K-1
Field Detectives 3-6
Finding Your Bearings 4-9
Floaters and Sinkers 5-9
From Head to Toe 5-9
Fun with Foods 5-9
Glide into Winter with Math & Science K-1
Gravity Rules! Activity Book 5-12
Hardhatting in a Geo-World 3-5
It's About Time K-2
Jaw Breakers and Heart Thumpers 3-5
Just for the Fun of It! 4-9
Looking at Lines 6-9
Machine Shop 5-9
Magnificent Microworld Adventures 5-9
Math + Science, A Solution 5-9
Mostly Magnets 2-8
Multiplication the Algebra Way 4-8
Off The Wall Science 3-9
Our Wonderful World 5-9
Out of This World 4-8
Overhead and Underfoot 3-5
Paper Square Geometry:
    The Mathematics of Origami
Puzzle Play: 4-8
Pieces and Patterns 5-9
Popping With Power 3-5
Primarily Bears K-6
Primarily Earth K-3

Primarily Physics K-3
Primarily Plants K-3
Proportional Reasoning 6-9
Ray's Reflections 4-8
Sense-Able Science K-1
Soap Films and Bubbles 4-9
Spatial Visualization 4-9
Spills and Ripples 5-12
Spring into Math and Science K-1
The Amazing Circle 4-9
The Budding Botanist 3-6
The Sky's the Limit 5-9
Through the Eyes of the Explorers 5-9
Under Construction K-2
Water Precious Water 2-6
Weather Sense:
    Temperature, Air Pressure, and Wind 4-5
Winter Wonders K-2

Spanish/English Editions
Brinca de alegria hacia la Primavera con las
    Matemáticas y Ciencias K-1
Cáete de gusto hacia el Otoño con las
    Matemáticas y Ciencias K-1
Conexiones Eléctricas 4-9
El Botanista Principiante 3-6
Los Cinco Sentidos K-1
Ositos Nada Más K-6
Patine al Invierno con Matemáticas y Ciencias K-1
Piezas y Diseños 5-9
Primariamente Física K-3
Primariamente Plantas K-3
Principalmente Imanes 2-8

All Spanish/English Editions include student pages in
Spanish and teacher and student pages in English.

Spanish Edition
Constructores II: Ingeniería Creativa Con Construcciones LEGO® (4-9)
The entire book is written in Spanish. English pages not included.

Other Science and Math Publications
Historical Connections in Mathematics, Vol. I 5-9
Historical Connections in Mathematics, Vol. II 5-9
Historical Connections in Mathematics, Vol. III 5-9
Mathematicians are People, Too
Mathematicians are People, Too, Vol. II
Teaching Science with Everyday Things
What's Next, Volume 1, 4-12
What's Next, Volume 2, 4-12
What's Next, Volume 3, 4-12

For further information write to:
AIMS Education Foundation • P.O. Box 8120 • Fresno, California 93747-8120
www.AIMSedu.org/ • Fax 559•255•6396

© 2002 AIMS Education Foundation

AIMS Duplication Rights Program

AIMS has received many requests from school districts for the purchase of unlimited duplication rights to AIMS materials. In response, the AIMS Education Foundation has formulated the program outlined below. There is a built-in flexibility which, we trust, will provide for those who use AIMS materials extensively to purchase such rights for either individual activities or entire books.

It is the goal of the AIMS Education Foundation to make its materials and programs available at reasonable cost. All income from the sale of publications and duplication rights is used to support AIMS programs; hence, strict adherence to regulations governing duplication is essential. Duplication of AIMS materials beyond limits set by copyright laws and those specified below is strictly forbidden.

Limited Duplication Rights

Any purchaser of an AIMS book may make up to *200 copies* of any activity in that book for use at *one school site*. Beyond that, rights must be purchased according to the appropriate category.

Unlimited Duplication Rights for Single Activities

An individual or school may purchase the right to make an unlimited number of copies of a single activity. The royalty is $5.00 per activity per school site.

Examples: 3 activities x 1 site x $5.00 = $15.00
9 activities x 3 sites x $5.00 = $135.00

Unlimited Duplication Rights for Entire Books

A school or district may purchase the right to make an unlimited number of copies of a single, *specified* book. The royalty is $20.00 per book per school site. This is in addition to the cost of the book.

Examples: 5 books x 1 site x $20.00 = $100.00
12 books x 10 sites x $20.00 = $2400.00

Magazine/Newsletter Duplication Rights

Those who purchase *AIMS*® (magazine)/*Newsletter* are hereby granted permission to make up to 200 copies of any portion of it, provided these copies will be used for educational purposes.

Workshop Instructors' Duplication Rights

Workshop instructors may distribute to registered workshop participants a maximum of 100 copies of any article and/or 100 copies of no more than eight activities, provided these six conditions are met:

1. Since all AIMS activities are based upon the *AIMS Model of Mathematics* and the *AIMS Model of Learning*, leaders must include in their presentations an explanation of these two models.
2. Workshop instructors must relate the AIMS activities presented to these basic explanations of the AIMS philosophy of education.
3. The copyright notice must appear on all materials distributed.
4. Instructors must provide information enabling participants to order books and magazines from the Foundation.
5. Instructors must inform participants of their limited duplication rights as outlined below.
6. Only student pages may be duplicated.

Written permission must be obtained for duplication beyond the limits listed above. Additional royalty payments may be required.

Workshop Participants' Rights

Those enrolled in workshops in which AIMS student activity sheets are distributed may duplicate a maximum of 35 copies or enough to use the lessons one time with one class, whichever is less. Beyond that, rights must be purchased according to the appropriate category.

Application for Duplication Rights

The purchasing agency or individual must clearly specify the following:
1. Name, address, and telephone number
2. Titles of the books for Unlimited Duplication Rights contracts
3. Titles of activities for Unlimited Duplication Rights contracts
4. Names and addresses of school sites for which duplication rights are being purchased.

NOTE: Books to be duplicated must be purchased separately and are not included in the contract for Unlimited Duplication Rights.

The requested duplication rights are automatically authorized when proper payment is received, although a *Certificate of Duplication Rights* will be issued when the application is processed.

Address all correspondence to: **Contract Division
AIMS Education Foundation
P.O. Box 8120
Fresno, CA 93747-8120**

**www.AIMSedu.org/
Fax 559•255•6396**

© 2002 AIMS Education Foundation